# Research Paradigms and Th Methodological Alignment in Social Sciences

*Research Paradigms and Their Methodological Alignment in Social Sciences* is a comprehensive guide addressing the common conceptions surrounding research paradigms. This practical book demystifies complex concepts, giving researchers a nuanced understanding of the significance of research paradigms. It offers detailed insights, examples, and strategies for selecting and applying appropriate research methods, aiming to enhance the rigour and impact of scholarly work.

This insightful guide meticulously explores the intricacies of research paradigms in the social sciences. It begins by unravelling the concept and historical development of research paradigm, emphasising its pivotal role in shaping the research process. The book elucidates major research paradigms, including positivism, interpretivism, transformative paradigm, postcolonial indigenous paradigm, and pragmatism. Each paradigm is dissected, unveiling philosophical underpinnings, methodological designs, and critical considerations. The chapters carefully align research questions with specific paradigms through illustrative case studies, offering practical guidance for researchers at all levels. Notably, the transformative paradigm and postcolonial indigenous perspective receive dedicated attention, addressing their unique methodological nuances and ethical dimensions. The exploration extends to pragmatism, seamlessly integrating theoretical foundations with real-world applications. The book strives to bridge the awareness gap in academic settings, fostering a profound appreciation for research paradigms and promoting a thoughtful, rigorous approach to scholarly inquiry.

This book caters to students, novice and experienced researchers, offering a comprehensive understanding of research paradigms. It's valuable for academia, aiding undergraduate and postgraduate students, educators, and researchers in various disciplines. Research organisations, academic institutions, and professionals in diverse fields engaged in research and development will also find it a valuable resource.

**Bunmi Isaiah Omodan** is an NRF-rated researcher at Walter Sisulu University in South Africa.

# Research Paradigms and Their Methodological Alignment in Social Sciences
A Practical Guide for Researchers

Bunmi Isaiah Omodan

Routledge
Taylor & Francis Group

LONDON AND NEW YORK

Designed cover image: AndreyPopov / Getty Images

First published 2024
by Routledge
4 Park Square, Milton Park, Abingdon, Oxon OX14 4RN

and by Routledge
605 Third Avenue, New York, NY 10158

*Routledge is an imprint of the Taylor & Francis Group, an informa business*

© 2025 Bunmi Isaiah Omodan

The right of Bunmi Isaiah Omodan to be identified as author of this work has been asserted in accordance with sections 77 and 78 of the Copyright, Designs and Patents Act 1988.

All rights reserved. No part of this book may be reprinted or reproduced or utilised in any form or by any electronic, mechanical, or other means, now known or hereafter invented, including photocopying and recording, or in any information storage or retrieval system, without permission in writing from the publishers.

*Trademark notice*: Product or corporate names may be trademarks or registered trademarks, and are used only for identification and explanation without intent to infringe.

*British Library Cataloguing-in-Publication Data*
A catalogue record for this book is available from the British Library

ISBN: 978-1-032-77625-5 (hbk)
ISBN: 978-1-032-77624-8 (pbk)
ISBN: 978-1-003-48406-6 (ebk)

DOI: 10.4324/9781003484066

Typeset in Optima
by KnowledgeWorks Global Ltd.

# Contents

*Author's Biography* x
*Justification and Chapter Overview* xi

1 Understanding Research Paradigm 1

 *Chapter Synopsis 1*
 1.1 Concept of Research Paradigm 1
 1.2 Importance of Research Paradigm 2
 1.3 The Historical Development of Research Paradigms 4
 1.4 Major Research Paradigms: Brief Overview and Comparison 6
 1.5 The Philosophical Foundations of Research Paradigms 8
     1.5.1 Epistemology 8
     1.5.2 Ontology 9
     1.5.3 Axiology 10
     1.5.4 Methodology 12
 1.6 Aligning Research Questions and Paradigms 13
     1.6.1 Case Studies on How to Align Research Questions With Paradigms 14
 1.7 Navigating the Complexities of Research Paradigms 18
 1.8 Summary 21

2 Positivist Paradigm and Methodological Alignment 23

 *Chapter Synopsis 23*
 2.1 Concept of Positivist Paradigm 23
 2.2 The Evolution of Positivism Paradigm 24
 2.3 Philosophical Foundations of Positivism Paradigm 25
     2.3.1 Epistemology of Positivist Paradigm 25
     2.3.2 Ontology of Positivist Paradigm 26
     2.3.3 Axiology of Positivist Paradigm 26
     2.3.4 Methodology of Positivist Paradigm 27

2.4 Key Concepts and Assumptions of Positivist Paradigm  27
2.5 Methodological Designs in Positivist Research  29
2.6 Aligning Research Questions with Positivist Paradigms  33
    2.6.1 Case Studies on How to Align Research Questions with Positivist Paradigm  36
    Case Study 1: The Impact of Technology Use on Student Academic Performance  36
    Case Study 2: Factors Influencing Employee Job Satisfaction  37
    Case Study 3: The Effect of Mobile Banking on Economic Development in Africa  38
    Case Study 4: The Relationship between Urbanisation and Air Quality in the Global North  38
2.7 Characteristics of Data Collection Methods in Positivist Research  39
    2.7.1 Methods of Data Collection Within the Positivism Paradigm  41
2.8 Characteristics of Data Analysis and Interpretation in Positivist Research  45
    2.8.1 Methods of Data Analysis within Positivist Paradigm  47
2.9 Critiques and Debates in Positivist Research  52
    2.9.1 Reductionism and Oversimplification  52
    2.9.2 Objectivity and Value Neutrality  53
    2.9.3 Quantitative Bias  54
    2.9.4 Generalisability and Contextual Understanding  54
    2.9.5 Power Dynamics and Researcher Dominance  55
    2.9.6 Limited Emphasis on Subjective Experience  55
    2.9.7 Ethical Considerations  56
2.10 Balancing Objectivity and Subjectivity in Positivist Research  57
2.11 Summary  58

3 Interpretive/Constructive Paradigm and Methodological Alignment     59

Chapter Synopsis  59
3.1 Methodological Designs of Interpretive Paradigm  60
3.2 Concept of Interpretive Paradigm  63
3.3 The Evolution of Interpretive Paradigms  64
3.4 Key Concepts and Assumptions  65
3.5 The Philosophical Foundations of Interpretive Paradigm  67
    3.5.1 Epistemology of Interpretive Paradigm  67

Contents   vii

      3.5.2   Ontology of Interpretive Paradigm  68
      3.5.3   Axiology of Interpretive Paradigm  68
      3.5.4   Methodology of Interpretive Paradigm  69
3.6   Aligning Research Questions with Interpretive Paradigms  69
      3.6.1   Case Studies on How to Align Research Questions with Interpretive Paradigm  71
      Case Study 1: Exploring Subjective Experiences of Work-Life Balance in a Multinational Corporation  71
      Case Study 2: Understanding the Construction of Online Self-Identity in Social Media Platforms  72
      Case Study 3: Navigating Diversity and Inclusion in Contemporary African Workplaces  73
3.7   Data Collection Methods in Interpretive Research  74
3.8   Data Analysis and Interpretation in Interpretive Research  78
3.9   Critiques and Debates in Interpretive Research  82
3.10  Balancing Subjectivity in Interpretive Research  84
3.11  Summary  86

## 4  Transformative Paradigm and Methodological Alignment    87

*Chapter Synopsis 87*
4.1   Concept of Transformative Paradigm  87
4.2   The Evolution of the Transformative Paradigm  88
4.3   Key Concepts and Assumptions  89
4.4   The Philosophical Foundations of the Transformative Paradigm  92
      4.4.1   Epistemology in the Transformative Paradigm  92
      4.4.2   Ontology in the Transformative Paradigm  93
      4.4.3   Axiology in the Transformative Paradigm  93
      4.4.4   Methodology of Transformative Paradigm  94
4.5   Transformative Paradigm and Qualitative Research  94
4.6   Transformative Paradigm and Mixed-Methods Research  96
4.7   Methodological Designs in Transformative Research  97
4.8   Aligning Research Questions with the Transformative Paradigm  100
      4.8.1   Case Studies on Aligning Research Questions With Transformative Paradigm  103
      Case Study 1: LGBTQ+ Mental Health and Access to Healthcare  103
      Case Study 2: Community Development and Indigenous Land Rights  104

Case Study 3: Women's Empowerment and Microfinance
in Sub-Saharan Africa  104
4.9 Data Collection Methods in Transformative Research  105
4.10 Data Analysis and Interpretation in Transformative
Research  110
    4.10.1 Transformative Justification of the Data
Analysis Methods  114
4.11 Critiques and Debates in Transformative Research  115
4.12 Balancing Research Rigour and Social
Justice in Transformative Research  116
4.13 Summary  118

5 Postcolonial Indigenous Paradigm and
Methodological Alignment     119

  Chapter Synopsis  119
  5.1 Concept Postcolonial Indigenous Paradigm  119
  5.2 The Evolution of the Postcolonial Indigenous
Paradigm  120
  5.3 Key Concepts and Assumptions  121
  5.4 The Philosophical Foundations of the
Postcolonial Indigenous Paradigm  123
    5.4.1 Epistemology of the Postcolonial Indigenous
Paradigm  123
    5.4.2 Ontology of the Postcolonial Indigenous Paradigm  124
    5.4.3 Axiology of the Postcolonial Indigenous Paradigm  124
    5.4.4 Methodology of the Postcolonial Indigenous
Paradigm  124
  5.5 Methodological Designs in Postcolonial Indigenous
Research  125
  5.6 Aligning Research Questions with the
Postcolonial Indigenous Paradigm  128
    5.6.1 Case Studies on How to Align Research Questions
With the Postcolonial Paradigm  129
    Case Study 1: Researching Indigenous Food Sovereignty
in Collaboration with a Community  129
    Case Study 2: Examining Indigenous Language Revitalisation
through Collaborative Research  130
    Case Study 3: Revitalising Indigenous Agricultural
Practices for Rural African Empowerment  131
  5.7 Data Collection Methods in Postcolonial Indigenous
Research  132

5.8 Data Analysis and Interpretation in
     Postcolonial Indigenous Research 136
 5.9 Critiques and Debates in Postcolonial Indigenous
     Research 139
 5.10 Balancing Empowerment and Ethical Issues
     in Postcolonial Indigenous Research 141
 5.11 Summary 142

6 Pragmatism Paradigm and Methodological Alignment 144

 Chapter Synopsis 144
 6.1 Concept of Pragmatism Paradigm 144
 6.2 The Evolution of Pragmatism Paradigm 145
 6.3 Key Concepts and Assumptions 146
 6.4 The Philosophical Foundations of the Pragmatism
     Paradigm 149
     6.4.1 Epistemology of the Pragmatism Paradigm 149
     6.4.2 Ontology of the Pragmatism Paradigm 150
     6.4.3 Axiology of the Pragmatism Paradigm 151
     6.4.4 Methodology of the Pragmatism Paradigm 151
     6.4.5 Pragmatism Paradigm and Qualitative Research 152
 6.5 Pragmatism Paradigm and Mixed-Methods Research 154
 6.6 Methodological Designs in Pragmatism Paradigm 156
 6.7 Aligning Research Questions with the Pragmatism
     Paradigm 159
     6.7.1 Case Studies on How to Align Research
           Questions With Pragmatism Paradigm 164
     Case Study 1: Understanding Obesity Prevention
           Efforts 164
     Case Study 2: Analysing Education Technology
           in Rural Schools 164
 6.8 Data Collection Methods in Pragmatism Paradigm 165
 6.9 Data Analysis and Interpretation in Pragmatism
     Paradigm 168
 6.10 Critiques and Debates in Pragmatism Paradigm 171
 6.11 Balancing Flexibility and Practicality in Pragmatism
     Paradigm 174
 6.12 Summary 175

 References 177
 Index 193

# Author's Biography

**Bunmi Isaiah Omodan** is an NRF-rated researcher. He holds a PhD in Education Management and Leadership, a Master's degree in Educational Management, and a BA Ed in English Language. He is the Editor-in-Chief of the *Interdisciplinary Journal of Rural and Community Studies*, the *Interdisciplinary Journal of Education Research* and the *Interdisciplinary Journal of Sociality Studies*. He also serves as an editorial member and guest-edited in various accredited journals. He is currently a member of the South African Education Research Association (SAERA), the Higher Education Learning and Teaching Association of Southern Africa (HELTASA), the British Education Leadership, Management and Administration Society (BELMAS), the Nigeria Association for Educational Administration and Planning (NAEAP), and the Commonwealth Council for Educational Administration and Management (CCEAM). Bunmi Omodan has supervised many postgraduate students, published edited books, and published numerous articles in various local and international journals, chapters-in-books, and conference proceedings. His research focus includes, but is not limited to, qualitative and quantitative research approaches, social and Africanised pedagogy, and conflict management.

# Justification and Chapter Overview

The concept of a paradigm in the field of research is often perceived as an intricate and challenging aspect, particularly among students and novice researchers. Unfortunately, this misunderstanding can lead to a lack of appreciation for its true significance. Some students and researchers, perhaps intimidated or confused by the complexity of paradigms, tend to overlook or underestimate its importance. They may assume that focusing on a research paradigm is an unnecessary or even pedantic step when crafting their theses, projects, and other academic publications. This misconception is prevalent among most young scholars, leading to an underestimation of the fundamental role that paradigms can play in guiding and shaping research. Consequently, this lack of focus on what can be a vital element in the structure and success of scholarly works can result in research that is not as robust, coherent, or as insightful as it could be. This book has been written to provide a comprehensive understanding of research paradigms in response to this pervasive issue. It does more than simply define the term; it emphasises paradigms' indispensable role in the entire research process. By demystifying the subject and breaking it down into accessible components, the book seeks to make paradigms approachable and relevant for all researchers, regardless of their level of experience. It offers detailed explanations, examples, and guidance on selecting and applying appropriate research methods suitable for various research paradigmatic contexts. The objective is to inform, educate, and empower researchers, encouraging them to recognise the value of paradigms and utilise appropriate methods in their work.

Ultimately, this book aims to bridge the gap in awareness that often exists in academic settings, fostering a greater appreciation for the intricacies and utility of research paradigms and promoting a more thoughtful, rigorous approach to scholarly inquiry. Therefore, the book's six chapters contribute to a higher standard of research and a deeper, more nuanced understanding of the subjects under investigation.

Chapter 1 meticulously unpacks the concept of the research paradigm, delineating its importance and providing a historical exploration of its development. It presents a comprehensive overview and comparison of major research paradigms, thereby laying a foundational understanding for the reader.

Furthermore, the chapter delves deeply into the philosophical foundations of research paradigms, elucidating the integral roles of epistemology, ontology, axiology, and methodology within this context. This includes highlighting the crucial connection between research questions and paradigms, supported by carefully selected case studies that demonstrate how to align research questions with specific paradigms. Additionally, the chapter engages with critiques and debates surrounding research paradigms, shedding light on diverse perspectives and the ongoing intellectual dialogues within the field. The chapter also provides invaluable guidance for navigating the inherent complexities of research paradigms. This includes a range of practical strategies and approaches designed to assist researchers in effectively manoeuvring through the intricacies of their chosen paradigm, with the ultimate goal of achieving rigorous and impactful research outcomes. Serving as a vital resource for researchers at various stages of expertise, this chapter aims to inform and empower, demystifying the concept of research paradigms and emphasising their critical role in academic inquiry.

Chapter 2 provides an in-depth exploration of the positivist and post-positivist paradigms, examining their methodological implications within the context of research. The chapter commences by uncovering valuable insights into the foundations, assumptions, and evolution of both positivism and post-positivism, elucidating how these paradigms fundamentally shape our understanding and approach to studying the world. It begins by thoroughly contextualising the positivist paradigms, clearly explicating the key concepts and assumptions inherent to positivism. Moreover, the chapter critically presents the critiques and modifications that have significantly contributed to the evolution of post-positivism. This includes carefully examining the methodological approaches employed within this paradigm and guidance on aligning specific research questions with the appropriate paradigm. The chapter also delves into the practical aspects, such as data collection methods typical in positivist research, and addresses the nuances of data analysis and interpretation within these paradigms. Alongside this, it discusses the critiques and debates prevalent in the field, providing a balanced view of the arguments. Finally, the chapter thoughtfully explores the delicate balance between objectivity and subjectivity in research, reflecting on how this interplay manifests within the positivist and post-positivist frameworks. Through a rigorous and methodical approach, Chapter 2 serves as a comprehensive guide to these essential paradigms, enriching the reader's understanding and facilitating a more nuanced approach to research.

Chapter 3 systematically presents the foundations, methodologies, and key considerations that characterise the interpretive research paradigm. This paradigm, known for emphasising the understanding of subjective meanings, social interactions, and the socially constructed nature of reality, requires a profound exploration of individuals' interpretations, experiences, and the context-specific understanding of social phenomena. The chapter elaborates on various research designs and methods that are commonly employed in interpretive research, including but not limited to ethnography, phenomenology, grounded theory, narrative research, and case study research. Furthermore, it underscores the importance of appropriately aligning research questions with the interpretive paradigm and offers illustrative examples of how to accomplish this alignment. Delving into the specialised methods of data collection, analysis, and interpretation specific to interpretive research, the chapter emphasises approaches such as thematic analysis, narrative analysis, and discourse analysis. It also addresses the critiques and debates that surround the interpretive research paradigm, focusing on intricate topics such as subjectivity, generalisability, and ethical considerations that may arise during the research process. The chapter culminates by emphasising the significance of reflexivity and transparency and the thoughtful balancing of subjectivity in interpretive research. These principles are essential for enhancing the rigour and credibility of findings, ensuring that the research not only resonates with the lived experiences of the subjects but also meets the scholarly standards of academic inquiry. Through its comprehensive and nuanced presentation, Chapter 3 serves as an essential resource for those seeking to engage with the interpretive paradigm in a methodologically sound and ethically responsible manner.

Chapter 4 embarks on an in-depth exploration of the transformative paradigm, also recognised as the critical paradigm, setting it as the central focus of examination. The chapter initiates its discussion by delving into the intricate contextual framework of the transformative paradigm, followed by a systematic examination of its philosophical underpinnings. This establishes a solid foundation, leading to a detailed exploration of key concepts and assumptions that make up this paradigm, aiming to equip readers with a comprehensive understanding. As the chapter unfolds, it proceeds to trace the evolutionary trajectory of the transformative paradigm, shedding discerning light on its development and maturation over time. Attention is then directed towards the methodological designs nestled within the transformative research framework, specifically emphasising effectively aligning research questions with the transformative paradigm. In a subsequent section, the chapter meticulously analyses the methods of data collection characteristic of Transformative Research, coupled with a detailed examination of the processes involved in data analysis and interpretation within this specific approach. Furthermore, the chapter delves into the critiques and debates that circulate around Transformative Research, providing a balanced and well-rounded perspective on its inherent strengths and potential weaknesses. It culminates by thoughtfully exploring the delicate balance between research rigour and the pursuit of social justice within the Transformative Research framework. In sum, Chapter 4 stands as a comprehensive and insightful dissection of the transformative paradigm and its multifaceted dimensions, serving as an essential guide for readers wishing to engage effectively and meaningfully with this particular research approach.

Chapter 5 offers a profound exploration of the Postcolonial Indigenous Paradigm, focusing on its methodological alignment and meticulously laying out a comprehensive understanding of its historical context, philosophical foundations, key concepts, and underlying assumptions. The chapter embarks on a detailed examination of the evolution of this paradigm, emphasising its intrinsic significance in the sphere of research. This includes a thoughtful inspection of the methodological designs, data collection methodologies, and data analysis techniques uniquely suited to the Postcolonial Indigenous research framework. A vital part of this discussion stresses the importance of ensuring that research questions are seamlessly aligned with the principles governing this paradigm. In addition to these core aspects, the chapter also addresses various critiques, debates, and ethical considerations that are pertinent when conducting research within this paradigm. This includes a nuanced focus on maintaining a delicate balance between empowerment and respecting Indigenous rights and protocols, a consideration that is paramount to ethical research practice within this framework. The chapter's introductory paragraph artfully sets the stage for a comprehensive and deeply insightful exploration of the Postcolonial Indigenous Paradigm. Doing so lays a solid foundation that paves the way for an enriched, in-depth understanding of its theoretical underpinnings and methodological approaches, ensuring that readers are well-equipped to engage with this complex and vitally important research perspective.

Chapter 6 offers an exhaustive and multifaceted exploration of the Pragmatism Paradigm, masterfully weaving together its inception, evolution, and key defining aspects. By delving into the underlying philosophical foundations, including the complex interplay of epistemology, ontology, and axiology, the text affords readers vital insights into the paradigm's methodological designs and the alignment of various research questions within this framework. Additionally, attention is judiciously devoted to the techniques employed in data collection and analysis and a comprehensive examination of the prominent debates and critiques that characterise this field of inquiry. Beyond theoretical considerations, the chapter sheds light on the alignment of the Pragmatism Paradigm with qualitative and mixed-methods research, considering the practicalities and nuances involved in employing this multifaceted approach. It further includes a thoughtful discussion of ethical considerations, underscoring their importance in the pragmatic approach. This extensive and meticulously crafted examination serves as a rich academic resource, furnishing readers with a profound and coherent understanding of pragmatism. It seamlessly bridges theoretical concepts with real-world applications, equipping scholars and researchers with the essential tools and perspectives necessary to engage effectively with this paradigm.

# 1 Understanding Research Paradigm

**Chapter Synopsis**

The chapter begins by unpacking the concept of research paradigm and its importance, exploring its historical development, and presenting an overview and comparison of major research paradigms. Furthermore, the chapter delves into the philosophical foundations of research paradigms, elucidating the role of epistemology, ontology, axiology, and methodology. It highlights the crucial link between research questions and paradigms, offering case studies that effectively illustrate how to align research questions with specific paradigms. Critiques and debates surrounding research paradigms are also addressed, shedding light on the diverse perspectives and ongoing discussions within the field. Additionally, the chapter provides invaluable guidance on how to navigate the complexities inherent in research paradigms. It offers a range of strategies and approaches to assist researchers in effectively manoeuvring through the intricacies of their chosen paradigm, ultimately leading to rigorous and impactful research outcomes. This chapter, therefore, serves as an essential resource for researchers alike, aiming to demystify the concept of research paradigms and emphasise their significance.

## 1.1 Concept of Research Paradigm

A paradigm is a worldview that forms the basis for understanding or interpreting a particular subject, phenomenon, or discipline. It represents a set of assumptions, concepts, values, and practices that shape how people think or view a given subject. It provides a framework for organising knowledge, conducting research, and solving problems within a specific field or discipline (Kivunja & Kuyini, 2017). That is, paradigm establishes the boundaries and methods for inquiry and guides the way individuals or communities understand and interpret reality. Therefore, paradigm shapes worldviews, influencing beliefs, assumptions, and actions. However, paradigms are not fixed or immutable; they can evolve and change over time as new evidence, ideas, or perspectives emerge. Thomas Kuhn, a philosopher of science, popularised the concept of paradigms in his book "The Structure of Scientific Revolutions."

DOI: 10.4324/9781003484066-1

He argued that scientific progress is not just a linear accumulation of knowledge but involves periods of revolutionary change when existing paradigms are challenged and replaced by new ones (Kuhn, 1997, 2012). This justifies that paradigms are worthy of note in various domains, including scientific disciplines, and even in everyday life.

In the research context, a paradigm provides a lens through which researchers view the world, conceptualise their research questions, select appropriate methods, and interpret their findings. According to Davies and Fisher (2018), it is a foundation that helps researchers make sense of their research and determine what knowledge is valid and valuable within their field. Research paradigm, therefore, specifically pertains to the application of a paradigmatic framework within the field of research. This resonates with Raines's (2013) argument that paradigm refers to the assumptions, beliefs, and methods researchers adopt when approaching their studies. One can then argue that research paradigms define what is considered acceptable or valid within a given discipline or field of study, which provides researchers with a shared language, theoretical foundations, and methodological principles that guide their investigations. In order words, it is a philosophical foundation that helps to shape the research questions, theoretical and methodological process and, data analysis techniques, and interpretations, ensuring that the research is aligned with the underlying philosophical and theoretical principles of the chosen paradigm.

## 1.2 Importance of Research Paradigm

Research paradigms play a fundamental role in shaping the landscape of research within social sciences and beyond. This is because they provide a framework for understanding and conducting research, influencing how researchers conceptualise their studies, gather and analyse data, and interpret their findings. In this section, I shed more light on the significance of research paradigms and their impact on the field of research in social sciences.

First and foremost, research paradigms serve as lenses through which researchers view the world by offering distinct perspectives, theoretical orientations, and assumptions that guide the research process (Park et al., 2020). Therefore, by adopting a particular paradigm, researchers align themselves with philosophical underpinnings shaping their knowledge-creation approach. This alignment helps researchers navigate the complex realities of social phenomena and enhances the rigour in the choice of research methods and designs as well as the validity of their investigations (Shah & Al-Bargi, 2013). Furthermore, research paradigms contribute to the advancement of social sciences by facilitating interdisciplinary dialogue and collaboration. While each paradigm offers a unique lens, they are not isolated entities. Researchers from different paradigmatic schools of thought exchange ideas and challenge one another's assumptions. This intellectual exchange fosters a richer understanding of social phenomena and encourages the development of innovative research approaches. The research paradigm, therefore, is argued to reflect an exercise that promotes intellectual growth and the expansion of knowledge in the social sciences.

Research paradigms also play a pivotal role in addressing practical societal challenges. They also highlight the importance of a research culture that supports knowledge society and the role of research in professional development and educational practice (Baporikar, 2015). For instance, a researcher employing a critical/transformative paradigm may delve into societal power structures and inequalities to propose transformative strategies for social change (Mertens, 2007). Conversely, a positivist researcher may examine causal relationships to inform policy decisions. Furthermore, an interpretive researcher may explore individuals' subjective meanings and lived experiences within a particular social context (Adil et al., 2022). Through interpretive research, researchers aim to illuminate the complex social processes, cultural norms, and social constructions that shape individuals' experiences, contributing to a nuanced understanding of the social world. In another example, a researcher embracing a postcolonial indigenous paradigm may examine the impacts of colonialism, imperialism, and the marginalisation of indigenous peoples (Chilisa, 2019). Research in this worldview usually aims to empower indigenous communities, reclaim cultural identities, and address issues such as land rights, self-determination, and cultural preservation. Through their work, the researcher seeks to redress historical injustices and contribute to the resurgence of indigenous knowledge and practices. Lastly, researchers employing the pragmatism paradigm might investigate urban poverty by combining quantitative data such as income levels with qualitative insights like personal experiences, thus providing a multifaceted understanding to inform policy decisions (Kaushik & Walsh, 2019). Similarly, in studying educational strategies, a pragmatic researcher could merge standardised test scores with teacher interviews and classroom observations, reflecting the paradigm's commitment to practical solutions and creating tailored interventions for specific community needs. Therefore, the choice of research paradigm reflects the researcher's commitment to making meaningful contributions to society.

Additionally, understanding research paradigms is crucial for students and researchers in the social sciences. This is because a solid grasp of different paradigms allows researchers to critically evaluate existing literature, comprehend the theoretical frameworks employed, and situate their research within the broader scholarly landscape. Furthermore, I argue that having adequate knowledge of the research paradigm enables researchers to identify gaps in knowledge, identify innovative research questions, and contribute to the ongoing dialogue in their field of study.

Despite the importance of research paradigms in knowledge development, research paradigms are not without their challenges and controversies. Debates exist regarding the superiority of one paradigm over another, with critics arguing for the limitations and biases inherent in each. Understanding these critiques (as discussed in subsequent chapters) is essential for researchers, as it encourages reflexivity and encourages individuals to critically assess their own assumptions and biases. In a null shell, research paradigms form a necessary foundation for social science researchers by shaping how researchers approach their studies, engage in interdisciplinary dialogue, address societal challenges, and contribute to knowledge creation. Therefore, by recognising the importance of research paradigms, researchers can create a zealous interest towards navigating the complexities of social research more effectively and make meaningful contributions to their respective fields of study.

### 1.3 The Historical Development of Research Paradigms

The historical development of research paradigms is a testament to the evolution of knowledge production in the social sciences. Understanding this development is crucial for researchers to appreciate the context and evolution of different paradigms. In this section, I delve into the historical trajectory of research paradigms and their key milestones with reference to five major paradigms: positivist paradigm, interpretivism paradigm, transformative paradigm, postcolonial indigenous paradigm, and pragmatist paradigm.

However, the roots of research paradigms can be traced back to ancient civilisations, where philosophical inquiry laid the foundation for understanding the social world. The works of philosophers like Plato and Aristotle introduced foundational ideas about knowledge, truth, and the nature of reality, which continue to shape contemporary research paradigms. However, significant advancements were made in scientific inquiry and empirical research during the Renaissance and the Enlightenment periods.

The positivist paradigm emerged as a dominant force during the 19th century, heavily influenced by thinkers such as Auguste Comte and Emile Durkheim (Nickerson, 2022; Panayotova & Panayotova, 2020). According to Rehman and Alharthi (2016), positivism emphasises the application of scientific methods to social research, seeking to uncover universal laws governing social phenomena. This period witnessed the rise of quantitative methods, hypothesis testing, and the establishment of social sciences as disciplines. In contrast to positivism, the 20th century witnessed the emergence of interpretivism as a reaction to the limitations of purely objective and quantitative approaches. Influential figures like Max Weber and Alfred Schutz emphasised the importance of understanding social action and subjective meanings attributed by individuals to their experiences (Rasid et al., 2021). Hence, the interpretive paradigm stresses the need for qualitative methods, such as ethnography, interviews, and textual analysis, to capture the complexity and depth of human behaviour (Yanow, 2017).

During the latter half of the 20th century, the critical paradigm, otherwise called the transformative paradigm, emerged as a significant development in research paradigms. Influenced by scholars like Karl Marx, Herbert Marcuse, and Jurgen Habermas, critical theory focused on challenging power structures, inequality, and social injustices (Corradetti, 2012; Morley et al., 2020).

This paradigm sought to uncover hidden power dynamics and emancipate marginalised groups by examining social, economic, and political systems through a critical lens. Critical paradigm encouraged researchers to question prevailing assumptions, reveal underlying power imbalances, and propose transformative strategies for social change (Chilisa, 2019).

Another significant development in recent decades has been the rise of postcolonial and indigenous paradigms. Stemming from the experiences of colonised peoples, these paradigms aim to decolonise knowledge production and centre indigenous perspectives. Scholars such as Linda Tuhiwai Smith, Vine Deloria Jr, and Bagele Chilisa highlighted the importance of indigenous knowledge systems, cultural revitalisation, and self-determination (Chilisa, 2019; O'Neal, 2015; Smith et al., 2018). Postcolonial indigenous paradigms, in its principles challenge dominant Western frameworks, engage in knowledge co-creation with indigenous communities, and aim to address the legacies of colonisation and cultural erasure.

Lastly, pragmatist paradigm also emerged in the late 19th and early 20th centuries in the United States and was heavily influenced by philosophers like Charles Sanders Peirce, William James, and John Dewey (Kaushik & Walsh, 2019; Maxcy 2003), among others. Pragmatism rejects the idea that there is a single, absolute truth, emphasising instead the usefulness and practical consequences of beliefs and theories. The paradigm encourages a flexible and pluralistic approach to research, incorporating both qualitative and quantitative methods, and is often associated with mixed-methods research (Creswell & Clark, 2017; Morgan 2014). It has been applied across various fields, including philosophy, education, social sciences, and more.

Hence, it is important to note that these paradigms have not existed in isolation but rather have influenced and interacted with one another. Researchers from different paradigms have engaged in critical dialogue, borrowing concepts and methodologies from one another. This interdisciplinary exchange has led to the emergence of mixed-methods research, which seeks to integrate quantitative and qualitative approaches, recognising the complementary strengths of each paradigm. Therefore, the historical development of research paradigms reflects the dynamic nature of knowledge production in the social sciences. From the positivist emphasis on scientific objectivity to the interpretivism focus on subjective meanings and the critical examination of power structures, to postcolonial and indigenous view on people's emancipation and pluralistic approach tendency of pragmatist paradigm, research paradigms have evolved to accommodate changing theoretical and methodological landscapes. Therefore, understanding the historical development of research paradigms is instrumental for researchers, as it allows adequate appreciation of the intellectual lineage of their work. While it also offers researchers a framework to engage in informed dialogue with fellow scholars and academics, and a lens through which they can navigate the complexities of knowledge creation in the social sciences. This historical perspective enriches their approach, enabling them to choose methodologies that are grounded in well-established traditions, while also remaining receptive to new innovations and approaches that reflect the evolving nature of scholarly inquiry.

## 1.4 Major Research Paradigms: Brief Overview and Comparison

Research paradigms serve as worldviews that shape how researchers approach and conduct their studies. This section briefly overviews the major research paradigms, including positivism, interpretivism/constructivism, critical/transformative, postcolonial indigenous and pragmatism paradigms. I also compare these paradigms, highlighting their essential characteristics and differences.

- **Positivism:** The positivist paradigm is rooted in the belief that knowledge can be acquired through direct observation, measurement, and the application of scientific methods. It emphasises objectivity, causality, and the search for universal laws (Aliyu et al., 2014). The aim of this paradigm is to test hypotheses, employ quantitative methods, and gather empirical evidence to explain and predict social phenomena. The researchers in this worldview strive for generalisability and value replicable findings. The emphasis on objectivity and detachment from the research subject distinguishes this paradigm from others. See Chapter 2 for a comprehensive conceptualisation and analysis of the positivist paradigm.
- **Interpretivism/Constructivism:** The interpretive paradigm, otherwise called the constructivist paradigm, places importance on understanding the subjective meanings and social contexts in which individuals experience the world (Adil et al., 2022). Researchers adopting this paradigm believe that reality is socially constructed and that interactions negotiate meanings (Thanh & Thanh, 2015). They utilise qualitative methods such as interviews, participant observation, and textual analysis to explore the complexity of human experiences. Interpretive researchers seek to capture the richness of social phenomena, highlight multiple perspectives, and emphasise context and individual agency. See Chapter 3 for a comprehensive conceptualisation and analysis of the interpretivist paradigm.
- **Critical/Transformative:** The critical paradigm, otherwise known as transformative paradigm, focuses on power structures, social inequality, and emancipation. Researchers adopting this paradigm aim to uncover hidden power dynamics, challenge oppressive systems, and work towards social change (Omodan, 2022a). They also engage in critical analysis, critique existing structures, and advocate for the marginalised (Romm, 2015). This paradigm draws from critical theory and employs interdisciplinary approaches to illuminate structural inequalities and encourages reflexivity, actively involving participants and fostering collaboration with communities impacted by social injustices (Mertens, 2007). See Chapter 4 for a comprehensive conceptualisation and analysis of the transformative paradigm.

- **Postcolonial Indigenous Paradigm:** The paradigm emerged from the experiences of colonised peoples and the recognition of the need to decolonise knowledge production. It centres indigenous communities' perspectives, voices, and knowledge, challenging Western dominance in research (Chilisa, 2019). Postcolonial indigenous researchers prioritise cultural revitalisation, self-determination, and recognising diverse ways of knowing. They engage in collaborative and community-based research, acknowledging indigenous knowledge systems and advocating for the rights and well-being of indigenous peoples. See Chapter 5 for a comprehensive conceptualisation and analysis of the postcolonial indigenous paradigm.
- **Pragmatism:** The pragmatist paradigm focuses on practicality and integrating methods that best answer the research question (Morgan, 2013). Unlike the positivist paradigm, which emphasises objectivity and the use of quantitative methods, or the interpretivist paradigm, which values subjective meaning and employs qualitative techniques, pragmatism allows for the use of both qualitative and quantitative approaches. This paradigm recognises that different types of data can provide complementary insights and is more concerned with the problem to be solved than the methods used to solve it (Kaushik & Walsh, 2019). The pragmatist researcher is often more flexible, adapting to the needs of the research rather than adhering to strict philosophical positions. This contrasts the critical paradigm's focus on power structures and the postcolonial indigenous paradigm's emphasis on decolonising knowledge. In pragmatism, the emphasis is on finding what works to answer specific questions and solve problems, reflecting a practical, real-world orientation that is willing to use any available methods, techniques, or theories. See Chapter 6 for a comprehensive conceptualisation and analysis of the pragmatist paradigm.

When comparing these paradigms, several vital distinctions emerge. Positivism prioritises objectivity, quantitative methods, and causal relationships, seeking to uncover generalisable laws. Interpretivism/constructivism values subjectivity, qualitative methods, and context, emphasising the role of human agency in constructing social reality. Critical/transformative paradigms focus on power dynamics, inequality, and social change, employing interdisciplinary approaches and challenging dominant structures. While postcolonial indigenous paradigms emphasise decolonisation, centring marginalised voices and indigenous knowledge systems, and fostering collaborative and community-based research and pragmatism, which focus on flexibility, adapting to the needs of the research rather than adhering to protocol. It is important to note that these paradigms are not mutually exclusive, and researchers often draw on multiple paradigms or employ mixed-methods approaches. The choice of paradigm depends on the research questions, the nature of the phenomena under investigation, and the researcher's philosophical and methodological orientations. Therefore, understanding the distinctions and compatibilities between these paradigms enables researchers to make informed choices and select appropriate methods that align with their research goals.

Therefore, major research paradigms such as positivism, interpretivism/constructivism, critical/transformative, postcolonial indigenous and pragmatism paradigms provide distinct lenses for understanding and conducting research in the social sciences. While each paradigm has its own philosophical foundations and methodological preferences, they collectively contribute to advancing knowledge by addressing different aspects of the social world. Hence, recognising the similarities and differences between these paradigms allows researchers to engage in interdisciplinary dialogue, make informed methodological choices, and navigate the complexities of social research.

## 1.5 The Philosophical Foundations of Research Paradigms

This section discusses the philosophical foundations of research paradigms: epistemology, ontology, axiology, and methodology. These philosophical pillars form the basis for building research paradigms, guiding researchers' understanding of knowledge, reality, values, and the methods they employ. These foundations offer researchers the underlying knowledge of the assumptions and perspectives that shape their research approaches. Therefore, they are essential for researchers as they conduct research and make conscious choices regarding their paradigmatic stance, research design, data collection methods, and interpretation of findings. Consequently, researchers can critically engage with their assumptions and reflexive practices and meaningfully contribute to paradigmatic dialogue within their respective fields.

### 1.5.1 Epistemology

Epistemology in research paradigms pertains to the study of knowledge and how it is acquired, justified, and understood within a particular framework. It explores the underlying assumptions and beliefs about the nature of knowledge, the methods of inquiry, and the criteria for establishing truth claims (Tuli, 2010). That is, epistemology is an essential aspect of research paradigms that influences the researcher's approach to knowledge creation.

Different research paradigms have distinct epistemological perspectives. In the positivist paradigm, epistemology is rooted in the belief that knowledge is obtained through objective observation and empirical evidence (Godwin et al., 2021). This is because positivist researchers aim to uncover generalisable laws and causality, utilising quantitative methods and emphasising replicability and reliability (Dieronitou, 2014). In contrast, interpretivist paradigms embrace a subjective and socially constructed view of knowledge (Adil et al., 2022). Epistemologically, this paradigm emphasises the importance of understanding subjective meanings, social contexts, and the multiple perspectives of individuals. Researchers adopting interpretive paradigms employ qualitative methods, such as interviews, observations, and textual analysis, to capture the complexity and richness of human experiences.

The critical and transformative paradigm takes an epistemological stance that acknowledges the influence of power structures on knowledge production. Epistemologically, critical researchers aim to uncover hidden power dynamics, challenge oppressive systems, and promote social change (Mertens, 2007). They critically analyse social, economic, and political systems to unveil structural inequalities, engaging in interdisciplinary approaches and advocating for marginalised groups. In the postcolonial indigenous paradigm, epistemology recognises the importance of decolonising knowledge production and centring indigenous perspectives (Chilisa, 2019). It emphasises the revitalisation of indigenous knowledge systems, self-determination, and the inclusion of diverse ways of knowing and understanding the world.

In the pragmatism paradigm, the epistemological stance is characterised by a flexible approach that recognises the complementary strengths of objective and subjective inquiry methods (Kaushik & Walsh, 2019). Pragmatism values practical solutions and real-world applications, often integrating quantitative and qualitative approaches to develop a more comprehensive understanding. The focus is on solving specific problems, and truth is what works best in terms of practical outcomes. This alignment with practicality allows pragmatism to bridge other paradigms, seeking the most suitable methods for the research question at hand.

Therefore, the epistemological foundations of research paradigms enable researchers to make informed choices regarding research design, methods, and interpretation of findings. By implication, epistemological underpinnings also allow researchers to engage in intellectual dialogue and produce knowledge consistent with the chosen paradigm's philosophical foundations.

### 1.5.2 Ontology

Ontology in research paradigms refers to the philosophical study of the nature of reality and existence. It explores and guides researchers on fundamental questions about the nature of social phenomena, entities, and the relationship between the researcher and the *researched* (Chilisa & Phatshwane, 2022). Ontology examines the assumptions that underlie different research paradigms and their implications for knowledge creation, influencing researchers' perspectives on whether social phenomena are socially constructed or have an objective and independent existence.

Ontological perspectives can range from realism, which posits an objective reality that exists independently of human perception, to social constructionism, which views reality as a product of social and cultural processes. The researcher's ontological stance shapes the choice of research design, data collection, and interpretation of findings. For example, in a positivist paradigm with a realist ontology, the researcher may aim to discover and uncover objective truths about the social world using methods that emphasise external validity and generalisability (Al-Saadi, 2014). In contrast, within an interpretive paradigm with a social constructionist ontology, the researcher may focus on understanding the diverse perspectives and meanings attributed by individuals, employing qualitative methods to capture the subjective nature of reality (Adil et al., 2022).

In a transformative paradigm, the researcher acknowledges that reality is shaped by social, political, cultural, economic, and gender values (Romm, 2015). A study guided by this paradigm might investigate the systemic barriers that marginalised communities face in accessing education, recognising that these barriers are both real and historically constructed. Within a postcolonial indigenous paradigm, the researcher understands that reality is interconnected and often defined by relationships between people, culture, nature, and the spiritual world (Chilisa & Phatshwane, 2022). An example of research in this paradigm might involve exploring indigenous communities' relationship with their ancestral lands, among others.

In the pragmatism paradigm, which is often associated with a pluralistic ontology, the researcher recognises that reality is complex and multifaceted, as discussed above. This paradigm allows for the integration of different ontological stances to solve real-world problems (Creswell & Clark, 2017; Morgan, 2014). For example, a pragmatist researcher might study urban transportation issues by combining objective data on traffic patterns (realist ontology) with subjective experiences of daily commuters (social constructionist ontology). The result might be a comprehensive understanding that leads to practical solutions, such as redesigned traffic flow or increased public transportation options. By embracing multiple realities, the pragmatism paradigm provides a flexible approach to knowledge construction and complex social phenomena.

Therefore, understanding ontology in research paradigms allows researchers to critically reflect on their assumptions about the nature of reality and social phenomena. And it helps researchers to navigate the complexities of knowledge creation by aligning their ontological stance with their research questions and methods. Hence, recognising the ontological underpinnings of research, researchers can make informed choices that are consistent with their philosophical and theoretical perspectives.

### 1.5.3 Axiology

Axiology in research paradigms pertains to the study of values and ethics, exploring the role of values in the research process and the researcher's stance towards objectivity, subjectivity, and the ethical responsibilities associated with conducting research. Axiology addresses questions of value neutrality, moral considerations, and the ethical implications of research (Khatri, 2020). That is, axiology acknowledges that research is not value-free and recognises the influence of the researcher's values, beliefs, and biases on the research process (De Monticelli, 2018) which involves reflecting on the ethical dimensions of research and considering the potential impacts on participants, communities, and society. One could, therefore, argue that axiological considerations involve transparency, fairness, respect for human dignity, privacy, and informed consent.

Different research paradigms have distinct axiological orientations. For instance, value neutrality and objectivity are emphasised in positivist paradigms, aiming to minimise personal biases and ensure impartiality in the research process (Killam, 2013). Researchers strive to maintain distance from the research subject and focus on objective data collection and analysis. In contrast, interpretivism recognises knowledge's subjectivity and embraces the researcher's subjective perspective. Researchers in these paradigms are more likely to acknowledge their values and subjectivity and actively engage in reflexivity to understand their impact on the research process. Axiology also plays a significant role in the transformative paradigm. Researchers adopting these paradigms often commit to social justice and aim to challenge power structures and address social inequalities (Mertens, 2007). Ethical considerations are central to their work as they navigate issues of power, representation, and advocacy for marginalised communities. They prioritise the ethical treatment of participants, collaboration with communities, and ensuring that research outcomes contribute to positive social change.

In the postcolonial indigenous paradigm, axiology is deeply rooted in indigenous cultures' values, ethics, and beliefs (Chilisa & Phatshwane, 2022). Researchers working within this paradigm are committed to decolonising research methods and honouring indigenous knowledge systems. An example might involve a study of traditional agricultural practices within an indigenous community. The researcher would actively engage with community members, respecting their wisdom and cultural values, and work collaboratively to ensure that the research process and outcomes align with the community's needs and interests. The pragmatism paradigm, on the other hand, emphasises practical outcomes and problem-solving. Axiologically, pragmatist researchers are often guided by what works best in a particular context rather than adhering to rigid philosophical or ethical stances (Kaushik & Walsh, 2019). For example, in a study of environmental conservation, a pragmatist researcher might combine different methodologies, such as scientific measurements of pollution levels and community interviews about local attitudes towards conservation. The researcher's values would be oriented towards finding the most effective and practical solutions to the environmental challenges at hand, even if it means transcending traditional boundaries between qualitative and quantitative methods.

Hence, understanding axiology in research paradigms is crucial for researchers as it guides them in making ethical decisions throughout the research process. It encourages researchers to critically reflect on their values, biases, and the potential impact of their research on participants and society. Axiological considerations inform the researcher's approach to data collection, analysis, and dissemination of findings, ensuring that research is conducted with integrity and aligns with ethical standards. Therefore, by recognising the axiological dimensions of research, researchers can navigate ethical complexities and contribute to knowledge creation in an ethically responsible manner.

### 1.5.4 Methodology

Methodology refers to the systematic approach and principles used to guide the research process within a particular paradigm. It encompasses the overall framework, procedures, and techniques researchers employ to collect, analyse, and interpret data (Patel & Patel, 2019), including the ontological, epistemological, and axiological underpinnings of a research paradigm that influence methods in any research process.

In positivist paradigms, methodology emphasises rigorous and standardised quantitative methods. Researchers employ experimental designs, surveys, and statistical analysis to collect numerical data and test hypotheses (Park et al., 2020). The focus is on objectivity, generalisability, and establishing causal relationships. Park et al. (2020) further argue that positivist methodology emphasises reliability and validity, ensuring the research findings are replicable and accurately reflect the phenomena under investigation. In interpretive paradigms, methodology shifts towards qualitative approaches, emphasising understanding subjective meanings and social contexts. Researchers employ methods such as interviews, observations, and textual analysis to capture the richness, complexity, and nuances of human experiences. Therefore, these premises confirm that interpretive methodology focuses on in-depth exploration, emphasising contextual understanding and capturing participants' perspectives and lived experiences (Frechette et al., 2020).

Transformative paradigms employ diverse methodologies that reflect their commitment to social justice and challenging power structures. Researchers within these paradigms often utilise participatory action research, collaborative methods, and critical discourse analysis. They engage with communities, giving voice to marginalised groups and involving them in the research process. Methodology within transformative paradigms is designed to empower participants, challenge existing norms, and contribute to social change (Mertens, 2007). In the postcolonial indigenous paradigm, the methodology also encompasses diverse approaches that align with its goals of decolonisation, cultural revitalisation, and empowering indigenous communities. Researchers within this paradigm may utilise community-based participatory research, oral histories, and storytelling methodologies, emphasising collaboration, indigenous knowledge systems, and the recognition of diverse ways of knowing.

In the pragmatism paradigm, the methodology is not confined to a strict tradition but combines quantitative and qualitative methods, reflecting practical problem-solving needs. For example, a study on educational policy might use standardised testing to measure achievement and interviews to understand perceptions. By employing a mixed-methods approach, the researcher provides a comprehensive understanding of the issue, harnessing the strengths of both paradigms. The pragmatism methodology emphasises actionable insights, aligning research design with the specific questions being asked, and is driven by a desire to inform policy and practice.

Therefore, methodology is a crucial component of research paradigms as it guides the researcher in systematically collecting, analysing, and interpreting data. It helps researchers address their research questions, align their methods with the philosophical foundations of their paradigm, and ensure the validity and reliability of findings. Hence, methodological choices should be consistent with the paradigm's epistemological, ontological, and axiological assumptions, allowing researchers to produce rigorous and meaningful research outcomes. Understanding the methodology within the chosen paradigm enables researchers to make informed decisions about research design, data collection methods, and data analysis techniques.

## 1.6 Aligning Research Questions and Paradigms

Methodology and methods are crucial components of the research process, shaping how researchers approach and investigate their research questions within a specific paradigm. The alignment between research questions and paradigms is essential to ensure coherence and rigour in the research design and to generate meaningful and relevant findings. This section explores the importance of aligning research questions with the appropriate methodology and methods within different research paradigms.

The choice of methodology depends on the paradigm's underlying epistemological and ontological assumptions (Omodan, 2022b). For example, in a positivist paradigm, research questions may focus on causal relationships and the generalisability of findings. Therefore, quantitative methods such as surveys, experiments, and statistical analysis would be appropriate to gather and analyse data. On the other hand, the interpretivist paradigm emphasises understanding subjective meanings and social contexts. Research questions within these paradigms might explore individuals' lived experiences and perspectives, necessitating the use of qualitative methods such as interviews, observations, and textual analysis. In a transformative paradigm, research questions may focus on social inequalities and the promotion of social justice. Therefore, methods such as participatory action research, collaborative methods, or critical discourse analysis would be appropriate to engage and empower marginalised communities. Also, in the postcolonial indigenous paradigm, research questions may explore indigenous knowledge, rights, or cultural heritage. Therefore, methodologies like community-based participatory research, oral histories, and storytelling would be suitable, emphasising collaboration with indigenous communities. And lastly, in a pragmatism paradigm, research questions could aim at practical problem-solving or integrating different viewpoints. Therefore, a mixed-methods approach, combining quantitative techniques like surveys and qualitative methods like interviews, would be appropriate to comprehensively understand the problem.

The alignment between research questions and methodology also ensures that researchers can effectively address their research objectives. This is in line with the argument of Ramsay-Jordan et al. (2022) that a well-crafted research question provides clarity and direction, guiding researchers in selecting the appropriate methodology and methods to obtain the desired insights. For instance, a research question that aims to explore the impact of a social intervention program on a specific community's well-being would benefit from a mixed-methods approach. This could involve collecting quantitative and qualitative data to measure outcomes to understand the participants' lived experiences and subjective perspectives. Most importantly, the alignment between research questions and paradigms contributes to the overall coherence and integrity of the research. This means that a mismatch between the research question and the chosen paradigm can lead to inconsistencies and potential limitations in the research design and findings. For example, attempting to answer a research question about individual experiences using a purely positivist paradigm might overlook the richness and complexity of human subjectivity.

Furthermore, aligning research questions and paradigms allows researchers to leverage the strengths and advantages of each paradigm (Järvinen, 2000). Different paradigms offer unique perspectives and methodologies that can shed light on different aspects of the research question. Hence, it is essential to note that alignment between research questions and paradigms does not imply rigid adherence or exclusivity to a single paradigm. Researchers often adopt mixed-methods approaches or draw on multiple paradigms to address complex research questions. This interdisciplinary approach enables researchers to triangulate findings, enrich their understanding, and explore different facets of the research topic.

Therefore, aligning research questions with the appropriate methodology and methods within a specific research paradigm is crucial for conducting rigorous and meaningful research towards ensuring coherence, integrity, and relevance in the research design and facilitating the generation of valuable insights. By considering the paradigm's underlying epistemological and ontological assumptions and research objectives, researchers can select the most suitable methodology and methods to effectively address their research questions. The overall argument is that alignment between research questions and paradigms enhances the quality of research, fosters interdisciplinary engagement, and contributes to the advancement of valid knowledge.

### 1.6.1 Case Studies on How to Align Research Questions With Paradigms

**Case 1:** To illustrate the process of aligning research questions with paradigms, let's consider a case study on the topic of gender inequality in the workplace.

Suppose a researcher aims to investigate the experiences of women in leadership positions and their strategies for overcoming barriers in a male-dominated industry. In this case, an interpretive paradigm may be appropriate to capture the subjective meanings and social contexts of women's experiences. The research question could be framed as follows: *"How do women leaders navigate and challenge gender-based barriers in the XYZ industry?"* This research question aligns with the interpretivist paradigm, as it seeks to understand women's lived experiences, perspectives, and strategies in the workplace. To align the research question with the paradigm, the researcher can select qualitative methods that emphasise understanding subjective meanings and capturing rich, contextual data. In this case, methods such as in-depth interviews with women leaders, participant observation in workplace settings, and analysis of relevant organisational documents could be employed. These methods allow the researcher to delve into the complexities of gender inequality, exploring the strategies employed by women leaders and the social dynamics within the industry. By aligning the research question with the interpretivist paradigm and selecting appropriate qualitative methods, the researcher can gain deep insights into the experiences of women leaders, the challenges they face, and the strategies they employ to overcome gender-based barriers. This alignment ensures that the research design and methods are consistent with the philosophical foundations of the chosen paradigm, leading to a comprehensive and nuanced understanding of the research topic.

Note that the case study provided is an example, and the choice of paradigm and methods should be carefully considered based on the specific research context, objectives, and available resources. The process of aligning research questions with paradigms requires thoughtful reflection and an understanding of the philosophical underpinnings of the paradigms to ensure a coherent and rigorous research design.

*Case 2:* Let's consider a case study exploring the impact of a specific teaching methodology on students' academic performance in a secondary school setting. The researcher aims to investigate whether the implementation of an inquiry-based learning approach leads to improved academic outcomes compared to traditional lecture-based instruction. To align the research question with the positivist paradigm, the researcher formulates the question as follows: *"What is the effect of implementing an inquiry-based learning approach on students' academic performance in a secondary school setting?"* This research question aligns with the positivist paradigm, which seeks to establish a cause-and-effect relationship between the teaching methodology and academic performance, focusing on measurable outcomes. To ensure the alignment of the research question with the positivist paradigm, the researcher would employ quantitative methods and collect data that can be objectively measured and analysed. For instance, the researcher may conduct pre- and post-tests to assess students' academic performance, comparing the scores of those who received inquiry-based instruction with those who received lecture-based instruction. This approach enables the researcher to gather numerical data that can be analysed statistically, allowing for testing hypotheses and drawing causal inferences. By aligning the research question with the positivist paradigm and employing appropriate quantitative methods, the researcher can obtain objective data on the impact of the teaching methodology on students' academic performance. The use of rigorous methods and statistical analysis contributes to the reliability and generalisability of the findings, as they are based on measurable outcomes and can be replicated in similar educational contexts.

Note that the case study provided is an example, and the choice of paradigm and methods should be carefully considered based on the specific research context and objectives. It is crucial to ensure that the research design aligns with the philosophical foundations of the positivist paradigm, emphasising objectivity, quantifiability, and the establishment of causal relationships.

*Case 3:* Let's consider a case study examining the experiences of individuals from marginalised communities in accessing healthcare services and the potential barriers they face. The researcher aims to explore the systemic factors that contribute to healthcare disparities and propose strategies for addressing these inequalities within the healthcare system. To align the research question with the transformative/critical paradigm, the researcher formulates the question as follows: *"What are the structural and systemic factors contributing to healthcare disparities among marginalised communities, and how can the healthcare system be transformed to promote health equity?"* This research question aligns with the transformative/critical paradigm as it seeks to critically analyse power structures, challenge existing systems, and propose transformative strategies for social change. To ensure the alignment of the research question with the transformative/critical paradigm, the researcher would employ a mix of qualitative and participatory methods. This may involve conducting interviews with individuals from marginalised communities, engaging in focus group discussions, and collaborating with community organisations and healthcare providers. These methods allow the researcher to explore the lived experiences, perspectives, and insights of marginalised individuals and stakeholders, ensuring their voices are heard and empowering them in the research process. By aligning the research question with the transformative/critical paradigm and employing participatory methods, the researcher can uncover the underlying power dynamics and systemic barriers contributing to healthcare disparities. The research aims to generate knowledge that can inform policy changes and transformative interventions within the healthcare system to promote health equity and social justice for marginalised communities.

Note that the case study provided is an example, and the choice of paradigm and methods should be carefully considered based on the specific research context and objectives. It is crucial to ensure that the research design aligns with the philosophical foundations of the transformative/critical paradigm, emphasising the critical analysis of power structures, engagement with marginalised communities, and the pursuit of social change.

*Case 4:* Let's consider a case study examining the impact of colonial policies on the cultural identity and well-being of indigenous youth in a specific community. The researcher aims to explore indigenous youth's experiences and perspectives and strategies for cultural revitalisation and empowerment. To align the research question with the postcolonial/indigenous paradigm, the researcher formulates the question as follows: *"How do colonial policies and practices impact the cultural identity and well-being of indigenous youth, and what strategies can be employed to promote cultural revitalisation and empowerment?"* This research question aligns with the postcolonial/indigenous paradigm as it seeks to centre the experiences and voices of indigenous youth, challenge colonial influences, and promote the decolonisation and empowerment of indigenous communities. To ensure the alignment of the research question with the postcolonial/indigenous paradigm, the researcher would employ a community-based and participatory research approach. This may involve collaborating with indigenous community members, elders, and youth to co-create the research process, ensuring their perspectives are central to the study. Methods such as storytelling, focus groups, and cultural mapping may capture the multifaceted nature of indigenous youth experiences and their cultural revitalisation efforts. By aligning the research question with the postcolonial/indigenous paradigm and employing community-based and participatory methods, the researcher can uncover the impacts of colonial policies on indigenous youth, highlight cultural strengths and resilience, and promote strategies for cultural revitalisation and empowerment. The research aims to contribute to the recognition and validation of indigenous knowledge systems, advocate for the rights and well-being of indigenous youth, and support efforts towards self-determination and decolonisation.

Note that the case study provided is an example, and the choice of paradigm and methods should be carefully considered based on the specific research context and objectives. It is crucial to ensure that the research design aligns with the philosophical foundations of the postcolonial/indigenous paradigm, emphasising the recognition of indigenous voices, cultural revitalisation, and the promotion of self-determination and decolonisation.

*Case 5:* Let's consider a case study that investigates the best methods for reducing waste and increasing recycling in urban environments. The researcher is interested in both the practical outcomes and the diverse perspectives of the residents and local authorities. They pose the research question: *"What combination of policies, community engagement, and technological innovations can effectively reduce waste and enhance recycling in an urban context?"* This research question aligns with the pragmatism paradigm as it seeks to solve a real-world problem, emphasising the integration of various methods and the collaboration between different stakeholders. To align with the pragmatist paradigm, the researcher may choose mixed methods, including surveys to quantify residents' recycling behaviours, interviews with policymakers to understand potential regulations and observations of waste management practices. The research could also involve a participatory design with community workshops to co-create waste reduction strategies. Therefore, by aligning the research question with the pragmatism paradigm and employing a blend of qualitative and quantitative methods, the researcher can generate a comprehensive understanding of the waste reduction challenge. They can create practical recommendations that consider both empirical evidence and the contextual and subjective experiences of those involved. This alignment ensures that the research design is consistent with the philosophical foundations of the pragmatism paradigm, emphasising practical solutions, the collaboration of various stakeholders, and the flexibility in the use of methods.

Note that the case study provided is an example, and the choice of paradigm and methods should be carefully considered based on the specific research context, objectives, and available resources. Ensuring that the research design aligns with the philosophical foundations of the chosen paradigm, leading to effective solutions to real-world challenges is crucial.

## 1.7 Navigating the Complexities of Research Paradigms

Research paradigms are multifaceted frameworks that encompass a wide array of philosophical, theoretical, and methodological perspectives. The complexities inherent within these paradigms require researchers to navigate them skilfully to conduct rigorous and meaningful research. This section explores the intricate nature of research paradigms by highlighting their ten associated complexities. These complexities include questions of objectivity and subjectivity, debates on validity and reliability, power dynamics and representation, ethical considerations, the role of theory and generalisability, the ongoing qualitative-quantitative debate, paradigm compatibility and integration, the influence of context and reflexivity, the dynamic nature of paradigms, and the impact of paradigms on research outcomes. Recognising these complexities is crucial for researchers as they embark on their research journey. A comprehensive list of strategies is provided to assist researchers in navigating these intricacies. These strategies encompass understanding the paradigm landscape, promoting reflexivity and self-awareness, embracing flexibility and openness, utilising methodological pluralism, engaging in collaborative and participatory research, pursuing continuous learning and professional development, considering ethical considerations, engaging in reflexive iteration, participating in scholarly dialogue and debates, and seeking mentorship and collaboration. Therefore, incorporating these strategies into research practice enables researchers to effectively navigate the complexities of research paradigms, ensuring that their research is robust, rigorous, and impactful.

Below are ten common complexities researchers face and provide strategies to navigate them.

1. **Ontological Assumptions**: Ontology refers to the researcher's assumptions about the nature of reality and what can be considered valid knowledge (Adil et al., 2022). Researchers encounter the complexity of different ontological perspectives, such as realism, constructivism, or pragmatism. To navigate this complexity effectively, researchers should critically reflect on their ontological assumptions and examine how these assumptions shape their research questions, methodology, and interpretation of findings. By explicitly stating their ontological stance, researchers can then ensure coherence and transparency in their research design, allowing readers to understand the philosophical foundation upon which their study is based.
2. **Epistemological Considerations**: Epistemology pertains to how knowledge is acquired, validated, and understood (Tuli, 2010). Researchers must grapple with questions such as how knowledge is constructed, the role of the researcher in knowledge production, and the nature of truth claims. To navigate this complexity, researchers should clarify their epistemological stance and identify the most appropriate methods for generating and validating knowledge within their chosen paradigm. For example, researchers adopting an interpretive paradigm may prioritise understanding subjective experiences through in-depth interviews or observations, while those adhering to a positivist paradigm may emphasise quantitative methods and statistical analysis to establish empirical generalisations.
3. **Methodological Choices**: Methodology encompasses the research approaches, methods, and techniques used to gather and analyse data (Patel & Patel, 2019). Researchers face the complexity of selecting the most suitable methods within their chosen paradigm. To navigate this, researchers should comprehensively review available methods and techniques, consider the fit between the research question and methodology, seek expert advice, and ensure that their chosen methods align with their paradigm's underlying assumptions and goals. Additionally, researchers should be aware of their chosen methods' limitations and potential biases and employ strategies to mitigate them, such as triangulation or member checking.
4. **Ethical Considerations**: Research ethics is a critical complexity that researchers must navigate. Ethical considerations encompass respecting participants' autonomy, protecting their privacy and confidentiality, minimising harm, and ensuring equitable treatment (Okeke et al., 2022). Researchers should familiarise themselves with ethical standards and guidelines specific to their field and seek institutional ethical review and approval. To navigate ethical complexities effectively, researchers should be mindful of power dynamics in the research process, obtain informed consent from participants, provide clear information about the study's purpose and procedures, and address any potential risks or discomfort that participants may encounter.

5. **Power Dynamics and Representation**: Power imbalances and the representation of diverse voices are significant complexities within research paradigms (Fitzgerald, 2004; Hardy & Clegg, 2006; Karnieli-Miller et al., 2009;). These issues are particularly pronounced in research with children, Indigenous communities, and diverse cultural and gender groups. The tension between power redistribution and methodological challenges in qualitative research further complicates these dynamics. Despite the potential of participatory research to address power imbalances, the gap between theory and practice remains a challenge. Gender dynamics in research teams can also influence the production of knowledge, highlighting the need for a more inclusive and equitable research process. Therefore, researchers should be aware of their own positions of power and strive to ensure fair representation and inclusion of marginalised or underrepresented groups. To navigate this complexity, researchers should seek diverse perspectives by purposefully sampling participants from different backgrounds, engaging in participatory research approaches involving participants as active partners, and promoting collaboration and dialogue with marginalised communities. By sharing power in the research process and involving participants in decision-making, researchers can foster a more inclusive and empowering research environment.

6. **Researcher Positionality**: Researcher positionality is critical in qualitative research, influencing the research process and findings (Holmes, 2020). It presents ethical and methodological dilemmas, particularly for "insider" researchers (Moore, 2012), and is a multi-dimensional and developmental concept, challenging the insider/outsider dichotomy (Lu & Hodge, 2019). Hence, researchers are expected to grapple with their own positionality, including their social, cultural, and personal backgrounds that may influence the research process and outcomes. Researchers should acknowledge their biases, be reflexive, and critically reflect on how their positionality may impact the research design, data collection, analysis, and interpretation. By engaging in reflexivity, researchers can actively examine how their personal experiences, beliefs, and values shape their research and ensure that they remain transparent about their positionality. Additionally, researchers should consider the potential impact of their positionality on participant engagement, data collection, and the interpretation of findings.

7. **Paradigm Compatibility and Integration**: Researchers may encounter challenges when integrating or bridging different research paradigms. To navigate this complexity, researchers should engage in interdisciplinary research collaborations and seek common ground between paradigms. This can involve exploring how different paradigms conceptualise similar phenomena, identifying shared assumptions or theoretical perspectives, or utilising mixed-methods approaches that leverage the strengths of multiple paradigms. By fostering dialogue and collaboration with researchers from different disciplines and paradigms, researchers can enrich their understanding, challenge their own assumptions, and expand their methodological repertoire.

## Understanding Research Paradigm 21

8  **Data Analysis and Interpretation**: Analysing and interpreting data within a specific research paradigm can be complex. Researchers should carefully consider the analytical techniques and interpretive frameworks that align with their chosen paradigm. They should engage in iterative data analysis, seeking peer feedback or external validation to ensure that their interpretations are consistent with their chosen paradigm and capture the richness of the data. Researchers should also consider the context in which the data was collected, reflect on their own biases, and critically examine alternative interpretations to ensure the robustness and validity of their findings.

9  **Theoretical Frameworks**: The selection and application of appropriate theoretical frameworks within a research paradigm have been a serious concern for young researchers, most especially students (Omodan, 2022b). Hence, researchers need to critically review existing theories, choose frameworks that align with their research questions and objectives, and explore how these theories can inform their research design, analysis, and interpretation. By carefully selecting and applying theoretical frameworks, researchers can enhance the theoretical underpinnings of their research and contribute to knowledge development in their field. It is essential to articulate how the chosen theoretical framework informs the research questions, guides the data collection and analysis process, and shapes the interpretation of findings.

10  **Researcher Bias and Objectivity**: Jukola (2015) and Mantzoukas (2005) both emphasise the importance of context and reflexivity in ensuring objectivity, with the latter arguing that bias cannot be excluded from the research process. Therefore, researchers must navigate the complexities of their own biases and strive for objectivity within their chosen paradigm. To address this complexity, researchers should be transparent about their potential biases and acknowledge them as part of the research process. Employing rigorous research design and methods, engaging in peer review or external validation, seeking diverse perspectives, and documenting the decision-making process can help mitigate personal biases and enhance the objectivity of the research. Researchers should be vigilant in critically examining their assumptions and interpretations to ensure that their findings are grounded in evidence rather than preconceived notions.

### 1.8 Summary

The chapter provides a comprehensive overview of research paradigms in the social sciences. It presents the importance of research paradigms, discusses the historical development of paradigms, and compares major paradigms. The chapter delves into the philosophical foundations of research paradigms, including epistemology, ontology, axiology, and methodology. It examines the complexities within research paradigms and offers strategies to navigate them effectively. The chapter emphasises the alignment of research questions with paradigms and provides case studies illustrating how different paradigms are applied. It concludes by highlighting the challenges and considerations in navigating research paradigms and the importance of continuous learning and critical engagement in advancing research in the social sciences. Most importantly, the chapter serves as a comprehensive guide for researchers seeking to understand the complexities of research paradigms to conduct rigorous and impactful social science research.

# 2 Positivist Paradigm and Methodological Alignment

**Chapter Synopsis**

In this chapter, in-depth exploration is undertaken to delve into the positivist and post-positivist paradigms and their methodological implications in research. The chapter uncovers valuable insights into the foundations, assumptions, and evolution of positivism and post-positivism, as these paradigms shape our understanding and approach to studying the world. It begins by contextualising the positivist paradigms and explaining the key concepts and assumptions underlying positivism. Furthermore, the chapter presents the critiques and modifications that have contributed to the evolution of post-positivism, explores methodological approaches employed within this paradigm, and examines how to align research questions with the appropriate paradigm. Additionally, it delves into the data collection methods utilised in positivist research, addresses data analysis and interpretation within these paradigms, discusses critiques and debates in the field, and finally explores the delicate balance between objectivity and subjectivity in research within the positivist and post-positivist frameworks.

## 2.1 Concept of Positivist Paradigm

The positivist paradigm is a research worldview emphasising objectivity, empirical evidence, and the search for universal laws governing phenomena. It is often associated with the natural sciences but is also applied to social sciences, which assumes that the world operates according to predictable patterns that can be observed and measured (Aliyu et al., 2014; Ochulor, 2005). In the positivist paradigm, researchers aim to study the world unbiased and value-free. In most cases, it relies on systematic observation data collection using quantitative methods (Crook & Garratt, 2005). The goal is to gather empirical evidence through controlled experiments or surveys and then analyse the data using statistical techniques.

Positivist researchers believe that knowledge can be acquired through the careful study of observable phenomena and the formulation of general principles or laws. They seek to uncover cause-and-effect relationships and

DOI: 10.4324/9781003484066-2

establish objective truths about the world (Arghode, 2012). This approach often involves breaking down complex phenomena into smaller, measurable units to facilitate analysis and prediction. One can then argue that it provides a clear framework for conducting research and ensures that findings are based on observable evidence rather than subjective opinions or personal biases. The emphasis on objectivity helps researchers maintain a level of impartiality in their observations and analysis, thereby enhancing the credibility and reliability of their research.

Furthermore, the positivist paradigm offers a range of quantitative methods that enable researchers to collect and analyse data systematically and standardised (Ryan, 2015). By employing controlled experiments or surveys, researchers can gather empirical evidence on a large scale, allowing for generalisations and predictions. This emphasis on quantification facilitates comparisons and statistical analyses, enabling researchers to identify patterns, trends, relationships, and differences within their data. Hence, the positivist paradigm provides researchers with a solid foundation for conducting research by emphasising objectivity, empirical evidence, and the search for universal laws. It offers a structured framework that ensures rigorous data collection and analysis, enhancing the credibility of research findings. However, researchers must be mindful of the paradigm's limitations and be open to employing alternative approaches when studying complex, subjective, or culturally embedded phenomena.

## 2.2 The Evolution of Positivism Paradigm

Positivism is a philosophical and scientific paradigm that emerged in the 19th century and profoundly impacted various disciplines, including sociology, philosophy, and the natural sciences (Halfpenny, 2014; Kaboub, 2008). At its core, positivism is based on the belief that knowledge should be derived from empirical observations and scientific methods, emphasising the use of reason and logic to understand the world (Goduka, 2012). This approach sought to establish a rigorous and systematic way of studying phenomena by relying on measurable and observable data. Auguste Comte, often regarded as the "father of sociology," played a crucial role in the development of positivism (Comte, 1975; Sarton, 1952). He introduced the term "positivism" and advocated for the application of scientific methods to the study of society, aiming to transform sociology into a legitimate scientific discipline.

However, positivism was not without its critics. As the 20th century dawned, scholars began to question the positivist assumption of value-free objectivity and the idea of a completely neutral observer. Logical positivism, a stage that emerged during this period, emphasised the verification of statements through logical and empirical means. The Vienna Circle, a group of philosophers and scientists, championed this approach, seeking to distinguish meaningful statements that could be empirically verified from those they deemed meaningless expressions of emotion or personal preference

(Stadler, 2015). As the 20th century progressed, post-positivism gained momentum as a response to the limitations of traditional positivism. Post-positivists acknowledged that researchers could not be entirely detached from the subjects they studied and that observable, objective facts did not solely determine social phenomena (Panhwar et al., 2017). This perspective incorporated some interpretive and critical elements into scientific research, recognising the role of interpretation, subjectivity, and context.

Despite the rise of post-positivism, elements of traditional positivism continue to persist in contemporary scientific research. Many scientists still emphasise the importance of empirical evidence, systematic observation, and the falsifiability of hypotheses. However, contemporary positivism tends to be more nuanced, integrating insights from other philosophical and scientific paradigms. It acknowledges the complexities of the human experience and the limitations of purely empirical approaches, recognising the value of considering social and cultural contexts in scientific inquiry.

In a null shell, the evolution of positivism has been marked by a gradual refinement of its core ideas and the incorporation of insights from other philosophical and scientific perspectives. Positivism's emphasis on empirical observation and logical reasoning has shaped the methods and approaches of many scientific disciplines. However, the following paradigms have recognised the limitations of strict positivism and sought to integrate more interpretive and critical elements into research. Ultimately, the legacy of positivism continues to influence modern science and social sciences, albeit in conjunction with other paradigms that recognise the importance of understanding human behaviour and society in a broader context, such as interpretive paradigm, transformative paradigm, postcolonial indigenous paradigm, and pragmatist paradigm (Chilisa & Phatshwane, 2022; Morgan, 2014; Potrac et al., 2014; Romm, 2015).

## 2.3 Philosophical Foundations of Positivism Paradigm

The philosophical foundations of the positivist paradigm encompass its epistemology, ontology, axiology, and methodology, shaping its approach to research and knowledge production.

### 2.3.1 Epistemology of Positivist Paradigm

Epistemology within the positivist paradigm, which is fundamentally grounded in empiricism, emphasises the acquisition of knowledge through direct observation and measurable phenomena. Positivists assert that empirical evidence is the cornerstone for understanding the natural and social world and that through systematic observation and quantitative methods, researchers can detect patterns, causal relationships, and regularities (Dieronitou, 2014). This philosophy leads positivists to prioritise objective, replicable data that can be precisely measured (Godwin et al., 2021). In the eyes of positivists, the scientific method stands as the epitome of reliable knowledge acquisition, enabling the careful and controlled testing of hypotheses and the systematic accumulation of evidence to support or debunk theories. Such a research process aims to discover universal truths or principles that govern phenomena, fostering a generalisable and reliable understanding. Therefore, the positivist paradigm thus shapes a rigorous and objective pathway to knowledge, excluding subjective or unobservable aspects from its realm of inquiry.

### 2.3.2  Ontology of Positivist Paradigm

Ontology within the positivist paradigm is anchored in a realist perspective, asserting that an objective reality exists outside of human perception, operating according to predictable patterns that can be systematically investigated. This conviction leads positivists to contend that the underlying causes and regularities of social and natural phenomena can be identified, analysed, and understood through rigorous, methodical research. By embracing a realist ontology, positivists are committed to the discovery of objective truths about the world, relying heavily on empirical observation and principles of objectivity (Park et al., 2020). This ontological standpoint forms the bedrock of the positivist research approach, emphasising an unwavering search for universal laws or principles that are applicable across varying contexts (Goduka, 2012). Therefore, the positivist paradigm rejects subjective interpretations or personal insights, instead focusing on a stable, consistent understanding of the world grounded in observable, measurable facts. This perspective underlines the positivist emphasis on the external, physical reality as something that can be apprehended with precision through scientific inquiry, laying the foundation for a structured and empirical approach to knowledge.

### 2.3.3  Axiology of Positivist Paradigm

Within the positivist paradigm, axiology emphasises a stringent commitment to value neutrality and objectivity in research, essentially divorcing personal values, beliefs, and biases from the investigative process (Aliyu et al., 2015). Positivists contend that research should be an unadulterated pursuit of facts, grounded in empirical evidence and logical analysis, devoid of the influences of personal opinions or moral judgements (Bahl & Milne, 2007). They advocate for an objective stance, diligently working to minimise or eradicate subjective biases that may otherwise compromise the integrity of the findings. By staunchly maintaining a value-neutral approach, positivists aim to ensure that research outcomes are reliable and untainted by the subjective preferences or perspectives of the individual researcher. This alignment with objectivity and empirical rigour is not only consistent with but central to the positivist goal of uncovering knowledge that stands on its own merits, independent of human interpretation or emotion. Therefore, the axiological perspective within the positivist paradigm serves as a fundamental guiding principle, reinforcing the pursuit of universal truths through methodical observation and measurement.

### 2.3.4 Methodology of Positivist Paradigm

Methodology within the positivist paradigm revolves around using quantitative methods and statistical analysis. Positivists employ systematic and structured approaches to collect and analyse data to uncover cause-and-effect relationships and establish generalisable laws or principles (Park et al., 2020). They prioritise the use of controlled experiments, surveys, or other systematic observations to gather data that can be quantified and analysed using statistical techniques. The goal is to produce objective and replicable findings that can be applied across different contexts. Within quantitative methods, positivists aim to reduce subjective biases and enhance the reliability of the research outcomes. According to McGregor and Murnane (2010), this methodology is rooted in the belief that numerical data and statistical analysis provide a more rigorous and objective foundation for knowledge production. The systematic and quantitative approach within the positivist paradigm allows for the identification of patterns, trends, and relationships that contribute to the understanding of the phenomena under investigation.

## 2.4 Key Concepts and Assumptions of Positivist Paradigm

The foundations of positivism encompass a set of key concepts and assumptions that underpin this research paradigm. These foundations provide the philosophical and methodological basis for the positivist approach to studying the world. Understanding these concepts and assumptions is crucial for researchers seeking to adopt the positivist paradigm in their research endeavours. The concepts and assumptions are discussed below:

- **Objectivity:** Within the positivist paradigm, objectivity is a crucial principle. Positivists posit that an objective reality exists independently of human perception (Karupiah, 2022). They strive to minimise subjective biases and personal interpretations, aiming for an objective understanding of the phenomena under study. Researchers following the positivist approach aim to observe and measure phenomena in a systematic and impartial manner, ensuring that personal biases or preconceived notions do not influence their findings.
- **Empiricism:** Positivism strongly emphasises empiricism, which refers to the reliance on empirical evidence derived from sensory experience as the primary source of knowledge (Clark, 1998; Ryan, 2018). That is, positivist researchers seek to collect data through direct observation or experimentation, employing methods that allow them to gather objective evidence to support or refute hypotheses and theories. By emphasising empiricism,

positivists aim to establish their research on observable and measurable data rather than subjective opinions or speculative interpretations.
- **Deterministic principles:** The positivist paradigm assumes that the world operates according to deterministic principles (Corry et al., 2019). This means that events and phenomena have underlying causes that can be identified through systematic investigation. Positivist researchers aim to discover and understand these causal relationships using rigorous scientific methods. By identifying these causes, they strive to establish generalisable laws or principles that can explain and predict the relationships between variables or phenomena.
- **Reductionism:** Reductionism is a concept embraced by the positivist paradigm (Yu, 2003). It involves breaking down complex phenomena into simpler, and more manageable parts for analysis. By reducing phenomena to their constituent elements, positivist researchers aim to uncover the underlying regularities and patterns that govern them. This reductionist approach allows researchers to focus on specific variables or factors that can be measured and manipulated, contributing to the overall understanding of the phenomenon under investigation.
- **Universality:** Positivism adopts a nomothetic approach, seeking to establish general laws or principles that apply universally (Konuralp, 2019). This approach is often associated with quantitative research methods and statistical analysis. That is, positivist researchers strive to identify patterns and regularities in data that can be generalised to broader populations or contexts. By identifying general laws or principles, positivism aims to provide explanations and predictions that are applicable beyond specific cases or contexts.
- **Value-free or neutral stance:** Positivism assumes a value-free or neutral stance in research (Dyzenhaus, 1983). Positivists argue that researchers should strive for objectivity by separating their personal values and beliefs from the research process. They advocate for researchers to maintain a detached, impartial perspective to minimise the influence of personal biases. The focus is on gathering and analysing data objectively without allowing personal values or preferences to sway the interpretation of the findings.
- **Realist ontology:** Positivism also adopts a realist ontology, asserting that an objective reality exists independently of human perception (Aliyu et al., 2014). Researchers within the positivist paradigm aim to uncover and understand this reality through empirical observation and measurement. They believe that adhering to scientific methods and systematic observation can gain valid insights into the underlying reality that exists irrespective of individual perspectives or interpretations.
- **Deductive approach:** Positivism assumes a deductive approach to research (Ryan, 2018). Researchers formulate hypotheses or theories based on existing knowledge, often derived from established theories or empirical evidence. These hypotheses are then tested through empirical investigation, collecting data to support or refute the hypotheses. The deductive

reasoning employed in positivism allows researchers to make predictions and draw conclusions based on the collected data, thereby contributing to the accumulation of scientific knowledge.

## 2.5 Methodological Designs in Positivist Research

Positivist research incorporates diverse methodological designs that strongly align with the paradigm's core principles of objectivity, empirical evidence, and the pursuit of generalisable laws or principles. These carefully structured designs predominantly employ quantitative methods to collect and analyse data, emphasising systematic observation and rigorous analysis. Some key methodological designs within the positivist framework include experimental design, cross-sectional design, longitudinal design, quasi-experimental design, true experimental design, case study design, comparative design, correlational design, factorial design, and Ex post facto design. Each of these designs serves distinct purposes and allows researchers to investigate different aspects of the phenomena under study while adhering to the positivist principles of systematic inquiry and empirical validation. Here are key methodological designs in positivist research and how they align with the positivist paradigm.

i **Experimental Design:** Experimental design stands as a hallmark of positivist research, epitomising its core principles through the systematic manipulation of independent variables, measurement of their effects on dependent variables, and control of extraneous factors (Kirk, 2009; Rogers & Revesz, 2019). By aiming to establish causal relationships through controlled observations and comparisons between groups, experimental designs align perfectly with the positivist paradigm's emphasis on deriving knowledge from empirical observations and scientific methods. Replicability further enhances the positivist nature of experimental design, as the ability to reproduce results strengthens the generalisability of findings and contributes to the establishment of objective and generalisable laws. Emphasising objectivity in research, experimental designs minimise bias and personal interpretation, focusing on the collection and analysis of data impartially, all while reinforcing the positivist belief in an external reality that can be objectively studied and understood through empirical means. Thus, experimental design is critical in advancing scientific knowledge within the positivist framework by providing a rigorous and systematic approach to researching and comprehending the world.

ii **Survey Research Design:** Survey design is a prevalent and valuable tool extensively used in positivist research for gathering data from a large and diverse sample of participants. Typically employing standardised sets of questions, surveys are administered through questionnaires, interviews, or online platforms, providing a structured framework for data collection (Fowler, 2013; Young, 2015). This structured format and predefined response options facilitate quantitative analysis, enabling researchers to discern patterns, relationships, and statistical associations within the data. Such an emphasis on empirical data collection and the application of statistical techniques to generalise findings to broader populations aligns survey research seamlessly with the positivist paradigm. By adhering to the positivist principles of objectivity, systematic observation, and the belief in an external reality that can be studied through empirical means, surveys contribute significantly to the rigorous and objective investigation of various phenomena, allowing researchers to derive reliable and generalisable knowledge about the world.

iii **Cross-Sectional Design:** Cross-sectional design is a valuable and frequently employed approach in positivist research, where data is collected from different individuals or groups at a single point in time to explore the relationships between variables (Wang & Cheng, 2020). This design allows researchers to simultaneously examine various factors and characteristics within a population, providing a snapshot of the phenomenon under investigation. Cross-sectional designs are particularly well-suited for studying population characteristics, exploring correlations between variables, and generating descriptive statistics (Spector, 2019). Cross-sectional designs align closely with the positivist paradigm's central objective of identifying patterns and establishing statistical associations among variables by focusing on a single time point. This alignment is rooted in the positivist belief in the objective reality that can be studied and understood through empirical observations and systematic data analysis. By employing cross-sectional designs, researchers can derive valuable insights into the interrelationships and characteristics of the studied population, contributing to the advancement of empirical knowledge and informing evidence-based decision-making in various fields of inquiry.

iv **Longitudinal Design:** Longitudinal designs represent a robust research deign involving the collection of data from the same individuals or groups over an extended period, enabling researchers to explore changes, stability, or development of variables over time (Gustafsson, 2010; Schaie, 2014). By systematically gathering data at multiple time points, longitudinal designs closely align with the positivist paradigm's emphasis on rigorous and objective data collection. This allows researchers to examine temporal dynamics, identify causal relationships, and investigate how variables evolve over time. The insights provided by longitudinal designs are invaluable for understanding the direction and magnitude of change, contributing to the establishment of generalisable principles and patterns within the studied phenomena. Through their ability to track changes over time and provide a deeper understanding of complex processes, longitudinal designs are pivotal in advancing scientific knowledge and generating evidence-based conclusions within the positivist framework.

v **Quasi-Experimental Design:** Quasi-experimental designs play a critical role in research when a random assignment of participants to different conditions is not feasible or ethical. In these designs, according to Fife-Schaw (2012), researchers compare groups that naturally differ in their exposure to an independent variable or intervention. While lacking the rigorous control of true experimental designs, quasi-experimental aims to establish causal relationships by carefully controlling for confounding factors through participant selection, matching, or statistical adjustments. By aligning with the positivist paradigm's core principles, quasi-experimental designs seek to identify and understand causal links between variables, even when complete experimental control is impossible due to practical or ethical constraints. Despite these limitations, the systematic and careful approach of quasi-experimental designs contributes significantly to advancing empirical knowledge and establishing causal relationships within the positivist framework.

vi **True Experimental Design:** True experimental design is a design that falls within the positivist paradigm, emphasising control, manipulation, and the establishment of causal relationships between variables. This rigorous method involves the manipulation of an independent variable to observe its effect on a dependent variable while also employing the random assignment of participants to different groups to minimise bias (Lee & Whalen, 2007). By systematically varying the independent variable and using random selection, researchers ensure that any observed differences in the dependent variable are attributable to the manipulation of the independent variable rather than other extraneous factors. Therefore, implementing a true experimental design aligns closely with the positivist paradigm's core principles of empirical data collection and the pursuit of causal relationships. Through its focus on control and systematic inquiry, true experimental designs contribute to the establishment of generalisable laws or principles, enhancing the external validity of research findings and providing a robust foundation for advancing scientific knowledge within the positivist framework.

vii **Comparative Design:** Comparative designs constitute a vital research approach involving the comparison of various groups, populations, or contexts to discern similarities and differences (Bloemraad, 2013). These designs frequently encompass cross-national or cross-cultural studies, delving into how variables or phenomena vary across diverse settings. Comparative designs closely align with the positivist paradigm's fundamental tenets by seeking to identify generalisable laws or principles applicable across multiple contexts. These designs enable researchers to detect patterns, establish statistical associations, and formulate broader principles that transcend specific cases. Emphasising the systematic examination of multiple settings, comparative design contributes significantly to advancing empirical knowledge, shedding light on the underlying mechanisms that govern phenomena across diverse populations and contexts, thus enriching our understanding of the world comprehensively and scientifically rigorously.

viii **Case Study Design:** Case study design entails conducting an in-depth examination of a single case, which could be an individual, organisation, or event (Harrison et al., 2017). Researchers employ various data collection methods, including interviews, observations, documents, and artefacts, to gather extensive information about the case. While case studies are typically associated with qualitative research, a positivist case study design also emphasises the collection of quantitative data within a single case. By adopting this approach, researchers can explore complex phenomena in real-world contexts while still adhering to positivist principles of rigorous data collection and analysis. This design provides valuable and rich insights into the intricacies of the case under study, enabling researchers to uncover underlying patterns, relationships, and generalisable principles, even within the confines of a singular case. Thus, positivist case study designs serve as a powerful tool to deepen our understanding of phenomena in specific real-life settings, contributing to the comprehensive and systematic advancement of scientific knowledge.

ix **Correlational Design:** According to Devi et al. (2022), correlational design is a research design that examines the relationship between variables without establishing causality. In this design, researchers measure the variables of interest and analyse the degree and direction of their association using statistical techniques. With emphasis on the use of quantitative data and statistical analysis, correlational design closely aligns with the positivist paradigm's core principles, which emphasise the rigorous and objective study of empirical data. This design is valuable for investigating associations between variables and generating hypotheses for further research (Cavallo et al., 2016). Although correlational studies do not establish cause-and-effect relationships, they are crucial in identifying patterns and relationships between variables, providing valuable insights into the complex interplay of factors in various phenomena. By revealing associations and potential links between variables, correlational design contributes to the advancement of scientific knowledge and informs future research directions within the positivist framework.

x **Factorial Design:** According to Anderson et al. (2023), factorial design is a method that enables researchers to explore the effects of multiple independent variables on one or more dependent variables. By manipulating different levels of each independent variable and combining them to create various experimental conditions, researchers can systematically investigate the main effects of each independent variable and also explore potential interaction effects between them. This controlled and systematic approach to studying the impact of multiple variables aligns seamlessly with the principles of the positivist paradigm, emphasising the importance of rigorous and objective data collection and analysis (Collins et al., 2009). Factorial design plays a crucial role in establishing generalisable principles by providing valuable insights into how various factors interact and influence outcomes. By examining the complex interplay of independent variables, researchers can gain a deeper understanding of the underlying mechanisms that govern phenomena, thus contributing to the advancement of scientific knowledge within the positivist framework.

xi **Ex Post Facto Design:** Ex post facto design, also referred to as retrospective or causal-comparative design, is a research method that investigates relationships between variables after they have naturally occurred (Bais & Amechnoue, 2023). In this design, researchers identify groups exposed to different conditions or experiences and analyse the effects on the dependent variable. Although ex post facto designs do not establish causality due to their non-experimental nature, they closely align with the positivist paradigm by employing quantitative data and statistical analysis to examine associations and identify potential causal relationships. By utilising this method, researchers can gain valuable insights into the impact of variables in real-world settings where experimental manipulation may not be feasible or ethical. Ex post facto designs contribute significantly to the rigorous and systematic examination of phenomena, allowing researchers to explore and understand the relationships between variables within the constraints of practical and ethical considerations, thus advancing scientific knowledge within the positivist framework.

Please note that there are many other designs within the principle of positivism. However, these methodological designs in positivist research align with the paradigm's principles of objectivity, empirical evidence, and the search for generalisable laws or principles. They emphasise the use of quantitative methods, structured data collection techniques, and statistical analysis to ensure reliable and replicable findings. By employing these designs, researchers within the positivist paradigm aim to generate evidence-based knowledge that can be applied beyond specific cases or contexts, contributing to the advancement of scientific understanding. It is essential to acknowledge that these designs have their limitations and assumptions, and researchers should carefully consider their appropriateness based on the research questions, constraints, and ethical considerations specific to their study.

## 2.6 Aligning Research Questions with Positivist Paradigms

Formulating research questions that align with the positivist paradigm is of utmost importance to maintain consistency and coherence between the research approach and the underlying principles of positivism. When research questions are grounded in the positivist paradigm, researchers can effectively employ suitable methods and techniques that prioritise objectivity, empirical evidence, and the exploration of generalisable laws or principles. That is, adhering to the fundamental tenets of the positivist paradigm, researchers can design studies that emphasise systematic data collection, rigorous analysis, and the pursuit of causal relationships. Moreover, aligning research questions with positivism enables researchers to contribute to advancing scientific knowledge by generating evidence-based findings that are valid within specific contexts and have broader applicability across diverse populations and settings. Therefore, a strong alignment between research questions and the positivist paradigm ensures that the research is conducted in a manner that adheres to sound scientific principles and contributes to the rigorous and objective understanding of phenomena in the pursuit of generalisable knowledge.

Here are some factors that make research questions traceable to the positivist paradigm:

i **Quantifiability:** Positivist research questions often involve variables that can be measured and quantified. Using numerical data, they focus on observable phenomena and seek to establish relationships or associations between variables. Research questions that can be answered through quantitative analysis, statistical testing, and measurement are more likely to align with the positivist paradigm.

   **Example 1:** "What is the impact of exercise duration (measured in minutes) on cardiovascular fitness (measured by heart rate recovery) among sedentary adults?"

   **Example 2:** "Is there a significant correlation between customer satisfaction ratings (measured on a 5-point scale) and repurchase intentions (measured on a 7-point scale) in the hospitality industry?"

ii **Generalisability:** Positivist research aims to identify patterns and establish generalisable laws or principles. Research questions that seek to uncover relationships or principles that apply beyond a specific case or context are aligned with the positivist paradigm. They focus on understanding phenomena in a broader population or across different settings.

   **Example 1:** "What is the relationship between teacher experience (measured in years) and student academic achievement (measured by standardised test scores) across multiple schools in a specific district?"

   **Example 2:** "How does leadership style (measured using a standardised questionnaire) influence employee job satisfaction (measured on a 5-point Likert scale) in various industries?"

iii **Causality:** Positivist research often seeks to establish causal relationships between variables. Research questions exploring cause-and-effect relationships and identifying the influence of independent variables on dependent variables are traceable to the positivist paradigm. These questions require experimental or quasi-experimental designs to establish causality.

   **Example 1:** "Does a new teaching method (independent variable) significantly improve students' reading comprehension scores (dependent variable) compared to a traditional teaching method?"

   **Example 2:** "To what extent does advertising expenditure (independent variable) impact consumer brand preference (dependent variable) in the smartphone industry?"

iv **Objectivity:** Positivist research questions prioritise objectivity and strive to minimise subjective interpretations. Research questions that focus on understanding phenomena in an unbiased and value-neutral manner align with the positivist paradigm. They seek to uncover objective truths and avoid personal biases.

**Example 1:** "What is the relationship between employee job satisfaction (measured using a standardised scale) and employee turnover rates in a specific industry, controlling for demographic factors?"

**Example 2:** "How does product price (measured in dollars) affect consumer purchase decisions in the fashion industry, accounting for demographic variables and brand reputation?"

v **Empirical Evidence:** Positivist research questions emphasise the collection of empirical evidence derived from systematic observation or experimentation. Research questions that can be answered through data collection and analysis, preferably using quantitative methods, align with the positivist paradigm.

**Example 1:** "What is the impact of social media usage (measured by hours per day) on self-esteem levels (measured using a validated self-report questionnaire) among teenagers?"

**Example 2:** "How does employee training intensity (measured by hours of training) affect productivity levels (measured by units produced per hour) in a manufacturing setting?"

By considering these factors, researchers can carefully craft research questions that align with the positivist paradigm, thus ensuring consistency between their research approach and the underlying principles of positivism. Such research questions allow for the selection and application of appropriate methodologies, data collection techniques, and statistical analyses, which are essential for generating reliable and generalisable findings. These questions guide researchers towards conducting rigorous and systematic investigations prioritising objectivity, empirical evidence, and the search for general laws or principles.

However, it is essential to acknowledge that not all research questions will be well-suited for the positivist paradigm. There are research inquiries that necessitate alternative paradigms, particularly when studying subjective experiences, cultural phenomena, or complex social interactions. For instance, questions about individuals' perceptions, meanings, or experiences might require a more interpretive worldview, leading to a qualitative approach that delves into the subjective nuances and contextual intricacies of the phenomena under investigation. Similarly, questions exploring the influence of cultural factors or social constructions may benefit from alternative paradigms that emphasise understanding social processes and the construction of reality.

Hence, researchers should exercise discernment and critical thinking when formulating research questions, ensuring that the chosen paradigm aligns with the nature of the research problem, the goals of the study, and the phenomena being examined. This thoughtful consideration allows researchers to select the most appropriate paradigm, whether it is positivist, interpretive, critical, or another paradigm, to shed light on the research questions at hand. Doing so makes researchers embark on their investigations with a clear and intentional methodological direction, optimising the potential for producing meaningful and valuable contributions to knowledge within their specific fields of study.

### 2.6.1 Case Studies on How to Align Research Questions with Positivist Paradigm

This section presents case studies that exemplify the alignment of research questions with the principles of the positivist paradigm. These case studies serve as practical illustrations of how researchers can effectively formulate research questions in a manner that adheres to the positivist approach, emphasising objectivity, empirical evidence, and the pursuit of generalisable laws or principles. By understanding these case studies, readers can gain valuable insights into how to formulate research questions that systematically collect and analyse data while maintaining coherence with the fundamental principles of positivism.

---

**Case Study 1: The Impact of Technology Use on Student Academic Performance**

**Research Question:** Does the use of educational technology (independent variable) significantly impact student academic performance (dependent variable) in a specific grade level?

**Alignment with Positivist Paradigm**

i **Quantifiability**: The research question focuses on measuring the impact of technology use on student academic performance, which can be quantified through various metrics such as grades, test scores, or standardised assessments.
ii **Generalisability:** The research question aims to establish a relationship between technology use and student academic performance, allowing for potential generalisations to a broader population of students.
iii **Causality:** The research question explores the causal link between technology use and academic performance, which can be investigated using experimental or quasi-experimental designs to establish cause-and-effect relationships.

Positivist Paradigm and Methodological Alignment 37

iv **Objectivity:** The research question approaches the topic objectively and value-neutrally, seeking to examine the impact of technology use on academic performance, irrespective of personal beliefs or opinions.
v **Empirical Evidence:** The research question emphasises the collection of empirical evidence through quantitative data, enabling the application of statistical analysis to determine the extent of the impact of technology use on student academic performance.

**Case Study 2: Factors Influencing Employee Job Satisfaction**

**Research Question:** What are the key factors (independent variables) that significantly influence employee job satisfaction (dependent variable) in a specific industry?

**Alignment with Positivist Paradigm**

i **Quantifiability:** The research question involves identifying and quantifying the factors that influence employee job satisfaction, enabling researchers to measure these factors and their impact numerically.
ii **Generalisability:** The research question seeks to identify key factors influencing employee job satisfaction, allowing for potential generalisations to other employees in the same industry or organisational contexts.
iii **Causality:** The research question explores the causal relationship between independent variables (factors) and the dependent variable (job satisfaction), aiming to establish cause-and-effect links through quantitative analysis and statistical modelling.
iv **Objectivity:** The research question maintains an objective perspective by identifying objective factors influencing employee job satisfaction rather than subjective interpretations or individual opinions.
v **Empirical Evidence:** The research question emphasises the collection of empirical evidence through quantitative data, such as survey responses or structured interviews, to determine the significance and direction of the influence of different factors on employee job satisfaction.

**Case Study 3: The Effect of Mobile Banking on Economic Development in Africa**

**Research Question:** How does the use of mobile banking (independent variable) affect economic development (dependent variable) in rural communities in Africa?

**Alignment with Positivist Paradigm**

i **Quantifiability:** This research question allows for the quantification of the impact of mobile banking on economic development. Metrics such as changes in income levels, savings rates, or business growth can be used as quantifiable indicators.
ii **Generalisability:** The study aims to identify patterns or principles that could be generalised to other similar rural communities in Africa, adhering to the positivist goal of finding broader applicability.
iii **Causality:** The research question explores the causal relationship between the adoption of mobile banking services and economic development, which can be investigated using statistical methods to establish cause-and-effect relationships.
iv **Objectivity:** The approach to this question is objective, aiming to study the impact of mobile banking without bias or subjective interpretation, focusing solely on empirical data.
v **Empirical Evidence:** The emphasis is on collecting empirical evidence through quantitative data such as economic indicators, usage rates of mobile banking, and other relevant statistics.

**Case Study 4: The Relationship between Urbanisation and Air Quality in the Global North**

**Research Question:** What is the relationship between the rate of urbanisation (independent variable) and air quality (dependent variable) in major cities in the Global North?

**Alignment with Positivist Paradigm**

i **Quantifiability:** This research question involves quantifying urbanisation rates and measuring air quality indices, making it possible to analyse these variables numerically.

ii **Generalisability:** The aim is to identify a pattern or relationship that can be generalised to other urban areas in the Global North, in line with the positivist approach of seeking universal laws or principles.
iii **Causality:** The study focuses on establishing a causal link between urbanisation and changes in air quality, which can be explored through longitudinal studies or comparative analyses of different cities.
iv **Objectivity:** The research maintains an objective stance, free from personal biases, examining the relationship between urbanisation and air quality based on empirical data.
v **Empirical Evidence:** The emphasis is on the collection and analysis of empirical data, such as urbanisation statistics, air pollution levels, and health data, to understand the impact of urbanisation on air quality.

In all the case studies, the research questions are traceable to the positivist paradigm as they align with the paradigm's principles of objectivity, quantifiability, generalisability, causality, and the use of empirical evidence. These research questions guide researchers to adopt appropriate positivist methodologies, such as surveys, quantitative data analysis, and statistical techniques, to investigate the phenomena and generate reliable and generalisable findings.

## 2.7 Characteristics of Data Collection Methods in Positivist Research

Data collection methods in positivist research share several key characteristics that are in line with the paradigm's core principles. These methods prioritise objectivity, emphasising the use of empirical evidence and quantitative data. By adhering to these principles, researchers ensure that the data collected is reliable, measurable, and amenable to rigorous statistical analysis, ultimately contributing to the establishment of generalisable laws or principles within the positivist framework. Here are the main characteristics that can be expected in data collection methods in positivist research:

i **Standardisation:** Positivist research is characterised by its adherence to standardised data collection methods, where consistency in data collection is crucial across all participants or cases under investigation (Paré, 2004). By standardisation, researchers aim to minimise potential biases and improve the reliability of their findings. This is achieved through the use of structured questionnaires, interview protocols, or observation checklists, which offer clear instructions and predefined response options to ensure uniformity in data gathering. Therefore, adhering to these standardised methods, researchers can confidently draw conclusions and make generalisations based on the data collected, enhancing the credibility and robustness of their research outcomes. Ultimately, the emphasis on standardisation in positivist research fosters a more objective and systematic approach to studying phenomena, leading to valuable insights in various fields of study.

ii **Quantifiability:** Quantifiability is a fundamental aspect of positivist research, which prioritises the collection of measurable data (Tyson, 1992). By focusing on numerical information, positivist research ensures that the data can be subjected to rigorous statistical analysis. This facilitates the measurement of variables, calculation of frequencies or averages, and identification of statistical associations or patterns, all of which contribute to the establishment of reliable and objective findings. Through the application of statistical techniques, researchers can draw meaningful insights from the data, leading to generalisable conclusions that can be applied beyond the specific sample under investigation. The emphasis on quantifiability in positivist research enhances the rigour and objectivity of scientific inquiry, making it a valuable approach to understanding and explaining various phenomena across different fields of study.

iii **Objectivity:** Objectivity is a critical principle in positivist research, as it seeks to maintain the highest level of impartiality and minimise the impact of personal biases or interpretations on the data collection process (Ryan, 2018). By prioritising objectivity, researchers aim to gather information in a standardised and unbiased manner, ensuring that their own beliefs and values do not influence the results. This is often achieved through rigorous training of data collectors, providing them with unambiguous instructions on how to carry out the data collection procedures. Moreover, implementing quality control measures helps maintain consistency and reliability throughout the research process. Therefore, adhering to the principle of objectivity, positivist research aims to produce more reliable and credible outcomes, as it reduces the risk of introducing subjective elements that could compromise the validity of the findings. This commitment to objectivity strengthens the scientific rigour and validity of positivist studies, enabling researchers to draw robust and meaningful conclusions about phenomena under investigation.

iv **Reliability and Validity:** Reliability and validity are paramount in positivist research, as they underpin the credibility and trustworthiness of the findings. Reliability ensures that data collection methods are consistent and stable, meaning that similar results would be obtained if the research were repeated (Sürücü & Maslakci, 2020). This consistency strengthens the confidence in the accuracy of the conclusions drawn. On the other hand, validity guarantees that the data accurately measures what it is intended to measure (Rahardja et al., 2019), reflecting the true phenomenon under investigation. To enhance reliability and validity, positivist research utilises established measurement scales and tools that have been rigorously tested and proven to yield consistent and accurate results. Conducting pilot studies helps identify and rectify any potential issues with the data collection process before the main study. Additionally, appropriate sampling techniques are employed to ensure that the data collected is representative of the target population, further enhancing the validity of the research. Positivist research establishes a strong foundation for producing dependable and meaningful scientific knowledge in various fields by prioritising reliability and validity.

v **Large Sample Sizes:** In positivist research, large sample sizes play a crucial role in strengthening the reliability and generalisability of the findings (Polit & Beck, 2010). That is, by collecting data from a substantial number of participants or cases, researchers aim to increase the representativeness of the sample, making it more reflective of the entire population under study. This enhances the external validity of the research, allowing for a more confident extrapolation of the results to the broader population. Data collection methods in positivist research are designed to accommodate large-scale data gathering, employing techniques like random sampling or systematic sampling to ensure a diverse and unbiased representation of the population. The use of large sample sizes provides statistical power, enabling researchers to detect even small effects or associations with greater precision and confidence. Ultimately, the emphasis on large sample sizes in positivist research contributes to the robustness and credibility of the conclusions drawn, making the research findings more applicable and valuable in various real-world contexts.

From the above argument, positivist research data collection methods exhibit standardisation, quantifiability, objectivity, reliability and validity characteristics and often involve large sample sizes. These characteristics ensure that the data collected is reliable, measurable, and suitable for statistical analysis, aligning with the positivist paradigm's emphasis on objective and generalisable findings. By employing these methods, researchers can gather robust empirical evidence and contribute to the accumulation of scientific knowledge within their respective fields of study.

### 2.7.1 Methods of Data Collection Within the Positivism Paradigm

In quantitative research, numerous instruments are commonly used to collect data, and many of them are linked to the positivist paradigm. Some of these instruments include questionnaires, surveys, structured interviews, standardised tests, observations with predefined checklists, and experiments with control groups. These instruments align with the positivist paradigm, emphasising standardised data collection methods, quantifiability, objectivity, reliability, and validity, often requiring large sample sizes. They prioritise the use of numerical data that can be subjected to statistical analysis, enabling researchers to draw objective and generalisable conclusions. By employing these instruments, positivist researchers aim to minimise biases, establish causal relationships, and enhance the rigour and credibility of their findings. While there are other methods not covered here, these ten instruments demonstrate the strong link between data collection methods in quantitative research and the positivist paradigm's principles and objectives.

i **Questionnaires:** Questionnaires are a vital data collection method in positivist research, offering structured and standardised instruments to gather quantitative data from participants. These tools consist of a set of predefined questions that are administered consistently to all respondents, ensuring uniformity and reducing potential biases (Rowley, 2014). The numerical values assigned to the responses facilitate statistical analysis, enabling researchers to identify patterns, correlations, or trends within the data. Questionnaires are well-suited to large-scale studies as they can be distributed to a large number of participants efficiently, making them cost-effective and time-saving. Moreover, the standardised nature of questionnaires enhances the comparability of data across different studies and settings, promoting the accumulation of evidence and contributing to the establishment of generalisable findings. However, it is essential to design and pilot-test questionnaires carefully to ensure their validity and reliability. When appropriately executed, questionnaires are a powerful tool in the positivist research arsenal, providing valuable insights and quantitative data to investigate various phenomena in diverse fields of study.

ii **Surveys:** Surveys are a fundamental tool in quantitative research, reflecting a strong alignment with the positivist paradigm. These instruments involve the systematic administration of questionnaires to a sizable and representative sample of participants. Surveys are designed to gather quantifiable data, assigning numerical values to responses, which facilitates statistical analysis (Boeren, 2015). This allows researchers to identify patterns, correlations, or trends among the collected data. By employing surveys, researchers can approach their investigation in a standardised manner, ensuring consistency and minimising biases in data collection. The emphasis on quantifiable data and statistical analysis in surveys supports the positivist goal of objectivity and the establishment of generalisable findings. Surveys provide valuable insights into various topics, making them a versatile and powerful tool in quantitative research within the positivist paradigm.

iii **Rating Scales:** Rating scales are a valuable data collection method in quantitative research that strongly aligns with the positivist paradigm. These scales involve participants providing ratings or evaluations based on specific criteria, allowing researchers to quantify attitudes, perceptions, or opinions (Williamson & Hoggart, 2005). Common examples of rating scales include Likert scales, where respondents indicate their level of agreement or disagreement with a statement using a range of response options, and semantic differential scales, where participants rate a concept or item on bipolar adjectives (e.g., happy-sad, satisfied-dissatisfied). Using rating scales, researchers can easily convert qualitative responses into numerical data, which is amenable to statistical analysis. This quantification of data enables researchers to identify trends, patterns, and associations with objectivity, promoting the positivist goal of generating generalisable findings. Rating scales are versatile instruments that find applications in various domains, ranging from psychology and social sciences to marketing and customer satisfaction research, making them an indispensable tool for researchers operating within the positivist paradigm.

iv **Psychometric Tests:** Psychometric tests are essential tools in quantitative research, particularly in psychology and related fields, and they strongly align with the positivist paradigm. These tests are specifically designed to measure various psychological constructs, such as intelligence, personality traits, or emotional states, in a systematic and standardised manner (Kim, 2009). Through well-defined and consistent procedures, psychometric tests aim to gather quantifiable data, assigning numerical values to individuals' responses or performances. This emphasis on quantification allows researchers to apply statistical analysis, ensuring the reliability and validity of the data collected. Psychometric tests play a crucial role in establishing objective and replicable measures of psychological attributes, contributing to the positivist goal of generating generalisable findings. By adhering to rigorous psychometric principles, researchers can confidently draw conclusions about the psychological constructs under investigation, providing valuable insights into human behaviour and cognition.

v **Physiological Measures:** Physiological measures play a crucial role in quantitative research, particularly in fields like neuroscience, medicine, and psychology, and they strongly align with the positivist paradigm. Physiological measures offer quantifiable insights into the body's physiological processes by collecting objective data related to bodily functions or responses, such as heart rate, blood pressure, or brain activity (van Mersbergen & Patrick, 2022). Instruments like electrocardiograms (ECG) or electroencephalograms (EEG) allow researchers to obtain precise and standardised data, enabling statistical analysis to uncover patterns or relationships within the physiological responses. This emphasis on quantifiable data aligns with the positivist goal of objectivity and facilitates the establishment of reliable and generalisable findings. Physiological measures provide valuable insights into the functioning of the human body and brain, offering objective evidence to understand various physiological processes and their associations with behaviours, emotions, and cognitive functions.

vi **Observational Checklists:** Observational checklists are valuable instruments in quantitative research, particularly in fields like psychology, education, and social sciences, and they strongly align with the positivist paradigm. These checklists provide a structured and systematic approach to recording specific behaviours or events during observations, ensuring consistency and objectivity in data collection (Charlesworth et al., 1993).

Researchers use these tools to observe and quantify behaviours or occurrences of interest, assigning numerical values or scores based on predefined criteria. This quantification enables the application of statistical analysis, allowing researchers to identify patterns, associations, or trends within the observed data. By emphasising standardised data collection, observational checklists promote the positivist goal of objectivity and enhance the reliability of the findings. They are particularly useful when studying human behaviour in naturalistic settings, as they facilitate the measurement of observable phenomena, providing valuable insights into various aspects of human interactions and behaviour in a controlled and systematic manner.

vii **Experimental Apparatus:** Experimental apparatus plays a crucial role in quantitative research, particularly in experimental studies (Reif-Acherman, 2004), and strongly aligns with the positivist paradigm. These apparatuses are designed to manipulate independent variables and measure dependent variables under controlled and standardised conditions. By providing a controlled environment, experimental apparatuses ensure that the data collection process is consistent and minimises extraneous influences. This adherence to standardisation promotes objectivity in data collection and enhances the reliability and validity of the findings. Through precise measurement of variables, experimental apparatuses enable researchers to apply statistical analysis to establish cause-and-effect relationships between variables, which is a central goal of positivist research. These apparatuses are essential in conducting experiments that explore causal relationships between variables and contribute to the advancement of scientific knowledge in various disciplines.

viii **Digital Tracking Devices:** Digital tracking devices have become increasingly popular in quantitative research, especially in areas like sports science, health, and environmental studies, and they strongly adhere to the principles of the positivist paradigm. These devices, such as accelerometers that monitor physical activity levels (Vetter et al., 2023) or GPS trackers that record participants' location (Zhai et al., 2023), provide objective and accurate data without relying on self-reported information. Digital tracking devices offer a detailed and precise view of behaviour in naturalistic settings by collecting real-time data on participants' movements or activities. This objectivity in data collection aligns with the positivist goal of minimising biases and ensuring the reliability of the findings. Researchers can use statistical analysis to uncover patterns or associations within the data, gaining valuable insights into human behaviour, environmental interactions, or health-related outcomes. Digital tracking devices allow researchers to bridge the gap between controlled laboratory settings and real-world situations, providing a powerful means to study behaviour and phenomena with a level of accuracy and objectivity that was not easily achievable before.

ix **Standardised Tests:** Standardised tests are a prominent data collection method in quantitative research (Binns, 2023), particularly in the fields of education and psychology, and they strongly align with the principles of the positivist paradigm. These tests are designed to assess individuals' knowledge, skills, or abilities using uniform and consistent procedures, ensuring that all participants receive the same instructions and have equal opportunities to demonstrate their capabilities. The scoring criteria are predetermined, allowing for an objective and reliable evaluation of the responses. By generating quantifiable data, standardised tests enable researchers to apply statistical analysis, identifying patterns, trends, or relationships within the test scores. This emphasis on standardised procedures and quantification aligns with the positivist goal of objectivity, enhancing the reliability and validity of the test results. Standardised tests have broad applications in educational settings, psychological assessments, and various other domains, providing valuable insights into individuals' performance, abilities, and potential and serving as a vital tool in generating objective and generalisable findings.

x **Existing Databases:** Existing databases are valuable resources in quantitative research, offering a treasure trove of pre-collected data that aligns well with the positivist paradigm (Sexton et al., 1992). These databases, which may include government records, organisational datasets, or publicly available information, provide vast information that researchers can analyse to gain valuable insights. Accessing these large-scale datasets, researchers can apply statistical techniques to uncover patterns, trends, or associations within the data. The use of existing databases allows for efficient data collection without the need for additional time-consuming and costly data-gathering processes. Moreover, these datasets often cover many variables and long periods, enabling researchers to study trends and phenomena over time and across diverse populations. The quantifiable nature of the data in existing databases further aligns with the positivist goal of objectivity and the establishment of generalisable findings. By leveraging these databases, researchers can make substantial contributions to various fields, from social sciences and healthcare to economics and public policy, utilising existing data to answer important research questions and advance knowledge.

## 2.8 Characteristics of Data Analysis and Interpretation in Positivist Research

In positivist research, data analysis and interpretation play a crucial role as they involve the systematic examination and interpretation of collected data in a structured and objective manner. Adhering to the positivist paradigm, this approach emphasises applying quantitative methods and statistical techniques to rigorously analyse the data at hand. By employing this rigorous and objective framework, researchers can draw meaningful and unbiased conclusions, enhancing the reliability and validity of their findings. The systematic nature of the analysis ensures that data is thoroughly explored, allowing for a comprehensive understanding of the research phenomenon and facilitating the identification of patterns and relationships that might otherwise remain unnoticed. Consequently, positivist data analysis and interpretation contribute significantly to the advancement of knowledge and the overall scientific understanding of various phenomena. Below are the data analysis and interpretation characteristics that must be considered in positivist research.

i **Quantitative Analysis:** Quantitative analysis is a fundamental aspect of positivist research, leveraging numerical data collected through standardised methods and subjecting it to rigorous statistical examination. Researchers can delve deeply into the data by employing techniques like descriptive statistics, inferential statistics (Bettany-Saltikov & Whittaker, 2014; MacRae, 2019; Marshall & Jonker, 2010), correlation analysis, regression analysis, and hypothesis testing, uncovering patterns and relationships among variables. This objective approach allows for validating or rejecting research hypotheses based on concrete evidence. Through quantitative analysis, researchers can gain valuable insights and make informed interpretations, strengthening the validity and reliability of their findings. Ultimately, the utilisation of quantitative analysis in positivist research contributes to a more evidence-based and objective understanding of various phenomena, fostering advancements in knowledge and scientific understanding.

ii **Objectivity and Replicability:** In positivist research, data analysis embodies two crucial principles: objectivity and replicability (Kalelioğlu, 2021). Objectivity is achieved through an impartial and unbiased treatment of data, where researchers strive to minimise personal biases and subjective interpretations. Researchers can objectively examine the data by adhering to rigorous methodologies and standardised data analysis procedures, ensuring their conclusions are rooted in the evidence rather than preconceived notions. Replicability, on the other hand, ensures that the data analysis procedures employed in the study can be replicated by other researchers, providing an essential aspect of scientific rigour. When other researchers can independently reproduce the findings using the same data and analysis methods, it strengthens the reliability and trustworthiness of the research. To enhance both objectivity and replicability, researchers in positivist research employ predefined statistical tests, clear criteria for interpretation, and standardised analytical techniques, fostering an environment of transparency and accountability within the scientific community. This commitment to objectivity and replicability not only bolsters the validity of research findings but also allows for further advancement and refinement of knowledge through the cumulative efforts of multiple researchers.

iii **Statistical Interpretation:** In positivist research, statistical interpretation is a vital component that entails extracting meaningful insights from statistical results using established criteria and measures of statistical significance. Researchers carefully examine various statistical outputs, such as p-values, effect sizes, or confidence intervals, to discern the strength and direction of relationships or associations between variables (Perdices, 2018). By applying rigorous statistical analysis, researchers can draw well-informed conclusions based on objective evidence, distinguishing statistically significant findings from random fluctuations. This process of statistical interpretation not only supports the validation or rejection of research hypotheses but also contributes to the broader accumulation of knowledge within the specific research field. Through systematic and quantitative data exploration, positivist researchers can uncover meaningful patterns and relationships, enabling a more robust understanding of phenomena and facilitating evidence-based decision-making in various domains.

In summary, data analysis and interpretation in positivist research encompass the application of quantitative methods, statistical techniques, and the pursuit of objectivity. Using statistical analysis procedures, researchers analyse the collected numerical data to uncover patterns, relationships, or associations among variables. The objective interpretation of statistical results allows for drawing conclusions, supporting or refuting research hypotheses, and contributing to the empirical evidence within the positivist paradigm.

### 2.8.1 Methods of Data Analysis within Positivist Paradigm

This section focuses on the methods of interpreting and analysing quantitative data within the positivist research paradigm. As a research paradigm, positivism strongly emphasises empirical evidence and objective observations, using quantitative methods to study and understand phenomena. When it comes to quantitative data analysis, researchers apply structured and rigorous approaches to extract meaningful insights from numerical data collected through standardised procedures. Techniques such as descriptive statistics, inferential statistics, correlation analysis, regression analysis, and hypothesis testing are commonly employed to examine relationships between variables and draw objective conclusions. These systematic methods allow researchers to explore patterns, trends, and associations in the data, allowing them to validate or refute research hypotheses and contribute to advancing knowledge within the positivist paradigm. By adhering to these quantitative analysis methods, researchers can enhance the reliability and generalisability of their findings, further strengthening the validity of research outcomes in this empirical and data-driven research approach. Below are some of the methods of data analysis in the positivist paradigm.

i **Descriptive Statistics:** Descriptive statistics such as mean, median, mode, standard deviation percentiles, and quartiles play a crucial role in quantitative data analysis by providing a concise and informative dataset summary (Procheş, 2016). Researchers can effectively capture a variable's central tendency and variability under study through measures such as the mean, median, and standard deviation. For example, in the context of analysing individuals' heights, descriptive statistics would reveal the average height, the range of heights present in the sample, and the distribution of heights across the dataset. By employing descriptive statistics, researchers can objectively present and describe the essential characteristics of the data, which serves as a fundamental step in understanding the dataset's overall structure. These statistical measures offer a foundation for further analysis and interpretation, enabling researchers to gain valuable insights and make informed conclusions about the phenomenon being studied. Ultimately, descriptive statistics are invaluable tools in the positivist research paradigm, facilitating the systematic and objective examination of quantitative data to enhance the reliability and validity of research findings.

ii **Inferential Statistics:** Inferential statistics are a critical component of quantitative data analysis (Marshall & Jonker, 2011) within the positivist research paradigm, enabling researchers to extend their findings from a sample to a larger population. These statistical methods involve making inferences or generalisations based on the data collected from a sample. For example, through the use of a t-test, researchers can ascertain whether there is a statistically significant difference in test scores between two groups. By drawing conclusions from the sample data, researchers can make statements about the broader population, enhancing the external validity of their findings. For instance, in a study investigating the effectiveness of a new teaching method on student achievement, inferential statistics would determine if the observed improvement in test scores is not merely due to chance but is significant enough to be applied to a broader group of students. Thus, inferential statistics serve as a powerful tool in positivist research, allowing researchers to go beyond their specific sample and contribute meaningful insights to a broader context. Among them are:

   i **Correlation Analysis:** Correlation analysis is a valuable quantitative technique within the positivist research paradigm that explores the relationships between two or more variables (Asamoah, 2014). Researchers can assess the strength and direction of the association between the variables under investigation by calculating correlation coefficient. For instance, in a study examining the link between study hours and exam performance, correlation analysis can determine whether there is a significant correlation between these two variables. A highly positive correlation would indicate that as study hours increase, there is a corresponding improvement in exam performance. Through correlation analysis, researchers obtain a precise quantitative measure of the relationship between variables, enabling them to identify patterns and dependencies within the data. This statistical method is particularly useful in revealing meaningful connections between variables, supporting researchers in making evidence-based decisions and drawing important insights to inform future studies or interventions.

ii **Regression Analysis:** Regression analysis is a powerful statistical tool within the positivist research paradigm that enables researchers to investigate and understand the relationship between a dependent variable and one or more independent variables (Shi & Conrad, 2009). For instance, in a study exploring the connection between income and education level, regression analysis can be applied to assess how changes in education level influence income. Through this analysis, researchers can estimate the strength and direction of the relationship, examining whether higher levels of education are associated with higher incomes. By determining the significance of the independent variables, researchers can ascertain whether the observed relationships are statistically meaningful. Moreover, regression analysis allows for predictive modelling (Shipe et al., 2019), enabling researchers to make predictions about the dependent variable based on the values of the independent variables. This predictive capability enhances the applicability of the research findings in various contexts. Additionally, regression analysis aids in establishing causal relationships within the data, as it helps identify which independent variables directly impact the dependent variable. In summary, regression analysis provides valuable insights into the interplay between variables, empowering researchers to quantify the influence of different factors on the outcome of interest and contributing to evidence-based decision-making and policy formulation.

iii **Factor Analysis:** Factor analysis is a valuable statistical technique used in the positivist research paradigm to reveal underlying dimensions or factors within a set of observed variables. In studying personality traits, for instance, factor analysis can identify common factors such as extraversion, conscientiousness, and neuroticism, which represent latent constructs that underlie the observed data (Borkenau & Ostendorf, 1990). Hence, in analysing the interrelationships among variables, factor analysis helps simplify the data's complexity and uncovers the hidden patterns that explain the observed relationships. This process of dimension reduction allows researchers to gain a deeper understanding of the fundamental structure within the data, providing insights into the underlying factors that shape individuals' personality traits. Factor analysis is particularly useful when dealing with large datasets containing numerous variables, as it allows researchers to focus on the essential dimensions that contribute most to the observed variability. That is, factor analysis aids researchers in comprehending the latent constructs and fundamental dimensions that contribute to the observed variation in the data, leading to more precise and nuanced interpretations of the research findings.

iv **Cluster Analysis:** Cluster analysis is a technique in the positivist research paradigm that involves grouping similar cases or individuals together based on shared characteristics or dissimilarities in their attributes. In market research, cluster analysis can be applied to identify distinct consumer groups with similar preferences and purchasing behaviour (Morton et al., 2017). By categorising consumers into clusters based on their common characteristics, researchers can better understand consumer segments and develop targeted marketing strategies tailored to each cluster's specific needs and preferences. This process of objectively classifying data allows researchers to uncover meaningful subgroups or patterns within the dataset, providing valuable insights into the structure and diversity of the target population. Cluster analysis not only simplifies complex datasets but also aids in discovering hidden relationships and structures that might not be apparent through traditional data examination. Ultimately, cluster analysis empowers researchers to make informed decisions and develop more effective strategies by recognising and leveraging the unique characteristics of different consumer groups.

v **Analysis of Variance (ANOVA):** ANOVA is a statistical method within the positivist research paradigm that enables researchers to compare means across multiple groups or conditions to assess whether there are significant differences between them (Roberts & Russo, 2014). For instance, in an educational study comparing the effectiveness of three different teaching methods, ANOVA can be employed to determine if there is a statistically significant difference in student performance among the three groups. By objectively analysing and comparing group differences, ANOVA allows researchers to draw conclusions about the presence or absence of significant variation in the data, helping to identify which teaching method, if any, leads to better student outcomes. This method provides a robust and systematic approach to assessing the impact of various factors on the dependent variable and aids in making informed decisions based on statistical evidence. ANOVA is beneficial when dealing with studies involving multiple experimental conditions or groups, as it enables researchers to evaluate the significance of these differences and understand the effects of different treatments or interventions in a clear and objective manner.

vi **Multivariate Analysis of Variance (MANOVA):** MANOVA is an extension of ANOVA within the positivist research paradigm, enabling researchers to simultaneously analyse differences across multiple dependent variables (Haase & Ellis, 1987). In studies where different independent variables influence several outcome measures, MANOVA becomes invaluable. For instance, in a study comparing the effects of three different exercise programs on various health outcomes, MANOVA can be utilised to determine if there are significant differences in multiple dependent variables, such as weight loss, blood pressure, and cholesterol levels, among the exercise groups. Hence, researchers can comprehensively examine the combined effects of independent variables on multiple dependent variables, gaining a more holistic understanding of group differences and facilitating the interpretation of multivariate patterns. This method enhances the efficiency of data analysis and allows researchers to uncover complex relationships among various variables, leading to more nuanced and evidence-based conclusions. MANOVA is particularly useful in studies with multiple outcome measures, as it allows researchers to examine the collective impact of independent variables on multiple dimensions of interest, leading to a deeper insight into the overall effects of different treatments or interventions.

vii **Structural Equation Modelling (SEM):** SEM is a statistical technique within the positivist research paradigm that allows researchers to explore complex relationships among observed and latent variables (De Carvalho & Chima, 2014). For instance, SEM can be applied to test and refine a theoretical model representing these constructs in a study examining the interplay between job satisfaction, work engagement, and organisational commitment. By specifying the relationships among variables, SEM facilitates the evaluation of how well the model fits the data and enables researchers to draw conclusions about the hypothesised relationships. This quantitative approach provides researchers with a robust method to assess and validate theoretical frameworks, offering an objective means of examining relationships and testing hypothesised models. SEM is particularly advantageous when dealing with intricate and interconnected constructs, as it allows researchers to explore both direct and indirect effects, providing a more comprehensive understanding of the complex relationships within the data. By employing SEM, researchers can gain deeper insights into the underlying mechanisms that drive observed phenomena, leading to a more rigorous examination of theories and a refined understanding of the studied processes.

viii **Survival Analysis:** Survival analysis is a vital statistical technique within the positivist research paradigm that focuses on analysing time-to-event data, such as the time until an event occurs or the duration until a specific outcome is achieved (Harrell, 2015). In various fields, including medicine, economics, and social sciences, survival analysis is widely used to investigate and interpret event durations. For instance, in a medical study assessing the survival rates of patients with a particular disease, survival analysis can estimate survival probabilities over time, identify factors that influence patient outcomes, and assess the effectiveness of treatments or interventions. Therefore, employing survival analysis techniques, researchers can objectively examine and interpret data related to event durations, providing valuable insights into the temporal aspects of various phenomena. This approach offers a quantitative framework to analyse and model time-based outcomes, contributing significantly to our understanding of the time-dependent nature of events and facilitating evidence-based decision-making in diverse research areas.

In summary, these methods of data analysis fall under the positivist paradigm because the emphasis on objectivity, quantification, and systematic procedures characterises them. The positivist paradigm seeks to uncover empirical evidence and establish generalisable findings through the application of scientific methods. The data analysis methods discussed, such as descriptive statistics, inferential statistics, correlation analysis, and regression analysis, align with the positivist paradigm by employing rigorous quantitative techniques to analyse data and draw objective conclusions. These methods prioritise the quantification of data, statistical analysis, and the establishment of general laws or patterns governing phenomena, which are fundamental tenets of the positivist approach. By adhering to these methods, researchers within the positivist paradigm strive to minimise subjective biases and interpretations, providing objective evidence and contributing to the accumulation of scientific knowledge.

## 2.9 Critiques and Debates in Positivist Research

The positivist paradigm has faced critiques and debates over time, raising questions about its fundamental assumptions, research methodologies, and the very nature of scientific inquiry. Scholars and researchers have engaged in discussions that underscore key areas of concern within the positivist approach. Here are some key critiques and debates in the positivist paradigm.

### 2.9.1 Reductionism and Oversimplification

One critique often levied against the positivist paradigm is its inclination towards reductionism, whereby complex phenomena are broken down into simpler parts for analysis (Ryan, 2006). This reductionist approach may lead to an oversimplification of the complexity inherent in social phenomena, thus neglecting the intricate interplay of various factors at play. Critics argue that a comprehensive understanding of social phenomena cannot be achieved solely by isolating individual variables, as these variables are deeply intertwined within a larger social context. Social phenomena are multifaceted and influenced by a myriad of contextual factors, cultural dynamics, and subjective experiences. The argument is that reducing them to isolated variables, the positivist paradigm may fail to consider the broader social, cultural, and historical context that shapes human behaviour. For instance, studying the impact of educational attainment on income levels without accounting for structural inequalities or societal barriers overlooks the broader systemic factors that contribute to social disparities. Critics argue that social phenomena are better understood through a holistic approach that embraces the interconnectedness and complexity of the social world (Marsh & Furlong, 2002).

Moreover, the positivist paradigm's reductionist approach may overlook individuals' subjective experiences and interpretations. Human behaviour is influenced by individual perspectives, meanings, and emotions that cannot be easily quantified or reduced to measurable variables. The subjective dimensions of social phenomena require approaches that delve into the intricacies of human experiences, narratives, and interpretations. Critiques argue that qualitative research methods, such as interviews or ethnography, provide valuable insights into social phenomena' subjective realities and complexities, complementing the quantitative methods used within the positivist paradigm.

*2.9.2 Objectivity and Value Neutrality*

The positivist paradigm asserts the importance of objectivity and value neutrality in research, aiming to separate researcher biases and personal values from the research process. However, critics contend that achieving complete objectivity is inherently challenging, if not impossible, as researchers are influenced by their social and cultural contexts (Borrell & Boulet, 2005). They argue that the positivist paradigm may overlook critical social and cultural factors shaping human behaviour (Rogers, 2012), rendering the research incomplete or biased. Researchers bring their own values, beliefs, and biases to the research process, which can influence the formulation of research questions, study design, data collection methods, and interpretation of findings. Even when researchers strive for objectivity, their subjective influences may inadvertently shape their choices and decisions throughout the research journey. For example, researchers may unconsciously select certain variables to measure or interpret findings in a manner that aligns with their preconceived notions or societal biases. Critics also advocate for a more nuanced understanding of subjectivity and acknowledge the importance of reflexivity in research. Reflexivity entails researchers critically reflecting upon their assumptions, biases, and positions of power concerning the research topic and participants. By embracing reflexivity, researchers can acknowledge their own subjectivity and work towards minimising the impact of their biases on the research process.

Furthermore, critics argue for the inclusion of diverse perspectives, experiences, and voices in research. They contend that the positivist paradigm's insistence on value neutrality may overlook the insights and contributions of marginalised groups or underrepresented communities. By recognising the situated nature of knowledge and understanding, researchers can actively engage in dialogue and collaboration with research participants, allowing for multiple perspectives to shape the research process and findings. While the positivist paradigm promotes objectivity and value neutrality, critics highlight the challenges of achieving complete objectivity and argue for a more reflexive and inclusive approach to research. Acknowledging the influence of researcher biases and the role of social and cultural contexts is crucial in ensuring a more comprehensive and nuanced understanding of human behaviour and the social world. Researchers should actively reflect on their own subjectivity, engage in dialogue with diverse perspectives, and strive for transparency and inclusivity in their research endeavours.

### 2.9.3 Quantitative Bias

The positivist paradigm strongly emphasises quantitative methods and statistical analysis as primary tools for understanding the social world. However, critics contend that this emphasis on quantification may result in a bias towards measurable variables, thereby neglecting the qualitative aspects of human experiences (Borrell & Boulet, 2005). Quantitative methods prioritise numerical data, which can limit the exploration of the richness, depth, and complexities of subjective experiences, meanings, and interpretations. The positivist paradigm may overlook important nuances that contribute to a comprehensive understanding of social phenomena by focusing solely on quantifiable variables. Therefore, critics argue that a more holistic understanding of social phenomena requires an integration of both quantitative and qualitative methods. By combining the strengths of both approaches, researchers can gain a more comprehensive and nuanced understanding of the social world. This integration allows for the exploration of quantitative relationships while also capturing the rich qualitative aspects of human experiences.

Hence, while the positivist paradigm heavily relies on quantitative methods and statistical analysis, critics argue that this emphasis may neglect the qualitative aspects of human experiences. Therefore, one can suggest that by incorporating qualitative research methods alongside quantitative approaches, researchers can bridge this gap and gain a more comprehensive understanding of the complexities and nuances of social phenomena. This integration allows for a more holistic exploration of human experiences, meanings, and interpretations, enriching our understanding of the social world.

### 2.9.4 Generalisability and Contextual Understanding

The positivist paradigm strongly emphasises the establishment of generalisable laws or principles that can be universally applied. However, critics argue that social phenomena are intricately tied to specific social, cultural, and historical contexts. They assert that the positivist paradigm's emphasis on generalisability may overlook the uniqueness and specificity of different social settings, thereby limiting the transferability of research findings to diverse contexts (Lukka & Kasanen, 1995). Social phenomena are complex and multifaceted, influenced by a wide range of contextual factors that shape individuals' behaviours, beliefs, and experiences. The critique against generalisability within the positivist paradigm emphasises the importance of considering the specific contexts in which social phenomena occur. Different cultural norms, historical events, socioeconomic conditions, and power dynamics can significantly impact the dynamics of social phenomena and produce distinct outcomes. Thus, researchers should be cautious in assuming that findings from one context can be directly applied to other contexts without considering these contextual factors.

This critique highlights the need for researchers to embrace a more nuanced approach, acknowledging the contextual nature of social phenomena and exploring the specificities of different settings. Alternative paradigms, such as interpretivism or constructivism, emphasise the importance of context and advocate for in-depth, context-specific research that recognises and appreciates the unique characteristics of different social settings. By considering the complexities and variations across contexts, researchers can generate findings that have greater relevance and applicability to specific social contexts, fostering a more comprehensive understanding of the social world.

### 2.9.5 Power Dynamics and Researcher Dominance

Critics of the positivist paradigm raise concerns about the power dynamics inherent in traditional research practices, where researchers exert significant control over the research process, and participants are often treated as passive subjects from whom data is collected, preaching for a more participatory and collaborative approach that actively involves research participants in the research process (Prasad, 2015). These critics emphasise the importance of considering the perspectives and voices of research participants, particularly those from marginalised communities. They argue that research should be conducted on participants and with participants, recognising their agency, expertise, and lived experiences. This critique of power dynamics in the positivist paradigm calls for a shift towards more inclusive, participatory, and collaborative research practices. Such approaches aim to challenge the traditional researcher-participant hierarchy, elevate marginalised voices, and promote a more democratic and equitable research environment. By actively involving research participants and recognising their expertise, alternative paradigms seek to create more responsive, accountable, and socially just research.

### 2.9.6 Limited Emphasis on Subjective Experience

The positivist paradigm strongly emphasises objective measurement and quantification, which can neglect individuals' subjective experiences, meanings, and interpretations (Antwi & Hamza, 2015). Critics argue that this limitation overlooks the rich and diverse range of human experiences that cannot be easily captured through quantitative methods alone. Subjective experiences are complex and context-dependent, requiring qualitative approaches to delve into the depth and nuances of individual interpretations.

Quantitative methods prioritise numerical data and statistical analysis, focusing on observable and measurable variables. While these methods provide valuable insights into patterns and trends, they may fail to capture the subjective dimensions of human experiences. Qualitative methods, such as interviews, focus groups, or ethnography, offer researchers the opportunity to explore the subjective meanings individuals attribute to their experiences and the contextual factors that shape these interpretations. The integration of qualitative methods within the positivist paradigm enriches research by providing a more holistic understanding of the human experience. By acknowledging the importance of subjective interpretations and meanings, researchers can capture the individual perspectives that quantitative data alone may overlook. This integration allows for a more nuanced and comprehensive analysis, bridging the gap between objective measurements and subjective experiences and contributing to a more holistic understanding of human behaviour.

### 2.9.7 Ethical Considerations

The positivist paradigm has faced criticism for its limited attention to ethical considerations, particularly in experimental settings. Critics argue that the paradigm's focus on control and manipulation of variables may raise ethical concerns, such as the potential for harm to participants and the lack of informed consent (Lincoln & Guba, 1989). As a result, advocates stress the need for a more robust consideration of ethical principles and guidelines in research practices. Ethical concerns are fundamental to safeguarding the well-being and rights of research participants, and alternative paradigms emphasise the importance of conducting research ethically.

The positivist paradigm often prioritises the control of variables to establish cause-and-effect relationships, which can involve experimental designs with potentially intrusive interventions. Critics argue that such designs can expose participants to risks that need to be carefully evaluated and mitigated. Ethical principles, such as minimising harm, ensuring informed consent, and maintaining participant confidentiality, are crucial to protecting the rights and welfare of research participants. Alternative paradigms emphasise a more comprehensive consideration of ethical concerns, urging researchers to critically evaluate the potential risks and benefits associated with their methodologies and interventions.

Moreover, the positivist paradigm's emphasis on objectivity and detachment may downplay the significance of ethical considerations. Critics argue that ethical responsibility extends beyond adhering to formal ethical guidelines and regulations and necessitates ongoing ethical reflexivity throughout the research process. Ethical reflexivity involves continuously questioning the potential consequences of the research on participants and society, which may affect the research design and interpretation of findings.

To conclude this section, the critiques and debates surrounding the positivist paradigm have led to the emergence of alternative paradigms, such as interpretivism, constructivism, and critical theory. These paradigms offer different ontological and epistemological perspectives that challenge the positivist assumptions. They emphasise the importance of understanding social phenomena within their specific contexts, acknowledging the subjective nature of human experiences, and considering the role of power dynamics in research. Additionally, integrating qualitative and quantitative methods through mixed-methods research has gained attention, aiming to overcome the limitations of singular approaches and promote a more comprehensive understanding of social phenomena. Mixed-methods research combines the strengths of qualitative and quantitative approaches, allowing for a more nuanced understanding of complex phenomena and addressing the limitations of purely positivist perspectives.

## 2.10   Balancing Objectivity and Subjectivity in Positivist Research

Balancing objectivity and subjectivity is a crucial consideration in positivist research. The positivist paradigm, rooted in the pursuit of objective knowledge, emphasises the importance of minimising the influence of subjective biases. Researchers strive to approach their work in an impartial and unbiased manner, ensuring that their personal values and beliefs do not unduly influence the research process. In this context, objectivity involves maintaining a neutral stance in data collection, analysis, and interpretation to yield reliable and valid findings. That is, it is fostered through various practices within positivist research. For instance, researchers employ standardised protocols and methodologies to ensure consistency in data collection. By adhering to established procedures, researchers can reduce the potential impact of personal biases on the research outcomes. Additionally, employing statistical techniques helps to quantify and analyse data objectively, providing a structured and systematic approach to drawing conclusions.

However, it is important to acknowledge that complete objectivity may be unattainable. Researchers are not detached observers but rather active participants who bring their own perspectives, experiences, and subjectivities to their work. Recognising this, researchers must engage in self-reflection and reflexivity throughout the research process. Reflexivity involves critically examining one's assumptions, values, and biases and how they may shape the research process and findings. By acknowledging and addressing these influences, researchers can enhance the transparency and credibility of their work.

On the other hand, subjectivity cannot be entirely eliminated and should not be disregarded in positivist research. Subjectivity refers to the unique lens through which researchers view and interpret the world. While positivism seeks to minimise subjective influences, it is important to recognise that researchers play an active role in shaping the research process. Researchers decide on research questions, select methods, and interpret findings based on their perspectives and understandings. Therefore, it is essential to strike a balance between objectivity and subjectivity, ensuring that subjectivity is acknowledged and managed appropriately.

Triangulation is also an effective strategy for balancing objectivity and subjectivity in positivist research. Triangulation involves using multiple methods, data sources, or researchers to validate and corroborate findings.

By employing both quantitative and qualitative approaches, researchers can capture a more comprehensive understanding of the research topic. Quantitative data provides objective measurements and allows for statistical analysis, while qualitative data enables the exploration of subjective experiences, meanings, and interpretations. Triangulation, thus, enhances the validity and reliability of research findings by minimising the impact of individual subjectivity on the overall results.

Achieving a balance between objectivity and subjectivity is a critical endeavour in positivist research. While objectivity is emphasised within the paradigm, it is important to recognise and address the inherent subjectivity of researchers. Reflexivity, acknowledging the role of subjectivity, and employing triangulation are strategies that researchers can employ to ensure a balanced approach. By embracing these methods, researchers can navigate the complexities of objectivity and subjectivity, contributing to rigorous, transparent, and valid research within the positivist paradigm.

## 2.11  Summary

This chapter presents the positivist paradigm and its methodological implications in research. I discussed the philosophical foundations of the positivist paradigm, which comprises epistemology, ontology, axiology, and methodology. The key concepts such as objectivity, empiricism, deterministic principles, reductionism, universality, value-free stance, realist ontology, and deductive approach were also uncovered. Various methodological approaches within the positivist paradigm were uncovered, including experimental design, survey research, correlational research, and quasi-experimental design. To further explore the chapter, I discussed how research questions can be aligned with positivist paradigms and the factors to consider in ensuring their traceability. Additionally, data collection methods in both qualitative research, highlighting their linkages to the positivist paradigm, data analysis and interpretation in positivist research, discussing various methods such as descriptive statistics, inferential statistics, and regression analysis.

Throughout the chapter, I addressed critiques and debates surrounding the positivist paradigm, including reductionism, neglect of qualitative aspects, power dynamics, ethical considerations, and the balance between objectivity and subjectivity. I emphasised the importance of reflexivity, triangulation, and the inclusion of diverse perspectives in addressing these critiques. The main argument is that, by considering these aspects, researchers can conduct research within the positivist paradigm while also being cognisant of its limitations and actively engaging in a more comprehensive and well-aligned approach.

# 3 Interpretive/Constructive Paradigm and Methodological Alignment

**Chapter Synopsis**

The chapter begins by providing a contextualisation of the interpretive paradigm, setting the stage for a deeper understanding of its principles and applications. This includes the historical and theoretical foundations that underpin the interpretive paradigm, highlighting its philosophical underpinnings in terms of epistemology, ontology, axiology, and methodology. Understanding these foundational aspects is essential for comprehending the interpretive paradigm's unique approach to knowledge production. The chapter also delves into the key concepts and assumptions associated with the interpretive paradigm. This includes an examination of how interpretivist's view knowledge acquisition, the nature of reality, the role of values, and the preferred methodologies for conducting research within this paradigm. By exploring these concepts and assumptions, researchers gain insights into the interpretive paradigm's distinct perspective on social sciences research.

The evolution of the interpretive paradigm is also discussed, presenting an overview of how it has evolved over time, including the critiques and debates surrounding its theoretical and methodological underpinnings. This provides a deeper appreciation of the development and refinement of the interpretive paradigm in response to ongoing scholarly discussions and advancements in the field. The chapter further explores the methodological approaches within the interpretive paradigm, elucidating how researchers employing this paradigm design their studies, collect data, and analyse and interpret their findings. The alignment of research questions with the interpretive paradigm is examined, along with the presentation of case studies to illustrate the application of the paradigm in real-world research contexts. In addition, the chapter covers data collection methods, data analysis, and interpretation techniques that align with the interpretive paradigm. The unique considerations and approaches within this paradigm are explored to provide researchers with a comprehensive understanding of navigating and deriving meaning from qualitative data.

DOI: 10.4324/9781003484066-3

## 3.1 Methodological Designs of Interpretive Paradigm

The interpretive paradigm embodies a methodological orientation geared towards qualitative research designs, making it particularly well-suited for probing into subjective meanings, social interactions, and the construction of reality. Acknowledging the importance of context, individual perspectives, and the intricate complexity of social phenomena, this paradigm strives to encapsulate and interpret these multifaceted dimensions through its distinct methodological approach. By valuing these nuanced elements, the interpretive paradigm employs specific research designs that are adept at unveiling the subtle interplay of meanings and relationships within the social world. The research designs commonly utilised within this paradigm are discussed below, illuminating how they collectively contribute to a richer understanding of human experience and social dynamics.

- **Ethnography:** Ethnography is a research design that consists of embedding oneself in a particular social setting or community to comprehensively examine the cultural meanings, practices, and social interactions within that specific environment (Cunliffe & Karunanayake, 2013). This design is particularly suited to the interpretive research paradigm, as it resonates with the principles and objectives that guide this approach. By engaging in participant observation, researchers actively immerse themselves in the daily activities and interactions of community members, affording them the opportunity to observe behaviours, rituals, and social dynamics. This immersion provides a robust and detailed portrayal of the community's unique social context, capturing the subtle nuances and specific factors that influence individual actions and interpretations. The inclusion of interviews is an essential component of ethnography, allowing researchers to gather firsthand accounts that unveil the perspectives, beliefs, and experiences of community members. This technique aligns perfectly with the focus of the interpretive paradigm on exploring diverse realities and subjective interpretations. Complementing these methods, document analysis further enriches the understanding by offering historical and contextual insights through the examination of diaries, letters, photographs, and other pertinent materials. These documents provide a deeper grasp of the community's cultural fabric and historical background. Therefore, the inherently immersive character of ethnography, coupled with its reliance on participant observation, interviews, and document analysis, renders it an excellent fit for the implementation of interpretive research, enabling an intricate exploration of subjective meanings and the socially constructed nature of reality within particular social milieus.
- **Phenomenology:** This design aims to explore the lived experiences of individuals and uncover the subjective meanings they attribute to those experiences. Phenomenology is a research design that is highly suitable for conducting interpretive research because it aligns closely with the

interpretive paradigm's focus on understanding the subjective nature of reality and the diverse perspectives individuals bring to their social interactions. Phenomenology seeks to uncover the essence of a phenomenon as experienced by individuals, aiming to understand the underlying meanings they assign to their lived experiences (Neubauer et al., 2019). Through in-depth interviews and reflective analysis, researchers explore participants' rich and nuanced descriptions, allowing for a deep understanding of their subjective interpretations of the phenomenon.

Therefore, phenomenology is particularly relevant to interpretive research as it emphasises the importance of context and the influence of cultural, social, and historical factors on individuals' experiences and interpretations. It recognises that individuals construct their own meanings and interpretations of their experiences, which may differ from person to person. Phenomenological research aims to capture and interpret these diverse perspectives, enabling a deeper understanding of the complexity and subjectivity of social phenomena. Researchers employing phenomenology within the interpretive paradigm can gain insights into the subjective nature of reality and uncover the diverse ways individuals make meaning of their social interactions.

- **Grounded Theory:** The grounded theory research design is a method that emphasises the development of theories and concepts originating from the data itself rather than deriving from pre-existing models or preconceived notions (Hussein et al., 2014). It stands as a valuable methodology within the interpretive research paradigm, perfectly aligning with the paradigm's focus on understanding subjective meanings and interpretations. Using constant comparative analysis, researchers engaged in grounded theory methodically identify patterns, categories, and themes within the data. This analytical process allows them to construct theories firmly rooted in the participants' perspectives, offering insights that are genuinely reflective of their experiences. Unlike methods that might impose existing theories onto the data, grounded theory fosters an iterative data collection and analysis process that unveils and interprets the multifaceted and complex nature of subjective experiences and meanings. By constructing theories that are precisely informed by participants' unique perspectives, this approach facilitates a profound understanding of the diverse interpretations of social phenomena. Overall, Grounded Theory's commitment to developing theories that emerge organically from the participants' views and experiences makes it an instrumental tool for interpretive research, resonating strongly with the paradigm's objectives of delving into the nuanced subjective realities within social contexts.
- **Narrative Research:** This design examines the stories and narratives that individuals construct to make sense of their experiences (Cardona-Rivera et al., 2020). Researchers collect and analyse personal narratives through interviews or written accounts to understand how individuals construct their identities and make meaning of their lives. Narrative research is

highly relevant to implementing interpretive research. It examines the stories and narratives that individuals construct to make sense of their experiences, shedding light on how they construct identities and attribute meaning to their lives. Researchers collect and analyse personal narratives through interviews or written accounts to better understand individuals' subjective interpretations. It allows researchers to explore the complexities of subjective experiences and interpretations, aligning with the interpretive paradigm's focus on understanding subjective meanings. This approach provides insights into how individuals navigate their social worlds and negotiate their identities within specific contexts. Narrative research captures the richness and contextuality of social phenomena, enabling a deeper understanding of subjective meanings within the interpretive paradigm making it a valuable tool for implementing interpretive research.

- **Case Study:** The case study research design is a method that enables an in-depth investigation of a specific case or phenomenon, aligning impeccably with the interpretive paradigm's focus on exploring the subjective meanings, social interactions, and contextual intricacies of social phenomena. Characterised by an intensive examination of instances within a defined context, this design employs multiple data sources such as interviews, observations, and document analysis. Such a multifaceted approach facilitates a rich and comprehensive understanding of the case under study, allowing researchers to unearth the individuals' subjective interpretations, meanings, and experiences (Harrison et al., 2017). The case study method captures the unique aspects of a specific case and contributes to the development of nuanced interpretations that enhance our understanding of the underlying social processes and meanings. Therefore, the suitability of the case study research design for interpretive research lies in its capability to provide a profound insight into the complexities of social phenomena, reflecting the interpretive paradigm's emphasis on the exploration of subjective realities within specific social contexts.

- **Critical Ethnography:** This design combines elements of traditional ethnography with a critical lens. Under this design, researchers engage in a reflexive exploration of power structures, social inequalities, and oppressive systems within a specific community or social setting (Breda, 2013). Critical ethnography is highly relevant to interpretive research as it combines elements of traditional ethnography with a critical lens. Researchers engaging in critical ethnography reflexively explore power structures, social inequalities, and oppressive systems within a specific community or social setting. This design aligns closely with the interpretive paradigm's emphasis on understanding the subjective nature of reality and the socially constructed aspects of social phenomena. Critical ethnography goes beyond surface-level understanding to uncover the underlying mechanisms that contribute to social inequalities and perpetuate oppressive systems by critically examining the power dynamics and oppressive structures. It enables researchers to reveal the lived experiences of individuals within the context of power relations, shedding light on the complexities of social life. Additionally, critical ethnography embraces reflexivity, encouraging researchers to reflect on their own positionality and biases, recognising that they are active participants in the research process. Critical ethnography contributes to the interpretive paradigm's commitment to understanding and challenging dominant narratives, fostering a deeper understanding of social phenomena within specific contexts by addressing power imbalances and advocating for social justice.

## 3.2 Concept of Interpretive Paradigm

The interpretive paradigm, rooted in hermeneutic and phenomenological traditions, emphasises the construction and dynamic nature of meaning (Schwartz-Shea, 2014). It is particularly relevant in social science research, where it can provide a deeper understanding of social reality and human behaviour (Adil et al., 2022). The interpretive paradigm, also known as the constructivist paradigm, is a research worldview widely used in social sciences that focuses on understanding human experiences, meanings, and interpretations. It emphasises the subjective and contextual nature of social phenomena and aims to uncover the complexities of human behaviour by examining the social and cultural contexts in which it occurs. This paradigm recognises that individuals actively construct their own realities and that multiple interpretations can exist within a given social context (Goulding, 1999). In the context of the interpretive paradigm, researchers recognise that knowledge is not fixed or objective but rather socially constructed and shaped by individual and cultural perspectives. It rejects the notion of a single truth or universal laws governing human behaviour; instead, it emphasises the importance of context, cultural values, and individual experiences. Researchers operating within the interpretive paradigm seek to explore the subjective meanings and interpretations that individuals attribute to their experiences, focusing on understanding participants' unique perspectives (Pervin & Mokhtar, 2022).

Most notably, interpretive paradigm is rooted in a qualitative research approach, employing methods such as interviews, observations, and textual analysis to gather rich, in-depth data (Adil et al., 2022; Schwartz-Shea, 2014). These methods allow researchers to delve into the complexities and nuances of human experiences, capturing the depth and richness of the participants' perspectives. The interpretive paradigm places importance on the researcher's role as an active participant in the research process, engaging in dialogue and interpretation to make sense of the data collected. On the other hand, interpretive paradigm emphasises the idea of reflexivity, recognising that researchers bring their own perspectives and biases to the research process. Researchers actively reflect on their own assumptions and values, critically examining how their own positionality may influence the research design and interpretation of findings. According to Darawsheh (2014), reflexivity enhances the transparency and rigour of the research, enabling researchers to acknowledge and address their own biases and potential impacts on the research outcomes.

Based on this concept, one can then argue that the interpretive paradigm provides a framework for understanding social phenomena through the lens of subjective experiences, meanings, and interpretations. It highlights the importance of context, cultural values, and individual perspectives, offering a deeper understanding of human behaviour in its social and cultural context. Therefore, by adopting this paradigm, researchers can explore the complexities of human experiences and contribute to knowledge that reflects the diversity and richness of the social world.

## 3.3 The Evolution of Interpretive Paradigms

The evolution of the interpretive paradigm has been shaped by a range of factors, including advancements in social sciences, shifts in theoretical perspectives, and critical engagement with its underlying principles. Over time, the interpretive paradigm has undergone refinement and expansion, adapting to the changing landscape of research in social sciences. The roots of the interpretive paradigm can be traced back to hermeneutics, which focuses on the interpretation of texts and understanding the meaning embedded within them (Scholz, 2023; Tomkins & Eatough, 2018). In the early 20th century, scholars such as Max Weber and Alfred Schütz laid the groundwork for interpretive sociology, emphasising the importance of subjective understanding and the social context in understanding human behaviour (Fallace & Fantozzi, 2013; Pfadenhauer & Knoblauch, 2018; Schutz, 1972). The interpretive paradigm continued to evolve through the work of sociologists like George Herbert Mead and Erving Goffman, who explored the symbolic interactions and social construction of reality (Quist-Adade, 2019). These scholars emphasised the significance of symbols, language, and shared meanings in shaping human behaviour. The interpretive paradigm gained further momentum with the emergence of phenomenology and ethnomethodology, which focused on individuals' lived experiences and everyday practices.

In more recent decades, the interpretive paradigm has been influenced by postmodern perspectives. Postmodernism challenges the notion of singular truths and objective realities, emphasising the multiplicity of perspectives and the role of power in shaping knowledge. However, the evolution reflects a continuous engagement with philosophical, theoretical, and methodological advancements. It expands the understanding of human behaviour by focusing on the subjective and contextual aspects of social phenomena and embracing a more holistic and inclusive approach to knowledge production. As it evolved, researchers have become more attuned to the complexities of social phenomena, recognising the importance of exploring diverse perspectives and understanding the social, cultural, and historical contexts in which they arise. This evolution has been marked by a broader embrace of qualitative research methods, such as interviews, ethnography, and textual analysis, which allow for a more nuanced understanding of subjective experiences and interpretations.

## 3.4 Key Concepts and Assumptions

The interpretive paradigm encompasses several key concepts and assumptions that underpin its approach to understanding social phenomena. These concepts and assumptions guide researchers in their exploration of subjective meanings, social interactions, and the construction of reality. Therefore, understanding these key concepts and assumptions provides a framework for researchers to delve into the subjective and socially constructed aspects of social phenomena that enable a nuanced understanding of how individuals assign meanings to their experiences, how social reality is constructed, and how context shapes social interactions. The key concepts and assumptions are:

i **Subjective Meanings:** In embracing the interpretive paradigm, acknowledgement is given to individuals attributing subjective meanings to their experiences and interactions, as elucidated by Fallace and Fantozzi (2013). Central to this paradigm is the recognition that these meanings are not inherent but rather socially and culturally constructed, exhibiting variations across different individuals and contexts. Researchers aligned with the interpretive paradigm aim to uncover and interpret these subjective meanings, seeking to delve into the intricacies of individual perspectives and the contextual nuances that shape them. The emphasis lies in gaining a profound and nuanced understanding of the phenomena under investigation, with a keen awareness of subjective interpretations' dynamic and culturally embedded nature.

ii **Social Construction of Reality:** At the foundation of the interpretive paradigm is the belief that reality is not an objective thing but is actually constructed as a result of the interaction of people among themselves, as Otoo (2020) claims. With this paradigm, what is a critical component is the recognition that individuals have a very significant say in how they interact in their social world and the meaning they produce. This can only be achieved through reliance on shared meaning, cultural norms, and the history behind the specific explanation of the social concepts of time, race, family, or any other social concept. When one seeks to consider the ongoing process by which social reality becomes constructed and, just as significantly, "[negotiated]" (Otoo, 2020, p. 21), the interpretive paradigm underlines how that one aspect of social time means to someone or other individual social perceptions, or culture and history, are all present.

iii **Multiple Realities and Perspectives:** Within the interpretive paradigm, a fundamental acknowledgement exists that a given phenomenon can be subject to multiple valid interpretations, as highlighted by Erciyes (2020). This paradigm embraces the understanding that individuals, shaped by their distinct perspectives, experiences, and cultural backgrounds, contribute to a rich tapestry of diverse interpretations of the world. Researchers aligned with this paradigm actively seek to capture and interpret these multifaceted realities and perspectives, recognising the inherent complexity arising from the diverse ways individuals make sense of and engage with their surroundings. By valuing and exploring the plurality of valid interpretations, the interpretive paradigm encourages a comprehensive and nuanced approach to understanding the intricate interplay of individual perspectives in constructing meaning and reality.

iv **Contextual Understanding:** The interpretive paradigm underscores the pivotal role of context in shaping social phenomena, emphasising that the intricacies of social interactions and meanings are profoundly influenced by the specific cultural, historical, and situational contexts within which they unfold. This paradigm posits that a comprehensive understanding of social phenomena necessitates an exploration of the contextual factors that contribute to their construction and interpretation. Researchers aligned with the interpretive paradigm engage in a deliberate and nuanced examination of the multifaceted layers inherent in cultural, historical, and situational contexts, recognising that these elements play a crucial role in shaping the dynamics of social interactions and their meanings. Therefore, by prioritising the study of context, the interpretive paradigm seeks to unravel the complex interplay between external influences and the construction of social phenomena, fostering a more profound comprehension of the intricate tapestry of human experiences.

v **Reflexivity and Interpretation:** The interpretive paradigm advocates for reflexivity, urging researchers to engage in critical self-reflection on their own assumptions, biases, and values that have the potential to impact the research process and subsequent interpretations, as noted by Malaurent and Avison (2017). This paradigm acknowledges the dynamic role of researchers as active participants in the production of knowledge, embracing the notion that interpretations are inherently subjective. Within this framework, researchers partake in an iterative process of interpretation, continually engaging in dialogue and discussion to refine their understanding of social phenomena. Therefore, fostering a culture of self-awareness and critical introspection, the interpretive paradigm recognises the subjective nature of research. It promotes a continual refinement of perspectives, thereby enriching the depth and quality of the interpretations generated throughout the research process.

vi **Qualitative and Inductive Methods:** Within the interpretive paradigm, a preference is distinctly manifested for qualitative research methods, which facilitate a comprehensive and nuanced exploration of subjective meanings and interpretations, as highlighted by Thanh and Thanh (2015). Techniques like interviews, participant observation, and textual analysis are frequently employed under this paradigm, allowing researchers to delve deeply into the intricacies of individual perspectives. The paradigm places significant importance on the generation of rich descriptions and thick descriptions, recognising the value of qualitative methods in providing a contextual understanding of phenomena. In embracing these methodologies, the interpretive paradigm seeks to capture the essence and complexity of human experiences, acknowledging the multifaceted nature of subjective interpretations and emphasising the depth of insight that qualitative research can bring to the understanding of social phenomena.

vii **Value-Laden Nature of Research:** The interpretive paradigm acknowledges that research is value-laden and that researchers cannot be completely objective or value-neutral (Brown, 2019; Zyphur & Pierides, 2020). It emphasises the importance of transparency, ethical considerations, and respecting the voices and experiences of research participants. That is, there is an acknowledgement that research inherently carries value, rendering complete objectivity or value-neutrality unattainable for researchers. This paradigm recognises the crucial significance of transparency, ethical considerations, and the profound respect for the voices and experiences of the research participants. Consequently, researchers operating within this paradigm find themselves compelled to navigate the intricacies of their own values and biases, all while prioritising a commitment to transparency and ethical conduct in their research pursuits.

## 3.5 The Philosophical Foundations of Interpretive Paradigm

The interpretive paradigm, a vital approach to understanding social phenomena, is underpinned by four key philosophical foundations: epistemology, ontology, axiology, and methodology. Together, these elements form a comprehensive framework that guides the paradigm's distinct approach to research. Epistemology emphasises the subjective nature of knowledge formation, while ontology focuses on the socially constructed nature of reality. Axiology acknowledges the value-laden nature of research and the importance of ethical considerations, and the methodology outlines the qualitative techniques and collaborative processes utilised within this paradigm. The following section delves into these critical aspects, illustrating how they collectively shape the interpretive paradigm's unique approach to exploring and understanding the complex and multifaceted human experience.

### 3.5.1 *Epistemology of Interpretive Paradigm*

Within the interpretive paradigm, epistemology diverges significantly from the concept of objective knowledge, emphasising instead the inherent subjectivity in understanding and constructing knowledge. It acknowledges that individual perspectives, subtle biases, and varying cultural contexts intertwine, shaping the complex process of interpreting the world around us (Adil et al., 2022). Unlike approaches seeking universal and unchanging truths, the interpretive paradigm focuses on uncovering the diverse meanings and interpretations people assign to their experiences, grounded in their unique situations. This standpoint highlights the socially constructed nature of knowledge, born from fluid interactions and personal interpretations within specific temporal and spatial circumstances (Cuthbertson et al., 2020). In adhering to this paradigm, researchers skilfully utilise various methodological approaches, such as in-depth qualitative interviews, participant observation, and textual analysis. These tools serve to explore the rich, multifaceted subjective meanings and interpretations that form the essence of human cognition and experience.

### 3.5.2 Ontology of Interpretive Paradigm

Ontologically, the interpretive paradigm recognises the socially constructed nature of reality, rejecting the notion of an objective reality that exists independently of human perception. Instead, it emphasises that reality is actively and continuously constructed through social interactions, shared meanings, and individual experiences (Otoo, 2020). This ontological perspective views individuals not as passive observers but as active participants in the construction of their social worlds, influenced and shaped by their cultural, historical, and societal contexts. According to Erciyes (2020), the interpretive paradigm seeks to understand the multiple realities and varying perspectives within a given social setting, recognising that each individual's experience is uniquely situated. Within this framework, researchers engage in detailed, thick descriptions to uncover and articulate the subjective experiences, meanings, and interpretations that individuals attribute to their social interactions and phenomena. By delving into these complex layers of meaning, the interpretive paradigm provides a nuanced and holistic view of the social world, reflecting the intricate interplay of personal perspectives and shared cultural understandings.

### 3.5.3 Axiology of Interpretive Paradigm

In the axiology of the interpretive paradigm, there is an acknowledgement of the value-laden nature of research, embracing the fact that researchers cannot be entirely objective or value-neutral (Brown, 2019; Zyphur & Pierides, 2020). That is, researchers within this paradigm recognise that they inevitably bring their own unique perspectives, assumptions, and values to the research process, all of which can shape their interpretations and conclusions. Rather than trying to eliminate these influences, the interpretive paradigm encourages reflexivity, prompting researchers to critically reflect on and recognise their biases and assumptions (Kler, 2010). This includes being open about how these personal factors might affect the research process and its outcomes. This paradigm places significant emphasis on transparency, ethical considerations, and respecting the voices and experiences of research participants. Researchers strive to understand and fully acknowledge the ethical dimensions of their work, including the potential impact their research may have on the individuals and communities involved. This approach reflects a commitment to an empathetic and responsible research practice that values both the process of inquiry and the welfare of the research subjects.

*3.5.4 Methodology of Interpretive Paradigm*

Within the methodology of the interpretive paradigm, qualitative research methods such as interviews, observations, and textual analysis are typically employed, enabling an in-depth exploration of subjective meanings and interpretations (Darby et al., 2019; Frechette et al., 2020). This paradigm values context, detailed description, and a holistic understanding of the social phenomena under investigation. Through iterative data collection and analysis processes, researchers actively seek to uncover patterns, themes, and shared meanings, offering a rich and nuanced perspective. Emphasising the role of interpretation and dialogue in the production of knowledge, the interpretive paradigm recognises that multiple valid interpretations can coexist, reflecting the complexity of human experience. This encourages critical and reflexive conversations among researchers, fostering a collaborative and interpretive community of inquiry. In this way, the interpretive paradigm provides the methodological tools to delve into complex social realities and promotes a thoughtful and communal approach to understanding the intricacies of human life.

In summary, the interpretive paradigm is grounded in philosophical foundations that shape its epistemological, ontological, axiological, and methodological perspectives that embrace subjectivity, the socially constructed nature of reality, the value-laden nature of research, and qualitative methods to uncover subjective meanings and interpretations. These philosophical foundations provide a framework for understanding and interpreting social phenomena from a nuanced and contextual perspective.

## 3.6 Aligning Research Questions with Interpretive Paradigms

Aligning research questions with interpretive paradigms involves ensuring that the questions are rooted in the principles and perspectives of the interpretive paradigm. There are several factors that contribute to making research questions traceable to interpretive paradigms:

i **Subjective Meaning:** Research questions aligned with interpretive paradigms focus on exploring the subjective meanings individuals assign to their experiences and social interactions. They seek to understand how individuals interpret and make sense of the world around them.
   **Example 1:** How do individuals interpret and ascribe meaning to the experience of unemployment in their lives?
   **Example 2:** What are the subjective meanings that individuals attach to the concept of "success" in the context of a competitive work environment?

ii **Contextual Understanding:** Research questions traceable to interpretive paradigms emphasise the importance of understanding the social, cultural, and historical context in which phenomena occur. They consider how context shapes individuals' interpretations and interactions.

    **Example 1:** How do cultural beliefs and practices influence the decision-making process of families in healthcare choices for their elderly members?

    **Example 2:** In what ways do historical events and societal norms shape the experiences and perspectives of individuals in a postcolonial society?

iii **Multiple Realities and Perspectives:** Research questions within interpretive paradigms acknowledge the existence of multiple realities and perspectives. They aim to explore the diverse interpretations and experiences of individuals within a given social setting, recognising that different individuals may attribute different meanings to the same phenomenon.

    **Example 1:** How do different religious groups in a diverse community interpret and practice concepts of forgiveness and reconciliation?

    **Example 2:** What are the varying perspectives and interpretations of success among students from different socioeconomic backgrounds in an educational institution?

iv **Social Construction of Reality:** Research questions aligned with interpretive paradigms address how reality is socially constructed and negotiated. They seek to understand the processes through which individuals collectively create and interpret their social worlds.

    **Example 1:** How do individuals within a marginalised community collectively construct and negotiate their identities in response to societal stereotypes and discrimination?

    **Example 2:** In what ways do social media platforms influence the construction of self-image and identity among young adults?

v **Reflexivity and Interpretation:** Research questions traceable to interpretive paradigms encourage reflexivity and self-awareness on the part of the researcher. They explore how the researcher's own perspectives, biases, and values may shape the research process and interpretations.

    **Example 1:** How do the researcher's own cultural background and experiences shape their interpretation of cross-cultural communication in a multicultural workplace?

    **Example 2:** What role do the researcher's personal values and biases play in understanding and interpreting ethical dilemmas in medical decision-making?

By ensuring that research questions encompass these factors, researchers can align their inquiries with the principles and perspectives of the interpretive paradigm. This alignment enables a deeper exploration of subjective realities, contextual understanding, and the social construction of meaning within specific social phenomena.

## 3.6.1 Case Studies on How to Align Research Questions with Interpretive Paradigm

Here are some case studies that demonstrate how research questions can be aligned with the interpretive paradigm:

---

**Case Study 1: Exploring Subjective Experiences of Work-Life Balance in a Multinational Corporation**

**Research Question:** How do employees in a global organisation interpret and perceive workplace equality, considering the impact of diverse cultural factors on their understanding and experiences?

**Alignment with Interpretive Paradigm**

This research topic is designed to embrace critical tenets of the interpretive paradigm, ensuring a comprehensive exploration of the complex dynamics surrounding workplace equality within a global organisation. The research question and its considerations align with various aspects of interpretive paradigms, as indicated below.

- **Subjective Meaning:** The research question explicitly targets employees' subjective interpretations and perceptions regarding workplace equality. By asking, "How do employees interpret and perceive," the study aims to uncover the unique and personal meanings individuals attribute to workplace equality.
- **Contextual Understanding:** The research also strongly emphasises contextual understanding by acknowledging the impact of diverse cultural factors. It recognises that workplace equality is not a universal concept but is shaped by the specific social, cultural, and organisational context within a global setting.
- **Multiple Realities and Perspectives:** By considering the influence of diverse cultural factors, this case study inherently acknowledges the existence of multiple realities and perspectives. It explores how different individuals within the global organisation may perceive workplace equality differently based on their cultural backgrounds and experiences.
- **Social Construction of Reality:** The research question implicitly addresses the social construction of reality by investigating how individuals within the global organisation collectively create and interpret the concept of workplace equality. It recognises that perceptions of equality are socially constructed within the organisational context and influenced by broader cultural factors.

- **Reflexivity and Interpretation:** The case study also promotes reflexivity and interpretation by recognising the role of diverse cultural factors in shaping individuals' understanding and experiences of workplace equality. It implicitly encourages the researcher to reflect on their perspectives and biases, fostering a deeper understanding of the complexities involved in the study.

**Case Study 2: Understanding the Construction of Online Self-Identity in Social Media Platforms**

**Research Question:** How do individuals construct and negotiate their self-identity on social media platforms, considering the influence of cultural norms, self-presentation strategies, and interactions with online communities?

**Alignment with Interpretive Paradigm**

This research topic is designed to embrace critical tenets of the interpretive paradigm, ensuring a comprehensive exploration of the complex dynamics surrounding the construction of online self-identity within social media platforms. The research question and its considerations align with various aspects of interpretive paradigms, as indicated below.

- **Subjective Meaning:** The research question explicitly targets individuals' subjective interpretations and experiences regarding the construction of online self-identity. By asking, "How do individuals construct and negotiate," the study aims to uncover the unique and personal meanings individuals attribute to online self-identity.
- **Contextual Understanding:** The research also strongly emphasises contextual understanding by acknowledging the influence of cultural norms on the construction of online self-identity. It recognises that specific socio-cultural factors within the context of social media platforms shape online self-identity.
- **Multiple Realities and Perspectives:** By considering the influence of cultural norms, self-presentation strategies, and interactions with online communities, this case study inherently acknowledges the existence of multiple realities and perspectives. It explores how different individuals construct and negotiate their self-identity differently based on cultural backgrounds and online experiences.

*Interpretive/Constructive Paradigm and Methodological Alignment* 73

- **Social Construction of Reality:** The research question implicitly addresses the social construction of reality by investigating how individuals collectively create and negotiate their self-identity within social media platforms. It recognises that self-identity is socially constructed and influenced by broader cultural factors and online interactions.
- **Reflexivity and Interpretation:** The case study also promotes reflexivity and interpretation by recognising the role of cultural norms, self-presentation strategies, and online interactions in shaping individuals' understanding and experiences of online self-identity. It implicitly encourages the researcher to reflect on their perspectives and biases, fostering a deeper understanding of the complexities involved in the study.

**Case Study 3: Navigating Diversity and Inclusion in Contemporary African Workplaces**

**Research Question:** How do contemporary African workplaces navigate and promote diversity and inclusion, considering the influence of cultural, organisational, and societal factors on employees' experiences and perceptions?

**Alignment with Interpretive Paradigm**

This research topic is designed to embrace key tenets of the interpretive paradigm, ensuring a comprehensive exploration of the complex dynamics surrounding diversity and inclusion in contemporary African workplaces. The research question and its considerations align with various aspects of interpretive paradigms, as indicated below.

- **Subjective Meaning:** The research question explicitly targets employees' subjective interpretations and experiences regarding diversity and inclusion in contemporary African workplaces. By asking, "How do contemporary African workplaces navigate and promote diversity and inclusion?" the study aims to uncover individuals' unique and personal meanings of the concepts within their work environments.
- **Contextual Understanding:** The research strongly emphasises contextual understanding by acknowledging the influence of cultural, organisational, and societal factors. It recognises that specific sociocultural norms, organisational structures, and broader societal expectations shape diversity and inclusion efforts in African workplaces.

- **Multiple Realities and Perspectives:** By considering the influence of cultural, organisational, and societal factors, this case study inherently acknowledges the existence of multiple realities and perspectives. It explores how individuals within contemporary African workplaces may perceive and experience diversity and inclusion efforts differently based on their cultural backgrounds, organisational roles, and societal contexts.
- **Social Construction of Reality:** The research question implicitly addresses the social construction of reality by investigating how individuals within contemporary African workplaces collectively create and interpret diversity and inclusion. It recognises that perceptions of these concepts are socially constructed within the organisational context and influenced by broader cultural and societal factors.
- **Reflexivity and Interpretation:** The case study also promotes reflexivity and interpretation by recognising the role of cultural, organisational, and societal factors in shaping individuals' understanding and experiences of diversity and inclusion. It implicitly encourages the researcher to reflect on their own perspectives and biases, fostering a deeper understanding of the complexities involved in the study.

In all case studies, the research questions prioritise the exploration of subjective meanings, contextual understanding, multiple realities and perspectives, the social construction of reality and reflexivity and interpretation, which are fundamental aspects of the interpretive paradigm. By using qualitative methods and considering the complexities of the specific contexts, these studies align with the interpretive paradigm's objectives of understanding subjective experiences, diverse perspectives, and the socially constructed nature of phenomena.

### 3.7 Data Collection Methods in Interpretive Research

Data collection methods are integral to interpretive research, enabling researchers to amass rich, qualitative information that encapsulates individuals' subjective meanings and interpretations within particular social contexts. Aligning with the foundational principles of the interpretive paradigm, the methods below underscore the importance of comprehending diverse perspectives, social interactions, and the specific nature of various social phenomena. The interpretive paradigm's emphasis on multifaceted understanding is reflected in the utilisation of a broad array of data collection techniques. These methods, often numbering around ten prominent ones, are systematically deployed in interpretive research to delve into how each uniquely relates to and resonates with the core tenets of the interpretive paradigm.

By employing these specialised tools, researchers are able to construct a textured and nuanced understanding that honours the complexity and individuality inherent in social experiences.

- **Interviews:** Interviews, as a method of data collection, play a vital role in interpretive research by fostering open-ended and exploratory dialogues with participants (Gardner, 2010). This method is uniquely tailored to understand the subjective experiences, interpretations, and perspectives of those being studied, in line with the focus of the interpretive paradigm on grasping the multiplicity of human experience. By facilitating direct interaction with participants, interviews enable researchers to capture rich, nuanced insights, uncovering the unique subjective meanings and interpretations that individuals ascribe to social phenomena. Unlike more structured or quantitatively driven methods, the interview method in interpretive research is inherently flexible and responsive, allowing for an organic exploration of thoughts and feelings. This fosters a more empathetic and human-centred understanding of social contexts, reflecting the interpretive paradigm's commitment to complexity, diversity, and the deeply contextual nature of human experience.
- **Participant Observation:** Participant observation is a central method in interpretive research that requires researchers to immerse themselves in the examined social context, actively observing and engaging with participants. Unlike more detached data collection methods, participant observation enables a deep and intimate understanding of social interactions, behaviours, and cultural practices within a given context (Balsiger & Lambelet, 2014). It aligns closely with the goals interpretive paradigm by facilitating the exploration of subjective meanings and the complex dynamics that shape human interaction and community life. Through active participation in the everyday lives of those being studied, researchers can glean insights into how individuals construct and interpret their reality, capturing the nuances and subtleties that might otherwise go unnoticed. This hands-on method provides a rich, layered understanding of social phenomena, allowing for a more holistic and empathetic portrayal of human experience. In turn, it reinforces the interpretive paradigm's emphasis on the socially constructed nature of reality and the intricate interplay of individual perception, cultural norms, and communal practices.
- **Focus Group Discussion:** Focus group discussions, which assemble a small group of participants for a guided conversation around a specific subject, are particularly suited for interpretive research (Redman-MacLaren et al., 2014). This method offers an opportunity to capture collective perspectives and shared experiences, extending beyond individual viewpoints to the negotiation of meaning within a communal context. By engaging participants in dynamic conversation, researchers can observe and analyse group dynamics, understanding how social interactions shape perceptions and forge common understandings. This rich, collaborative process allows

for the exploration of diverse perspectives and the way meanings are constructed collectively. The shared insights that emerge from focus group discussions provide a window into the multifaceted nature of social reality and how it is continuously negotiated and reshaped by group members. It also emphasises the interpretive paradigm's concern with the complexity of social interactions and the context-specific nature of social phenomena. In focusing on the collective rather than solely the individual, focus group discussions enrich the interpretive research by providing a textured understanding of the social processes that underpin human experience and meaning making.

- **Document Analysis:** Document analysis, the scrutiny of written or textual materials such as official records, letters, diaries, or media artefacts, serves as an essential method within interpretive research (Davie & Wyatt, 2021). By examining these documents, researchers can delve into the cultural, historical, and discursive dimensions of the social phenomena they are investigating. This method allows for understanding the broader context within which individual and collective meanings are constructed. It can reveal how power dynamics shape narratives, how symbolic meanings are embedded within texts, and how social realities are portrayed and perpetuated through written expression. The interpretive paradigm, with its focus on understanding the subjective and context-specific nature of social phenomena, finds in document analysis a powerful tool for uncovering layers of meaning. By decoding the subtleties of text, researchers can glean insights into the complexities of human thought and interaction, exploring how societal values, norms, and histories are captured, conveyed, and often contested within documents. This method enriches interpretive research by offering a nuanced view of how social meanings are inscribed and how they resonate within specific social contexts.

- **Ethnographic Observation:** Ethnographic observation is a method that requires researchers to observe and document the everyday practices, interactions, and cultural meanings within a specific community or social setting (Conroy, 2017). By immersing themselves in the environment and paying close attention to context-specific behaviours, social norms, and cultural practices, researchers can understand how individuals' experiences and interpretations are shaped. This method aligns with the principles of interpretive research, focusing on the subjective meanings, cultural dynamics, and the unique context within which social phenomena occur. It allows researchers to see the world from the community members' perspective, uncovering the underlying assumptions, values, and beliefs that inform their everyday lives. Rather than imposing preconceived notions or theories, ethnographic observation facilitates a rich, ground-level understanding of human experience. It helps reveal the complexities and subtleties of social life, emphasising the intricate interplay between individuals and their social environment. By focusing on the lived realities of people within their specific contexts, ethnographic observation contributes to a

nuanced and holistic understanding of social phenomena within the interpretive paradigm.
- **Narrative Interviews:** Narrative interviews are a distinct method that involves the collection of participants' personal narratives and life stories, allowing them to construct and share their own accounts of experiences and interpretations (Küsters, 2022). This method goes beyond mere question-and-answer interactions; it empowers individuals to articulate their lives in their own words and ways, unveiling how they construct their identities, make meaning of their existence, and interpret various social phenomena. Narrative interviews are closely related to interpretive research, as they prioritise individuals' subjective voices and sense-making processes within their specific social contexts. Researchers can gain rich insights into the complexities of human experience, relationships, values, and beliefs by enabling participants to share their stories without strict constraints or predetermined categories. This method emphasises empathy, collaboration, and deep listening, fostering a research environment where participants feel heard and understood. The focus on personal narratives aligns with the interpretive paradigm's commitment to understanding diverse realities and subjective interpretations, allowing for a more nuanced and compassionate exploration of social life.
- **Visual Methods:** Visual methods in research encompass the utilisation of photographs, videos, drawings, or other visual artefacts as tools for exploration and expression (Guillemin & Drew, 2010). By allowing participants to convey their thoughts, feelings, and experiences through visual means, these methods provide a unique window into the subjective and often unspoken dimensions of social life. Unlike traditional text-based approaches, visual methods enable non-verbal communication, inviting participants to share their perspectives in ways that might be more intuitive or resonant for them. This approach aligns seamlessly with the interpretive paradigm, as it acknowledges the multifaceted nature of human experience and interpretation, recognising that meanings can be constructed and conveyed through symbols, images, and visual narratives. The emphasis on visuality and symbolism facilitates a deeper understanding of social phenomena' aesthetic, emotional, and cultural aspects, creating a rich tapestry of insights that might remain hidden in purely verbal or textual inquiries. Overall, visual methods extend the horizons of interpretive research, offering innovative avenues for engaging with participants and exploring the complex interplay of perception, imagination, and social reality.
- **Reflexive Journals and Field Notes:** Reflexive journals in data collection play a crucial role in qualitative research, particularly in understanding the experiences and perspectives of participants (Sherwood, 2011). In the same vein, field notes also provide rich contextual information that can be used for secondary analysis and meta-synthesis (Phillippi & Lauderdale, 2018). They both serve as vital tools in interpretive research, providing a space for researchers to record and critically examine their own thoughts,

feelings, biases, and interpretive lenses throughout the research process. This method goes beyond mere data collection, promoting continual self-reflection and scrutiny of the researcher's positionality, assumptions, and influence on the research context and interactions. By maintaining these reflexive records, researchers actively engage in a dialogical process with themselves, acknowledging the inherently subjective nature of qualitative inquiry and striving for a deeper, more nuanced understanding of their own role in the co-construction of meanings and interpretations. The practice of reflexivity accentuates the interpretive paradigm's emphasis on the complex interplay between researcher and subject, recognising that research is not a neutral or detached activity but is shaped by personal, social, and cultural dynamics. Through reflexive journals and field notes, interpretive researchers make their engagement with the research process transparent, thereby contributing to the ethical integrity, transparency, and rigour of the study. Overall, this practice serves as a foundational aspect of interpretive research, fostering a thoughtful, responsive, and ethically attuned approach to exploring social phenomena.

In summary, these methods of data collection in interpretive research encompass a range of qualitative approaches that enable researchers to explore subjective meanings, social interactions, and the context-specific nature of social phenomena. By employing these methods, researchers align their data collection practices with the principles and perspectives of the interpretive paradigm, facilitating a deeper understanding of the complexities and nuances within a specific social context. However, there are other methods not covered in this book.

### 3.8 Data Analysis and Interpretation in Interpretive Research

Data analysis and interpretation in interpretive research constitute a complex, iterative process aimed at uncovering the multifaceted subjective meanings, social interactions, and context-specific intricacies of a given social setting. Central to this endeavour are techniques that align with the interpretive paradigm's core principles, which prioritise an empathetic understanding of diverse perspectives, recognition of subjective realities, and acknowledgement of the socially constructed essence of social phenomena. Through careful and nuanced examination of qualitative data, interpretive researchers engage in a dialogue with the text, iteratively coding, categorising, and thematic development to reveal patterns and insights that resonate with participants' experiences and worldviews. This process is not about imposing an external framework or seeking objective truths but rather about co-constructing meaning with participants, allowing their voices to guide the interpretation, and appreciating the complexity and dynamism of human experience. The analysis is informed by continuous reflexivity, recognising the researcher's role and influence in the interpretive process and aiming for a rich, holistic

## Interpretive/Constructive Paradigm and Methodological Alignment 79

understanding that honours the context and lived realities of the research subjects. Therefore, data analysis and interpretation in interpretive research are vital in achieving the paradigm's goal of elucidating the depth and complexity of human experience, providing a valuable lens for exploring social phenomena with empathy, authenticity, and ethical sensitivity. Below are the notable methods of data analysis suitable for interpretive paradigm.

i **Thematic Analysis:** Thematic analysis, a vital method within interpretive research, involves a nuanced and methodical process of identifying, analysing, and interpreting patterns, themes, and recurring concepts found within qualitative data (Braun & Clarke, 2012). Researchers use systematic coding and categorising techniques to unearth underlying themes that encapsulate participants' narratives and lived experiences, offering profound insights into the social phenomena under scrutiny. The method's alignment with the interpretive paradigm is seen in its emphasis on exploring subjective meanings and social interactions, as well as its focus on identifying patterns that illuminate the social construction of reality. As articulated here, it is evidenced that thematic analysis moves beyond surface-level observation and delves into the rich, multifaceted data, allowing researchers to grasp the subtleties and complexities of participants' interpretations and lived experiences. This process affirms the interpretive paradigm's commitment to recognising the intricate, context-specific nature of human experience and social dynamics, thereby contributing to a comprehensive and empathetic understanding of the phenomena being investigated.

ii **Narrative Analysis:** Narrative analysis is a method of data analysis that centres around the examination of personal stories and narratives shared by individuals (Smith, 2016). Researchers conduct a detailed analysis of the structure, content, and interpretive elements within these narratives to gain a deeper understanding of both individual and collective experiences. Narrative analysis is highly relevant to interpretive research as it provides a means to explore subjective interpretations, the construction of identities, and the social dynamics embedded within narratives. By closely examining the narratives, researchers can uncover how individuals make sense of their experiences, shape their identities, and interact with others within specific social contexts. Through narrative analysis, researchers can delve into the intricate connections between personal stories and the broader social, cultural, and historical contexts in which they are situated. This method allows for a nuanced exploration of subjective realities, enabling researchers to gain valuable insights into the diverse perspectives, meanings, and social dynamics that emerge from the narratives shared by participants.

iii **Discourse Analysis:** Discourse analysis, a method prominently utilised in interpretive research, emphasises the critical examination of language use and the multifaceted interconnections of social, cultural, and power dynamics within it (Moser et al., 2013). By focusing on how language constructs and reflects social phenomena, identities, and power relations, researchers can uncover and dissect the intricate ways meaning is negotiated, constructed, and challenged through communicative practices. The significance of discourse analysis within the interpretive paradigm lies in its ability to explore the socially constructed nature of reality, illuminating how language serves both as a reflection of and a tool for shaping social interactions, power structures, and knowledge creation. This method allows researchers to delve into the underlying meanings, ideologies, and social norms embedded within language, thereby unearthing insights into how individuals and social groups are both influenced by and actively shape discourse. In this way, discourse analysis reveals the complexities and subtleties inherent in social phenomena and provides a lens through which the relationship between language and social reality can be critically and thoughtfully examined.

iv **Phenomenological Analysis:** Phenomenological analysis is a method of data analysis that delves into understanding individuals' essence and lived experiences (Eatough & Smith, 2017). Researchers engaging in phenomenological analysis aim to uncover the subjective meanings and interpretations that individuals attribute to their experiences, aiming to identify commonalities and shared themes among participants. This method aligns closely with interpretive research as it emphasises the exploration of subjective realities and the interpretation of experiences. By adopting a phenomenology, researchers seek to understand how individuals make sense of and interpret the world around them, considering the influence of their unique perspectives and contexts. Phenomenological analysis contributes to the interpretive paradigm's emphasis on subjective meanings, highlighting the importance of context and individual perspectives in shaping social phenomena. Through this method, researchers can uncover rich insights into the diverse ways in which individuals interpret their experiences, providing a contextual understanding of social phenomena within the interpretive framework.

v **Grounded Theory:** Grounded theory is a method of data analysis that centres on the development of theories and concepts that emerge directly from the data. Researchers employing grounded theory use constant comparative analysis to identify patterns, categories, and themes within the data, ultimately constructing a theory that is firmly grounded in the participants' perspectives. This method is closely related to interpretive research as it aligns with the focus on subjective meanings, the exploration of diverse perspectives, and understanding the social construction of reality through iterative data analysis. Grounded theory recognises the importance of capturing individuals' nuanced interpretations and experiences within a specific social context. Researchers can identify commonalities, variations, and emergent concepts by systematically comparing and analysing the data, providing insights into how participants construct meaning and navigate their social worlds. Grounded theory within the interpretive paradigm emphasises the active role of participants in shaping the research findings and contributes to the ongoing dialogue around subjective realities and the socially constructed nature of social phenomena.

vi **Interpretative Phenomenological Analysis (IPA):** IPA is a method of data analysis that aims to comprehend how individuals derive meaning from their experiences and how those experiences shape their worldviews (Eatough & Smith, 2017). Researchers employing IPA meticulously examine individual cases, identifying themes and interpretative processes within the data. IPA is closely aligned with interpretive research as it emphasises the exploration of subjective meanings, individual perspectives, and the context-specific interpretation of experiences. By delving into individuals' unique perspectives and interpretations, IPA provides a deeper understanding of how subjective realities are constructed and navigated within specific social contexts. It highlights the significance of context in shaping individuals' interpretations and allows for an in-depth exploration of the rich complexities and nuances embedded within their experiences. Through IPA, researchers contribute to the interpretive paradigm by capturing the subjective and contextual nature of human experiences, shedding light on the individual sense-making processes and the intricate connections between personal experiences and broader social phenomena.

vii **Content Analysis:** Content analysis is a valuable method of data analysis that entails a systematic examination and categorisation of textual or visual data (Huckin, 2003). Researchers employing content analysis identify themes, patterns, and symbolic meanings within the data to gain insights into the social construction of reality and cultural influences. This method is highly relevant to interpretive research as it enables the exploration of discursive practices, cultural norms, and the interpretation of symbols within a specific context. By closely analysing the content, researchers can uncover the discourses and narratives that shape social phenomena, providing a deeper understanding of the underlying meanings and cultural dynamics. Content analysis allows for the identification of recurring themes and patterns, which highlight the ways in which individuals make sense of their experiences and the broader social context in which they occur. It offers a valuable lens through which researchers can interpret and analyse individuals' textual or visual representations, thereby contributing to the interpretive paradigm's focus on understanding the subjective meanings, cultural influences, and discursive practices that shape social interactions and constructions of reality.

viii **Comparative Analysis:** Comparative analysis is a valuable method of data analysis that involves the systematic comparison and contrast of data across different cases, contexts, or time periods (Rihoux, 2006). Researchers engaging in comparative analysis aim to identify patterns, variations, and context-specific factors that emerge from the data. This method is highly relevant to interpretive research as it facilitates the exploration of diverse perspectives and the influence of context on interpretations. By comparing data across different cases or contexts, researchers can uncover similarities and differences in subjective meanings, social interactions, and the construction of reality. Comparative analysis enables researchers to understand the complexities and nuances of social phenomena within specific social settings, shedding light on the contextual factors that shape individuals' interpretations and experiences. By recognising the role of context in shaping social phenomena, comparative analysis contributes to the interpretive paradigm's commitment to understanding the socially constructed nature of reality and the contextual understanding of subjective meanings.

ix **Dialogical Analysis:** Dialogical analysis is a data analysis method that centres on examining interactions and discourses within a social context (Matusov et al., 2019). Researchers engaging in dialogical analysis analyse the dynamic exchanges, conversations, and negotiations of meaning to better understand how social realities are constructed and maintained. This method aligns closely with interpretive research as it explores the social nature of reality, emphasising the negotiation of meaning through dialogue and the influence of social interactions on subjective interpretations. By closely examining the dialogues and interactions, researchers can uncover the discursive practices, power dynamics, and social norms that shape individuals' interpretations and understanding of the world. Dialogical analysis within the interpretive paradigm allows researchers to investigate how social realities are co-constructed through ongoing dialogues, illuminating the intricate connections between language, social interactions, and the subjective interpretations of individuals. Dialogical analysis contributes to understanding how individuals interpret and construct their subjective realities within the broader social context by focusing on the social dynamics embedded in dialogue.

## 3.9   Critiques and Debates in Interpretive Research

Critiques and debates surrounding the interpretive research paradigm have proliferated over time, reflecting a range of perspectives and stimulating rich discussions within the field. These dialogues are marked by differing opinions and viewpoints that engage with interpretive research's core principles and methodologies. Three prominent critiques, in particular, have catalysed considerable debate within the interpretive research paradigm, leading to ongoing conversations and reevaluations. These critiques challenge certain assumptions and practices within the paradigm and contribute to a deeper and more nuanced understanding of the underlying philosophical and methodological foundations. The engagement with these critiques continues to shape the evolution and refinement of the interpretive approach, reinforcing its dynamic and reflective nature within the broader context of social research. They are discussed below.

i **Subjectivity and Generalisability:** One critique of interpretive research that has incited significant discussion centres on the issues of subjectivity and generalisability. Critics contend that the intrinsic focus on subjective meanings and interpretations within specific contexts limits the generalisability of findings, restricting the capacity to make broader claims or develop universal theories (Carminati, 2018; Garrick, 1999). They argue that this emphasis on individual perspectives and context-specific nuance may undermine the traditional scientific aims of replicability and wide-ranging applicability. However, proponents of interpretive research counter this critique by emphasising that the paradigm's strength lies precisely in its deep and detailed exploration of subjective realities within specific social contexts. For them, the objective is not to achieve sweeping generalisations but to illuminate the complexity and multifaceted nature of human experiences. They stress the value of understanding the situated nature of social phenomena, arguing that this approach yields valuable insights precisely because of their contextually grounded and individually tailored focus.

ii **Reliability and Validity:** Another critique centres around issues of reliability and validity in interpretive research. Critics argue that the lack of standardised procedures and the subjectivity of interpretations raise concerns about the reliability and validity of the findings (Kelliher, 2011; Mellinger & Hanson, 2020). They raise questions about the rigour and credibility of interpretive research, suggesting that the biases and preconceptions of researchers may influence interpretations. In response, advocates of interpretive research argue that the interpretive paradigm requires a different understanding of reliability and validity. They contend that interpretive research is focused on understanding subjective meanings and constructing rich and context-specific interpretations rather than adhering to traditional notions of reliability and validity. They emphasise the importance of transparency, reflexivity, and systematic methods to enhance the trustworthiness and credibility of interpretive research findings.

iii **Ethical Considerations:** A third critique that arises in the realm of interpretive research centres on ethical considerations, which often prove to be complex and nuanced (Tiselius, 2019). Critics assert that the profound engagement and interaction between researchers and participants inherent in interpretive methodologies may give rise to challenging power dynamics and ethical and conflict dilemmas. And in conflict situations, ethical research is further complicated by issues of power, consent, and trust (Zwi et al., 2006). These critics often point to potential issues such as securing informed consent, maintaining confidentiality, and avoiding undue influence or misrepresenting participants' perspectives. Concerns about the potential exploitation or manipulation of research subjects are not uncommon. However, advocates of interpretive research acknowledge these ethical quandaries and actively emphasise the necessity of ethical reflexivity throughout the research process. They argue that these challenges can be met through careful and transparent negotiation of power relations, active involvement of participants in the research design and execution, and ongoing dialogue about ethical considerations. Furthermore, they call for an approach that is acutely aware of the complexity of interpretive research and that steadfastly prioritises respect for participants' autonomy, dignity, and well-being.

Hence, the interpretive research paradigm has not been immune to critiques and debates. Discussions around subjectivity and generalisability, reliability and validity, and ethical considerations have fuelled ongoing conversations within the field. These critiques highlight important considerations and challenges, but they also provide opportunities for refining and strengthening the practice of interpretive research. Ultimately, navigating these critiques fosters a deeper understanding of the interpretive paradigm's unique strengths and limitations, contributing to its ongoing development and its ability to shed light on the subjective meanings, social dynamics, and complex realities of human experiences.

## 3.10 Balancing Subjectivity in Interpretive Research

Balancing subjectivity in interpretive research is an essential task that underpins the rigour and credibility of the research process. The inherent subjectivity in interpretive research, driven by its emphasis on understanding individual subjective meanings and interpretations, necessitates a careful equilibrium. Researchers are challenged to strike a balance that acknowledges the subjective nature of the inquiry and ensures transparency, reflexivity, and robust engagement with the research data. This balance demands a considered approach where researchers are aware of their own biases and actively engage in critical reflection. They must remain open to diverse perspectives and strive to represent the complexity of the subjects' experiences and interpretations. Through the points discussed below, researchers can achieve a balance that honours the subjective nature of interpretive research while upholding the principles of rigour and credibility.

- **Reflexivity:** Reflexivity is an essential practice in interpretive research, as it allows researchers to critically examine their own biases, assumptions, and preconceptions (Darawsheh, 2014). By engaging in ongoing reflection, researchers can become aware of how their subjectivity may shape the research process and findings. This self-awareness helps researchers make conscious decisions, mitigate the influence of their biases, and enhance transparency in the research. Reflexivity prompts researchers to continually question their interpretations and consider alternative perspectives, fostering a more balanced approach to subjectivity.

- **Triangulation:** Triangulation involves the use of multiple sources of data or methods to corroborate findings in interpretive research (Adami & Kiger, 2005). By integrating different perspectives, researchers can reduce the potential impact of individual subjectivity on the research outcomes. Triangulation enhances the validity and reliability of the interpretations by ensuring that multiple sources of evidence converge to support the findings. By incorporating diverse data sources and methods, researchers can capture a more comprehensive understanding of the phenomenon under study, minimising the dominance of any single perspective or interpretation.
- **Transparency in Analysis:** Transparency in analysis is crucial for addressing subjectivity in interpretive research. Researchers must provide a clear and explicit account of the analytical process, including the steps taken to identify themes, patterns, and conceptual frameworks. By documenting the decisions made during analysis, researchers allow others to scrutinise and assess the potential influence of subjectivity. Transparent reporting fosters credibility and trustworthiness in interpretive research by enabling readers to evaluate the researcher's interpretations and the potential impact of subjectivity on the findings.
- **Peer Review and Collaboration:** Engaging in peer review and collaboration is a valuable strategy to balance subjectivity in interpretive research. Researchers can benefit from diverse perspectives and critical insights by seeking feedback and input from colleagues or other experts. Peer review and collaboration provide an external check on the researcher's subjectivity and encourage constructive challenges to interpretations. By involving others in the research process, researchers can enhance the validity and reliability of the findings and gain a more balanced understanding of the phenomenon under investigation.
- **Participant Involvement:** Actively involving participants in the research process helps to balance subjectivity. By seeking input from participants, researchers can ensure that their perspectives are adequately represented and validated. Participant involvement can include member checking, where participants review and validate the interpretations, or co-creation of knowledge, where participants actively contribute to the analysis and interpretation of the data. By valuing and integrating participants' voices, researchers can enhance the trustworthiness and authenticity of the research outcomes, mitigating the potential impact of their own subjectivity.
- **Transparency in Reporting:** Transparent reporting is essential in interpretive research to address subjectivity. Researchers should provide a comprehensive account of the interpretive process and explicitly discuss their positionality, biases, and potential influence on the research outcomes. By openly acknowledging the subjectivity inherent in interpretive research, researchers promote transparency and allow readers to evaluate the research and its limitations critically. Transparent reporting enables a more nuanced understanding of the research findings and fosters dialogue and critical engagement with the interpretations presented.

The major argument here is that researchers can effectively balance subjectivity in interpretive research by embracing reflexivity, employing triangulation, promoting transparency in analysis and reporting, seeking peer review and collaboration, and involving participants. These practices ensure a more rigorous and nuanced approach to interpretation, enhance the credibility and trustworthiness of the research findings, and advance knowledge within the interpretive paradigm.

## 3.11 Summary

This chapter explores the interpretive research paradigm's foundations, methodologies, and key considerations. The interpretive paradigm emphasises understanding subjective meanings, social interactions, and the socially constructed nature of reality. It involves a deep exploration of individuals' interpretations, experiences, and the context-specific understanding of social phenomena. The chapter discusses various research designs and methods commonly used in interpretive research, including ethnography, phenomenology, grounded theory, narrative research, and case study research. It highlights the importance of aligning research questions with the interpretive paradigm and provides examples of how to do so. The chapter also delves into the data collection, analysis, and interpretation methods in interpretive research, emphasising approaches such as thematic analysis, narrative analysis, and discourse analysis. It addresses critiques and debates within the interpretive research paradigm, focusing on topics such as subjectivity, generalisability, and ethical considerations. The chapter concludes by emphasising the significance of reflexivity, transparency, and the balancing of subjectivity in interpretive research for enhancing the rigor and credibility of findings.

# 4 Transformative Paradigm and Methodological Alignment

**Chapter Synopsis**

This chapter explores the transformative paradigm, also known as the critical paradigm, which is the focal point of discussion. The chapter begins by delving into the transformative paradigm's contextual framework and its philosophical foundations. Furthermore, key concepts and assumptions are explored, providing readers with a comprehensive understanding of the paradigm. The chapter proceeds to discuss the evolutionary trajectory of the transformative paradigm, shedding light on its development over time. Methodological designs within the transformative research framework are then addressed, specifically focusing on how to align research questions with the transformative paradigm. The data collection method in transformative research is also analysed, followed by a detailed examination of data analysis and interpretation in this research approach. Additionally, the chapter delves into the critiques and debates surrounding transformative research, providing a well-rounded perspective on its strengths and weaknesses. The chapter concludes by exploring the balance between research rigour and social justice within the transformative research framework. Overall, this chapter serves as a comprehensive and insightful exploration of the transformative paradigm and its various dimensions, equipping readers with the necessary knowledge to effectively engage with this research approach.

## 4.1 Concept of Transformative Paradigm

The transformative paradigm, otherwise referred to as the critical paradigm, is a significant area of exploration within the field of research. This paradigm seeks to challenge and transform existing social structures and power dynamics to promote social justice and empower marginalised communities (Mertens, 2012). Understanding the transformative paradigm involves recognising its roots in critical theory and its application in various disciplines. At its core, the transformative paradigm is deeply influenced by critical theory, which emerged from the works of critical theorists such as Karl Marx, Max Horkheimer, and Theodor Adorno (Garlitz & Zompetti, 2023). According to these theorists, critical theory emphasises the examination of power relations, social inequality, and the impact of dominant ideologies on society. Within the transformative paradigm, researchers adopt a critical stance towards societal norms, questioning existing power structures and seeking to bring about transformative change (Mertens, 2007, 2012). Researchers in transformative school thought aim to uncover and challenge oppressive systems, advocate for social justice, and amplify the voices of marginalised individuals and communities (Mertens, 2010). One can then argue that this paradigm recognises that knowledge is not neutral but is shaped by societal contexts and power dynamics.

Scholars explore key concepts and assumptions underpinning this paradigm in the context of transformative research. Concepts such as empowerment, liberation, voice, and agency take centre stage as researchers strive to understand and promote these elements within their studies. Assumptions about the importance of reflexivity, acknowledging positionality, and engaging in collaborative partnerships with participants are also central to the transformative paradigm. However, understanding the transformative paradigm in context requires recognising its theoretical foundations, interdisciplinary nature, and its commitment to social justice and empowerment. By embracing critical theory, challenging dominant ideologies, and centring the voices of marginalised communities, researchers adopting this paradigm undoubtedly contribute to transformative change and the pursuit of a more equitable society.

## 4.2 The Evolution of the Transformative Paradigm

The evolution of the transformative paradigm has been a dynamic and iterative process, shaped by various intellectual and socio-political movements over time. This paradigm has undergone significant developments, expanding its scope and deepening its understanding of transformative change and social justice. The origins of the transformative paradigm can be traced back to critical theory, a school of thought that emerged in the mid-20th century. Scholars such as Karl Marx, Max Horkheimer, and Theodor Adorno laid the groundwork for critical theory, which focused on analysing power structures, social inequality, and the role of ideology in perpetuating oppression (Garlitz & Zompetti, 2023; Postone 2017). Critical theory's emphasis on challenging dominant norms and advocating for transformative change provided a strong foundation for the transformative paradigm.

In the 1970s and 1980s, critical theory began to influence various academic disciplines, leading to the emergence of critical pedagogy, critical psychology, and critical social work. These disciplines embraced the transformative potential of critical theory and applied it to their respective fields. For example, critical pedagogy sought to empower learners and challenge oppressive educational practices (Joseph & Gandolfi, 2022), while critical psychology aimed to address the socio-political factors influencing mental health (Trott, 2016). The transformative paradigm continued to evolve in the late 20th century and early 21st century, incorporating insights from postcolonial theory, feminist theory, and intersectionality. Scholars like Bell Hooks, Paulo Freire, Patricia Hill Collins, and Angela Davis contributed to the expansion and refinement of the paradigm. These thinkers emphasised the importance of intersectional analysis, recognising the interconnected nature of social identities and systems of oppression.

In recent years, the transformative paradigm has increasingly engaged with issues of globalisation, environmental justice, and digital technologies. Researchers within this paradigm have explored the impact of neoliberalism on social inequalities, the environmental consequences of capitalism, and the role of digital activism in transformative change. This expansion reflects the paradigm's responsiveness to emerging social, political, and technological challenges. Furthermore, the evolution of the transformative paradigm has been shaped by the voices and experiences of marginalised communities (Bridwell, 2013). Indigenous scholars, activists, and community leaders have contributed to the paradigm's development by foregrounding decolonisation, cultural revitalisation, and indigenous knowledge systems. Similarly, the contributions of Black, feminist, queer, and disability scholars have enriched the paradigm by highlighting the intersecting oppressions faced by marginalised groups.

Therefore, the evolution of the transformative paradigm can be understood as a progressive engagement with critical theory and its application in various disciplines. It has incorporated insights from diverse intellectual traditions and social movements, adapting to the changing socio-political landscape. By embracing intersectionality, engaging with globalisation and technology, and centring the experiences of marginalised communities, the transformative paradigm continues to evolve and contribute to the pursuit of social justice and transformative change.

### 4.3 Key Concepts and Assumptions

The transformative paradigm is grounded in a set of key concepts and assumptions that shape its approach to research. These concepts and assumptions guide researchers within this paradigm, informing their understanding of power dynamics, social justice, participation, intersectionality, and transformative change. Knowing these foundational elements, researchers within the transformative paradigm are prepared to challenge oppressive structures, empower marginalised communities, and create knowledge that leads to positive and equitable societal transformations. The key concepts and assumptions are as follows.

- **Power and Oppression:** At the heart of the transformative paradigm lies a profound recognition of power dynamics and their pervasive manifestations within systems of oppression. Researchers within this paradigm delve into a critical analysis of how power operates across various social, political, and cultural contexts, elucidating the mechanisms that result in social marginalisation and disempowerment of specific groups (Bridwell, 2013; Mertens, 2012). This approach is central to exploring key concepts such as power relations, privilege, and intersectionality. Through this exploration, researchers seek not only to comprehend the intricate ways oppressive structures are upheld but also to actively challenge and transform these structures. The transformative paradigm thus serves as a lens through which scholars scrutinise and address the root causes of systemic inequalities, fostering a commitment to social justice and empowerment as integral components of the research endeavour.

- **Emancipation and Social Justice:** Grounded in a resolute dedication to emancipation and social justice (Mertens, 2007), the transformative paradigm serves as a catalyst for the profound transformation of social structures and systems that perpetuate inequality. Its overarching goal is to pave the way for the creation of societies that are not only more equitable but also inherently just. Emancipation, a central tenet of this paradigm, denotes the liberation of individuals and communities from oppressive conditions, affording them the agency and voice necessary for self-determination. Rooted in fairness and equality principles, social justice is the guiding force behind the transformative approach, propelling researchers to advocate for systemic change and ardently challenge unjust power dynamics. In essence, the transformative paradigm positions itself as a proactive force in the pursuit of societal transformation, aiming to dismantle oppressive structures and foster the conditions conducive to genuine equity and justice.
- **Reflexivity and Positionality:** In embracing the transformative paradigm, researchers actively incorporate reflexivity into their methodology and conscientiously acknowledge their positionality within the research process. Reflexivity, a pivotal practice within this paradigm, entails the critical examination of one's own biases, assumptions, and social locations that inevitably influence the research journey (Darawsheh, 2014). This involves a profound recognition of the impact of the researcher's background, privileges, and social identities on the knowledge produced. By cultivating a heightened awareness of their positionality, researchers within the transformative paradigm strive to mitigate power imbalances inherent in the research dynamic. This intentional self-reflection not only contributes to the development of a more nuanced and contextually rich understanding of the research subject but also serves as a means to foster collaborative relationships, ensuring that the research process is inclusive and ethically grounded. Through their commitment to reflexivity, the transformative researchers actively contribute to the cultivation of research practices that align with principles of equity, inclusivity, and ethical engagement.
- **Participatory and Collaborative Research:** Central to the ethos of the transformative paradigm is the emphasis on participatory and collaborative

research approaches, acknowledging the pivotal role of participants as active agents in the research process (Omodan, 2022a). This paradigm advocates for the meaningful engagement of participants, involving them in decision-making processes, co-designing research questions, and valuing their expertise and lived experiences. The participatory nature of this research framework fosters a sense of empowerment among participants and promotes the co-creation of knowledge. By actively involving those being studied in the research design and implementation, the transformative paradigm ensures that the research is relevant to the communities affected and meaningful in addressing their unique perspectives and needs. This approach aligns with a commitment to inclusivity, empowering participants to contribute to shaping research narratives and outcomes, thereby embodying the transformative potential of collaborative research practices.

- **Intersectionality:** Intersectionality is a cornerstone concept within the transformative paradigm, acknowledging the intricate ways individuals and communities navigate multiple forms of oppression and privilege concurrently (Corus & Saatcioglu, 2015). This recognition highlights the intersection of various social categories, encompassing race, gender, class, sexuality, and ability. Researchers within the transformative paradigm operate with the understanding that systems of power and oppression are interconnected and, as such, necessitate a holistic analysis. By centring intersectionality, this paradigm endeavours to grapple with the complexities and nuances inherent in social inequality. Understanding that a convergence of factors shapes individuals' experiences, the transformative paradigm aims to unravel the interconnected web of oppressions and privileges, fostering a more comprehensive and nuanced comprehension of the diverse ways systemic inequalities manifest across different social dimensions. This intentional focus on intersectionality aligns with the transformative goal of addressing and dismantling intersecting forms of oppression within society.

- **Transformative Change:** At the core of the transformative paradigm lies the central assumption of transformative change, advocating for research that transcends mere observation and understanding to actively generate actionable knowledge capable of fostering positive social transformation (Mertens, 2007). Researchers within this paradigm perceive their work as more than a passive academic endeavour; instead, they see themselves as catalysts for change. Transformative researchers aspire to challenge oppressive systems, champion alternative perspectives, and contribute to the empowerment and well-being of marginalised communities. This paradigm embraces a proactive stance, where the ultimate goal is to unveil and comprehend societal injustices and actively engage in endeavours that bring about tangible and positive shifts in the social landscape. In essence, the transformative paradigm aligns research with a commitment to social change, envisioning a future where research serves as a potent force in the ongoing pursuit of justice, equity, and the betterment of society.

- **Ethical Considerations:** Ethics stands as a vital cornerstone in the transformative paradigm, guiding researchers within this framework to uphold principles that prioritise the well-being and dignity of participants. Within this paradigm, ethical considerations extend across various facets of the research process. Researchers are particularly attentive to issues such as informed consent, ensuring that participants fully understand and voluntarily agree to engage in the research. Confidentiality is carefully maintained to protect the identities and privacy of individuals involved, and potential harm or exploitation is rigorously considered and mitigated. Furthermore, ethical responsibilities extend to disseminating and utilising research findings, with a commitment to ensuring that the knowledge generated respects the communities involved and actively contributes to advancing social justice objectives. This ethical framework within the transformative paradigm reflects a profound dedication to conducting research that abides by stringent ethical standards and actively promotes the well-being, agency, and dignity of all those engaged in the research process.

## 4.4 The Philosophical Foundations of the Transformative Paradigm

The transformative paradigm is anchored in its profound philosophical foundations, encompassing epistemological, ontological, axiological, and methodological aspects. These core principles substantially guide the way researchers within this paradigm interact with and approach knowledge, reality, values, and various research methodologies. The complex interplay of these elements forms the distinctive characteristics of the transformative paradigm, a framework defined by its steadfast commitment to instigating transformative change and promoting social justice. Attaining an in-depth comprehension of these philosophical underpinnings is not just instrumental but vital in fully appreciating the transformative paradigm's unique nature and its unwavering dedication to the aforementioned ideals. These philosophical foundations are discussed below.

### 4.4.1 Epistemology in the Transformative Paradigm

The epistemology of the transformative paradigm starkly contrasts traditional positivist notions of knowledge, instead adopting a critical and reflexive stance that acknowledges the influence of social, cultural, and historical contexts (Mertens, 2007, 2010). Researchers operating within this paradigm recognise that knowledge is neither objective nor value-free but dynamically shaped by many factors. They emphasise the importance of multiple perspectives and situated knowledge, elevating the lived experiences of marginalised communities as legitimate and essential sources of understanding. This epistemological approach in the transformative paradigm underscores the co-construction of knowledge through collaborative and participatory methodologies, seeking to empower participants as co-researchers and valuing their unique insights and contributions (Jackson et al., 2018). It reflects a purposeful movement away from traditional power hierarchies in the research process, aiming to challenge existing power imbalances in knowledge production and fostering a more inclusive, emancipatory, and transformative approach to understanding.

### 4.4.2  Ontology in the Transformative Paradigm

The ontological foundations of the transformative paradigm fundamentally challenge the idea of a fixed and objective reality, opting instead for a perspective that views reality as socially constructed and heavily influenced by power dynamics (Romm, 2015). This paradigm does more than simply recognise the existence of multiple and intersecting social identities; it acknowledges that individuals and communities perceive and experience reality differently, contingent on their unique positions within complex systems of privilege and oppression. Within this framework, the voices and perspectives of marginalised communities are not merely acknowledged but are actively valued, and the paradigm itself seeks to highlight and confront the structural inequalities that shape their lived realities. The transformative paradigm embraces the dynamic, multifaceted nature of reality and the inherent potential for transformative change. Ontologically speaking, this paradigm underscores the urgency of challenging and dismantling oppressive structures, and it aligns itself with a committed pursuit of new pathways to social justice and equity, reflecting a foundational belief in the possibility of transformation within society.

### 4.4.3  Axiology in the Transformative Paradigm

The axiological foundations of the transformative paradigm are firmly anchored in a deep commitment to social justice and emancipatory values, forming the ethical backbone of a paradigm intent on challenging and dismantling oppressive systems (Mertens, 2007). Within this framework, researchers recognise a moral imperative to foster the well-being and empowerment of marginalised communities. Principles that resonate with ideals of equality, solidarity, human rights, and the thoughtful redistribution of power and resources are central to the axiological stance of the transformative paradigm. This approach advocates for acknowledging, recognising, and affirming diverse identities, experiences, and forms of knowledge, emphasising a holistic and inclusive view of society. In conducting their work, researchers within the transformative paradigm strive to align their research practices with these underlying values, acknowledging that ethical integrity goes hand in hand with scholarly rigour. Emphasising the importance of ethical considerations is not merely a theoretical stance but a practical mandate that infuses every aspect of the research process. Reflexivity, social responsibility, and mindful consideration of how research practices impact communities are fundamental to this axiological perspective. These principles guide researchers in pursuing transformative change, shaping both the process and outcomes of their work and further reinforcing the transformative paradigm's unwavering commitment to social justice and equity.

### 4.4.4 Methodology of Transformative Paradigm

The methodological foundations of the transformative paradigm are integral to its function and are carefully designed to align with its epistemological, ontological, and axiological principles. These methodological approaches underscore the need for research that is reflective of and actively embodies the paradigm's commitment to social justice, emancipation, and transformative change. Firstly, methodologies within the transformative paradigm are often characterised by a participatory and emancipatory orientation (Omodan, 2022a). This orientation demands close collaboration between researchers and participants, thereby decentralising traditional research authority and encouraging a more democratic and inclusive approach. Active participation from those being studied is encouraged and seen as essential to co-creating knowledge. By recognising and valuing participants' agency, researchers empower them to contribute to the research process, allowing their voices to be heard and their experiences to be honoured. This shift in dynamics fosters a more equal and meaningful partnership in the research process.

Inclusion is further emphasised through the prioritisation of marginalised voices, ensuring that the perspectives and experiences of those often overlooked or excluded are centred in the research. To achieve this, the transformative paradigm employs culturally sensitive and contextually appropriate methods, acknowledging the diversity of experiences and recognising that traditional methods may not be suitable or equitable for all communities. Sensitivity to cultural nuances and local contexts is crucial in crafting methodologies that resonate with participants and reflect their lived realities. Researchers within the transformative paradigm are acutely aware of their findings' potential impact and dissemination. Rather than conducting research for research's sake, they aim to create actionable knowledge that transcends academic boundaries and becomes a catalyst for change. Whether at the individual, community, or systemic level, the goal is to inform and inspire transformative change, aligning with the paradigm's broader goals of challenging oppression, fostering equity, and advancing social justice.

## 4.5 Transformative Paradigm and Qualitative Research

The transformative paradigm's compatibility with qualitative research methods arises from its intrinsic focus on exploring power dynamics, the advocacy for social justice, and the reverence for the lived experiences of marginalised communities. This alignment with qualitative research positions the transformative paradigm as a particularly fitting framework for conducting thorough investigations into intricate social phenomena and producing substantial and insightful findings.

Central to the alignment between the transformative paradigm and qualitative research is the shared emphasis on comprehending power dynamics and opposing oppressive structures (Mertens 2010). Researchers are empowered to delve into the personal experiences, viewpoints, and narratives of individuals and communities by employing qualitative techniques such as interviews, focus groups, and ethnographic observations. Through the transformative paradigm, a qualitative approach becomes instrumental in unearthing the multifaceted and context-specific nature of power relationships, significantly impacting marginalised populations' everyday realities. This profound understanding is indispensable in addressing social disparities and championing transformative alterations.

Moreover, the commitment to social justice (Mertens, 2007) that permeates the transformative paradigm resonates with qualitative research's objectives of magnifying the voices of marginalised sectors. By emphasising participant inclusion and empowerment, qualitative methods enable individuals to articulate their experiences, wisdom, and concerns in their authentic expressions. This alignment with the transformative paradigm ensures that the perspectives of underrepresented individuals and communities are acknowledged, esteemed, and integrated into the research process. Qualitative research within this paradigm fortifies social justice initiatives by prioritising marginalised voices, countering prevailing narratives and facilitating equitable knowledge production.

Additionally, the transformative paradigm acknowledges the crucial role of context and the situated nature of knowledge, a principle where qualitative research methods particularly excel. By employing techniques such as participant observation, detailed interviews, and document scrutiny, practitioners within the transformative paradigm can comprehensively understand the multifaceted dynamics that govern social relationships and power mechanisms within their specific cultural, historical, and social environments. Such contextual comprehension is vital in pinpointing systemic inequities and crafting interventions or policies that further the causes of social justice and transformational change.

Also, the transformative paradigm's affinity with qualitative research methods is strongly evidenced by its concentration on power dynamics, social justice advocacy, and the valorisation of marginalised voices (Ratts, 2009). This alignment fosters a profound insight into power structures, amplification of underrepresented voices, and an appreciation of the contextual intricacies of societal phenomena. By adopting qualitative research within the transformative paradigm, researchers position themselves at the forefront of transformative change, actively working against oppressive constructs, advancing social justice, and empowering marginalised communities.

In summary, the methodological foundations of the transformative paradigm are multifaceted and complex, reflecting a thoughtful and deliberate effort to create authentic, inclusive, and impactful research. By weaving together participatory, emancipatory, and culturally sensitive practices with a strong ethical commitment, methodologies within this paradigm exemplify its overarching principles. This alignment of method and values ensures that the research process not only reflects the transformative paradigm's core beliefs but also serves as an active tool in pursuing its social justice aims.

### 4.6 Transformative Paradigm and Mixed-Methods Research

The transformative paradigm can be considered a suitable framework for implementing mixed-methods research due to its emphasis on understanding complex social phenomena, promoting social justice, and generating actionable knowledge for transformative change (Mertens, 2010). According to Mertens (2007), combining qualitative and quantitative approaches, mixed-methods research within the transformative paradigm provides a more comprehensive understanding of the interconnected nature of social issues and contributes to transformative outcomes.

One justification for the suitability of the transformative paradigm for mixed-methods research lies in its focus on understanding and challenging power dynamics. Mixed-methods research allows for the exploration of both subjective experiences and objective measures of social phenomena (Migiro & Magangi, 2011). Qualitative approaches, such as interviews or focus groups, can capture rich narratives, perspectives, and lived experiences, providing insights into power imbalances and the effects of oppression on marginalised communities (Hollstein, 2011). On the other hand, the quantitative approach enables the collection and analysis of numerical data, allowing researchers to examine broader patterns, relationships, and structural inequalities (Quick & Hall, 2015). By integrating these approaches, mixed-methods research within the transformative paradigm can reveal the complexities and nuances of power dynamics, leading to a more comprehensive understanding of social issues.

Furthermore, the transformative paradigm's commitment to social justice aligns with the potential of mixed-methods research to inform transformative change. Mixed-methods research can generate findings that go beyond mere description or correlation by uncovering causal relationships and identifying effective interventions or policies. This combination of qualitative and quantitative data can inform evidence-based practices, policies, and interventions to challenge oppressive structures and promote social justice. By integrating diverse perspectives and engaging with stakeholders, mixed-methods research within the transformative paradigm has the potential to drive meaningful and sustainable social transformations.

Moreover, mixed-methods research within the transformative paradigm can enhance the participatory nature of the research process. The transformative approach values the voices and expertise of marginalised communities, seeking to involve them as active agents in the research process. That is, mixed methods allow researchers to collaborate with participants to co-design research questions, choose appropriate methods, and interpret findings. This participatory aspect strengthens the research's relevance, validity, and potential for transformative change, as it allows for the integration of diverse perspectives and ensures that the research addresses the needs and priorities of the communities involved. Therefore, by combining qualitative and quantitative methods, mixed-methods research within the transformative paradigm can provide a comprehensive understanding of social issues, inform transformative change, and promote the active participation of marginalised communities.

## 4.7 Methodological Designs in Transformative Research

Methodological designs play a crucial role in implementing transformative research, as they shape the approach and process of inquiry within the paradigm. The selection of the appropriate methodological designs is not merely a technical detail but an essential part of the process, effectively addressing the unique and ambitious goals of transformative research. These goals often include understanding power dynamics, promoting social justice, and engaging with marginalised communities, aims that require a carefully chosen approach to be realised successfully. In this complex landscape, certain methodological designs emerge as particularly suitable for implementing transformative research, and the following section will delve into these, highlighting their key features and benefits, thus offering insights into why and how they can be leveraged to advance the very specific objectives of this innovative form of research.

i *Participatory Action Research (PAR):* PAR is a methodological design that aligns closely with the principles of the transformative paradigm, emphasising collaboration and the active participation of community members in the research process. Rather than treating participants as mere subjects of study, PAR engages them as co-researchers, empowering them to be integral parts of the research, including identifying questions, collecting and analysing data, and participating in decision-making processes (Doucet et al., 2022). This democratic and inclusive approach aims to generate actionable knowledge and facilitate transformative change, thereby reflecting the theoretical commitments of the transformative paradigm and actively advancing them. By involving participants in all stages of the research, especially those from marginalised communities, PAR provides a platform for them to contribute their unique knowledge and experiences. This involvement goes beyond token participation, enabling the development of strategies and interventions that address social inequalities and promote social justice, thus leading to practical, real-world change that resonates with the core aims of the transformative approach.

ii *Critical Ethnography:* Critical ethnography is another methodological design suitable for implementing transformative research, reflecting a commitment to uncovering and challenging underlying power dynamics. Unlike traditional ethnography, this method goes beyond merely documenting a social group or community and strives to gain an in-depth understanding of their experiences, social dynamics, structural inequalities, and systems of oppression (Murtagh, 2007). By immersing oneself within the community and incorporating critical theory perspectives, researchers can critically examine power relations, thus probing more profound insights into societal structures (Breda, 2013). Extended periods of observation, interviews, and document analysis become tools to challenge dominant narratives and illuminate how power operates within the researched community. Critical ethnography's focus on these deeper layers allows researchers to capture the complexities and nuances of social phenomena that might otherwise be overlooked. Moreover, by promoting a more profound understanding of the lived experiences of marginalised communities, this methodological design supports the development of knowledge that can lead to transformative change, aligning with the broader goals of social justice and equality inherent to transformative research.

iii **Intersectional Analysis:** Intersectional analysis is a research design that resonates deeply with the principles of the transformative paradigm, as it recognises the intricate and intersecting nature of social identities and systems of oppression. Unlike more simplistic or reductionist approaches, intersectional analysis delves into how different forms of oppression, such as race, gender, class, and sexuality, interact and collectively shape individuals' experiences (Christensen & Jensen, 2012). This approach encourages researchers to consider the multidimensionality of social identities, investigating how various axes of power intersect to form complex and often hidden patterns of social inequality. Whether incorporated into qualitative interviews, surveys, or content analysis, an intersectional lens can reveal more nuanced insights, capturing the multifaceted reality of social experiences. By adopting this perspective, researchers within the transformative paradigm can uncover the interconnected systems of power and oppression, thereby contributing to a more comprehensive, context-rich understanding of social injustices. Such an understanding is vital for designing interventions and policies that accurately reflect the complex realities of marginalised communities, ensuring that efforts to promote social justice are both meaningful and effective.

iv **Action Research:** Action research is a methodological design that uniquely aligns with the transformative paradigm by fusing research and action to confront practical problems and endorse transformative change (Johnson, 2020). Unlike conventional research methods that might separate the study from its practical application, action research establishes a cyclical process that includes planning, action, reflection, and adaptation, fostering continuous improvement and responsiveness (Coghlan, 2019). This approach emphasises the active involvement of participants in identifying problems, implementing interventions, and reflecting on the outcomes, thereby turning the researched community into vital partners rather than mere subjects. By focusing on empowerment and collaboration, action research transcends mere theoretical study, positioning itself firmly within the realm of practical application and social innovation. The alignment of this design with the transformative paradigm's commitment to collaboration, empowerment, and tangible social change is evident, reflecting a concerted effort to bridge the gap between academic inquiry and real-world impact and underscoring the paradigm's potential to translate research into meaningful change in people's lives.

v **Participatory Case Study:** Participatory case study is a distinctive research design that merges the depth and richness of traditional case study research with a participatory approach, aligning closely with the principles of the transformative paradigm. Unlike more detached methods, this design involves working intimately with individuals or communities to delve into a specific case or issue of interest (Reilly, 2010). The participatory nature of this approach encourages active engagement of participants in various stages of the research process, including data collection, analysis, and interpretation. By inviting participants' perspectives and knowledge into the research, the participatory case study design acknowledges and validates their lived experiences, ensuring that they are not merely subjects of the research but active contributors. This method is particularly valuable within the transformative paradigm as it fosters genuine collaboration and centres the voices of marginalised communities. By prioritising the insights and experiences of those directly affected by the issue under study, this design promotes a deeper, more nuanced understanding and empowers communities, potentially leading to more effective and socially just interventions and policies.

vi **Community-Based Action Research (CBAR):** CBAR is a methodological design that stands out for its emphasis on collaborative research partnerships between researchers and community members, embodying the principles of the transformative paradigm (Omodan, 2022a). This method goes beyond traditional research methods by actively engaging community members in all stages of the research process, from defining the research questions to collecting and analysing data and even implementing interventions. CBAR focuses on community-identified issues, prioritising local needs and perspectives (Gullion & Tilton, 2020), ensuring the research is rooted in the real-world context of those it seeks to benefit. Recognising and valuing local knowledge fosters community capacity-building and empowerment, placing the community at the centre of the research rather than at its periphery. This alignment with the transformative paradigm creates a dynamic and participatory process that facilitates true collaboration, reflects community values, and can lead to transformative change. By breaking down traditional barriers between researchers and participants, CBAR offers a model for conducting research that is not only rigorous but also deeply connected to the needs and aspirations of the communities it serves.

vii **Participatory Action Learning Action Research (PALAR):** PALAR is an intricate design that amalgamates elements of action research, participatory learning, and transformative practices, making it highly compatible with the transformative paradigm. Unlike traditional research methods, PALAR is centred on creating collaborative spaces for collective learning, critical reflection, and transformative action (Zuber-Skerritt, 2015), and according to Zuber-Skerritt (2018) is a collaborative approach to knowledge generation and social change, rooted in principles of justice and democracy. The design encourages participants to engage in iterative learning, action, and reflection cycles, fostering an environment where new insights can emerge, assumptions can be challenged, and real change can be effected. This continuous cycle empowers participants, emphasising their active learning and transformation roles. By integrating participatory methods, experiential learning, and transformative principles, PALAR transcends conventional research boundaries, aligning closely with the transformative paradigm's empowerment, collaboration, and social justice objectives. The fusion of these elements within PALAR allows researchers and participants to explore complex social issues with depth and nuance, leading to a theoretical understanding and, actionable insights and genuine change within the communities involved.

Therefore, in implementing transformative research, this book acknowledges that many designs are not included here; hence, selecting the appropriate design requires careful consideration of a method that aligns with the goals and principles of the transformative paradigm. However, PAR, critical ethnography, intersectional analysis, action research, participatory case study, CBAR, and PALAR are some of the methodological designs suitable for conducting transformative research. These designs promote collaboration, engagement with marginalised communities, critical analysis of power dynamics, and a deeper understanding of social inequalities. By utilising these methodological designs, researchers can effectively address the objectives of transformative research and contribute to social justice and transformative change.

## 4.8 Aligning Research Questions with the Transformative Paradigm

When aligning research questions with the transformative research paradigm, several factors must be meticulously considered to resonate with the paradigm's overarching goals of challenging power dynamics, promoting social justice, and fostering transformative change. These considerations are not mere formalities but essential aspects that guide the research in a direction that aligns with transformative principles. For example, one crucial factor may involve the conscious inclusion of marginalised voices to ensure that the research questions are relevant to these communities and empower them, and another may be the deliberate examination of existing power structures to challenge and dissect them.

*Transformative Paradigm and Methodological Alignment* 101

Similarly, consideration of the methods and tools employed might involve selecting those that promote collaboration and participatory engagement or choosing methods that allow for a deeper investigation of social inequalities. Here are examples of factors to consider, along with two examples for each factor:

i **Centring Marginalised Voices**

When aligning research questions with the transformative research paradigm, it is essential to centre the perspectives and experiences of marginalised communities. This factor recognises the importance of amplifying voices that have historically been silenced or marginalised. By prioritising the voices of marginalised individuals, researchers can uncover unique insights and foster a more inclusive research process. For example, in exploring how LGBTQ+ youth navigate and resist societal norms and power structures in educational settings, the research question places the experiences and perspectives of LGBTQ+ youth at the forefront, allowing for a deeper understanding of their challenges, coping mechanisms, and strategies for empowerment. Similarly, in investigating the strategies employed by indigenous women leaders to challenge gender inequality within their communities, the research question acknowledges the agency and leadership of marginalised women, providing an opportunity to learn from their experiences and promote social justice. See below research question as an example:

- *Example 1:* How do LGBTQ+ youth navigate and resist societal norms and power structures in their educational settings?
- *Example 2:* What are the strategies employed by indigenous women leaders to challenge gender inequality within their communities and promote social justice?

ii **Critical Examination of Power Relations**

Critical examination of power relations is crucial in aligning research questions with the transformative research paradigm. This factor involves analysing how power operates in society, uncovering systems of oppression, and understanding their impact on marginalised communities. For instance, in examining how the media reinforces and perpetuates racial stereotypes, the research question probes the power dynamics within media representation, highlighting the need to challenge and transform these harmful narratives. Similarly, in investigating the power dynamics within healthcare systems that contribute to disparities in access to quality healthcare for low-income communities, the research question directs attention to the structural inequalities that perpetuate health inequities, providing an opportunity to explore strategies for disrupting and transforming these dynamics. See below research questions as examples:

- *Example 1:* How does the media reinforce and perpetuate racial stereotypes, and what are the strategies for challenging and transforming these representations?

- **Example 2:** What are the power dynamics within healthcare systems that contribute to disparities in access to quality healthcare for low-income communities, and how can these dynamics be disrupted and transformed?

iii **Addressing Structural Inequalities**

Addressing structural inequalities is a significant factor when aligning research questions with the transformative research paradigm. This factor recognises that social injustices often stem from underlying systemic factors. For example, in examining how policies and practices in the criminal justice system perpetuate racial disparities in sentencing, the research question seeks to uncover and understand the systemic factors that contribute to racial inequities, aiming to inform efforts to address and rectify these disparities. Likewise, in investigating the barriers faced by individuals with disabilities in accessing employment opportunities, the research question acknowledges the structural inequalities that hinder their inclusion in the workforce, providing an opportunity to identify strategies for promoting inclusivity and dismantling barriers to employment. See the below research questions as examples:

- **Example 1:** How do policies and practices in the criminal justice system perpetuate racial disparities in sentencing, and what strategies can be implemented to address these disparities?
- **Example 2:** What are the barriers faced by individuals with disabilities in accessing employment opportunities, and how can organisations and policymakers promote inclusivity and remove these barriers?

iv **Promoting Empowerment and Social Justice**

Promoting empowerment and social justice is central in aligning research questions with the transformative research paradigm. This factor recognises the transformative potential of research to drive positive change and advance social justice goals. For instance, in exploring community-based interventions that empower refugee women to overcome barriers and build economic self-sufficiency, the research question focuses on empowering marginalised individuals by understanding their unique needs and identifying effective interventions. Similarly, in investigating strategies for promoting inclusive educational practices that empower students from diverse cultural backgrounds, the research question acknowledges the transformative power of education in fostering equity and social justice, emphasising the importance of creating inclusive learning environments that empower all students. See the research questions as examples:

- **Example 1:** How can community-based interventions empower refugee women to overcome barriers and build economic self-sufficiency within their host communities?

- **Example 2:** What are the strategies for promoting inclusive educational practices that empower students from diverse cultural backgrounds and contribute to equitable outcomes?

Considering these factors when formulating research questions enables researchers to ensure that their studies are within the transformative research paradigm grounded in a commitment to centring marginalised voices, critically examining power relations, addressing structural inequalities, and promoting empowerment and social justice.

### 4.8.1  Case Studies on Aligning Research Questions With Transformative Paradigm

The following three case studies exemplify how researchers strategically align their research questions with the transformative paradigm, shaping the entire research process to foster positive social change.

---

**Case Study 1: LGBTQ+ Mental Health and Access to Healthcare**

**Research Question:** How do healthcare systems perpetuate barriers to mental health services for LGBTQ+ individuals, and what strategies can be implemented to address these disparities?

**Alignment with Transformative Paradigm**

Aligning with the transformative paradigm, this research question centres on the experiences and challenges faced by LGBTQ+ individuals in accessing mental health services. It acknowledges the power dynamics within healthcare systems that contribute to disparities and marginalisation. By exploring the systemic barriers, such as discrimination and lack of LGBTQ+-inclusive policies and training, the study aims to uncover the underlying structural inequalities that hinder equitable access to mental healthcare. The research process involves engaging LGBTQ+ individuals as co-researchers, giving voice to their experiences, and empowering them to actively contribute to the identification of strategies to address these disparities. The research findings can inform transformative change by advocating for policy reforms, LGBTQ+ competency training for healthcare providers, and the development of LGBTQ+-affirming mental health services.

### Case Study 2: Community Development and Indigenous Land Rights

**Research Question:** How can community-based approaches support indigenous communities in reclaiming and protecting their land rights, and what are the transformative outcomes of such efforts?

**Alignment with Transformative Paradigm**

In line with the transformative paradigm, this research question focuses on the empowerment and social justice of indigenous communities. By centring the experiences and perspectives of indigenous communities, the research aims to examine power dynamics related to land rights and how colonial legacies perpetuate structural inequalities. The study involves a PAR approach, collaborating closely with indigenous community members as co-researchers and engaging in collective decision-making. The research process incorporates indigenous knowledge systems and cultural practices, ensuring that the research respects and amplifies the voices of the community. The research outcomes can inform transformative change by supporting indigenous communities in their struggles for land reclamation, contributing to legal and policy advocacy, and fostering community-led sustainable development initiatives that promote self-determination and social justice.

### Case Study 3: Women's Empowerment and Microfinance in Sub-Saharan Africa

**Research Question:** How can microfinance initiatives empower women in Sub-Saharan Africa to overcome economic barriers and foster transformative change within their communities?

**Alignment with Transformative Paradigm**

This research question aligns with the transformative paradigm by centring on women's experiences and challenges in Sub-Saharan Africa. It acknowledges the power dynamics within economic systems that contribute to gender disparities and marginalisation. The research aims to explore the systemic barriers, such as limited access to financial resources and gender-based discrimination, that hinder women's economic empowerment. The study involves a participatory research approach, engaging women as co-researchers to ensure their voices are heard and empowering them to actively contribute to identifying strategies for economic empowerment. The research findings can inform transformative change by advocating for policies supporting women's access to financial resources, fostering entrepreneurship, and challenging gender-based inequalities within economic structures. The ultimate goal is to contribute to the empowerment of women, leading to positive social and economic changes within their communities.

These case studies exemplify how research questions aligned with the transformative paradigm can address systemic inequalities, empower marginalised communities, and contribute to transformative change. They reflect the principles of centring marginalised voices, critically examining power relations, addressing structural inequalities, and promoting empowerment and social justice within the research process and outcomes.

### 4.9 Data Collection Methods in Transformative Research

Data collection methods are central to the implementation of transformative research, as they shape the process of gathering vital information, insights, and perspectives from individuals and communities. Within the transformative research paradigm, the selection of these methods is not arbitrary but must thoughtfully align with the specific goals of challenging existing power dynamics, promoting social justice, and empowering marginalised communities. The decision must reflect a deep understanding of the complexities involved in the study of social phenomena, recognising the need to create spaces where marginalised voices can be heard and where existing structures can be critically analysed. In the context of transformative research, eight data collection methods have been identified as particularly relevant, each chosen for its potential to contribute meaningfully to transformative change required of transformative researchers.

> i *In-depth Interviews:* In-depth interviews, as a qualitative data collection method (Minhat, 2015), hold a significant place within the transformative research paradigm, enabling a profound exploration of individuals' experiences, perspectives, and lived realities. This method goes beyond surface-level questioning, engaging individuals in detailed and open-ended conversations that seek to uncover nuanced and contextualised insights. Particularly valuable for giving voice to marginalised individuals and communities, in-depth interviews create a safe and confidential space where participants can freely share their stories, challenges, and aspirations. This personal and direct engagement empowers participants,

allowing them to actively contribute to the research. It also provides researchers with a deeper understanding of the underlying power dynamics, social inequalities, and potential pathways for transformative change, aligning with the overarching goals of the transformative research paradigm. The use of in-depth interviews reflects a commitment to recognising and valuing the complexity of human experiences, advancing empathetic and impactful research.

ii **Focus Groups:** Focus groups, as a qualitative data collection method, offer a unique collaborative environment within the transformative research paradigm, bringing together a small group of participants to engage in facilitated discussions around specific topics or issues (Khosravi, 2011). Unlike individual interviews, focus groups foster collective learning, reflection, and the co-creation of knowledge. By creating a space where participants can openly share their perspectives, debate ideas, and build upon each other's insights, focus groups generate rich and diverse data that reflect a shared experience. This communal approach creates a sense of community among participants and empowers them by validating their experiences and amplifying their voices. Within the context of transformative research, this method serves not merely as a means to gather information but as a platform to uncover shared concerns, collective aspirations, and potential strategies for transformative action. The interactive and participatory nature of focus groups aligns well with the goals of challenging power dynamics and promoting social justice, making it a powerful tool for researchers aiming to engage with and understand complex social phenomena.

iii **Photovoice:** Photovoice is a participatory data collection method that combines photography and storytelling, and it holds particular resonance within the transformative research paradigm (Kile, 2022). By providing participants with cameras and encouraging them to capture images representing their lived experiences, challenges, and visions for change, Photovoice offers an alternative means of expression that goes beyond words. This visual engagement allows participants to articulate their perspectives in a way that is both personal and powerful, reflecting on social issues in a tangible form. Within group discussions and through narrative analysis of the photographs, participants are empowered to visually communicate their realities, challenge prevailing stereotypes, and actively advocate for social justice. In the context of transformative research, Photovoice is not merely a data collection tool but a means of facilitating a deeper understanding of the lived experiences of marginalised communities. By embracing the visual medium, it provides a unique platform for voices to be heard and seen, transforming research into a collaborative and creative endeavour that aligns with empowerment, empathy, and transformation goals.

iv **Participatory Mapping:** Participatory mapping is a collaborative and innovative data collection method that involves working with individuals and communities to create maps representing their experiences of place, resources, and power relations (Emmel, 2008). Unlike traditional mapping, participatory mapping actively involves participants in the process, allowing them to identify important locations, boundaries, and social relationships that might otherwise be overlooked. Within the transformative research paradigm, this method transcends mere cartography and provides a profound visual representation of how power operates spatially, uncovering hidden geographies of inequality. By giving a spatial dimension to the experiences of marginalised communities, participatory mapping promotes spatial justice and fosters an understanding that is both tangible and contextual. Furthermore, this method goes beyond mere analysis, enabling community empowerment and transformative action by facilitating community-led initiatives for change. By highlighting the spatial dimensions of social injustices, participatory mapping aligns seamlessly with the transformative goals, creating an active platform for engagement, advocacy, and change and putting the power of mapping into the hands of those whose lives and experiences are being mapped.

v **Observational Methods:** Observational methods, including participant observation, are foundational approaches within qualitative research that involve systematically observing and documenting social phenomena in their natural settings (Fry et al., 2017). Unlike other methods that might rely on respondents' reflections or representations, observational methods require the researcher to immerse themselves within the community or group being studied, actively participating, and observing daily activities. Within the transformative research paradigm, this approach offers a unique and first hand understanding of power dynamics, social interactions, and the nuanced contextual factors that influence and shape social inequalities. By engaging with subjects in their everyday environments, researchers can capture rich, descriptive data that delves into the complexities of lived experiences. This method goes beyond mere observation, enabling the identification of transformative practices, resistance strategies, and the everyday realities that characterise the lives of marginalised communities. Observational methods thus provide a robust and intricate perspective that aligns with the goals of the transformative research paradigm, allowing researchers to navigate the complexities of social phenomena with an empathetic and engaged approach, actively witnessing and interpreting the world through the eyes of those being studied.

vi **Document Analysis:** Document analysis is a method that encompasses the review and critical analysis of various written or visual materials, ranging from policy documents and media articles to historical records (Danilovic, 2021). This method takes on a particular significance within the transformative research paradigm as it allows researchers to delve into the underlying power structures, ideologies, and discourses that shape and influence social realities. Rather than accepting documents at face value, researchers employing this method critically analyse texts through a transformative lens, seeking to uncover hidden biases, structural inequalities, and the often subtle ways in which power dynamics are maintained and reproduced. This analytical approach identifies opportunities for transformative change by revealing the underlying narratives and assumptions that may perpetuate injustice. In doing so, document analysis contributes to a more profound understanding of power relations and the development of strategies for challenging oppressive systems. Whether used alone or in conjunction with other research methods, document analysis within the transformative research paradigm becomes a powerful tool for inquiry, advocacy, and action, shedding light on the often unseen forces that shape our world.

vii **Digital Ethnography:** Digital ethnography represents a contemporary and increasingly relevant data collection method that centres on understanding social interactions and practices within digital spaces, such as online communities, social media platforms, or virtual environments (Borkovich & Middle, 2022). Within the context of the transformative research paradigm, digital ethnography is particularly significant as it recognises the growing influence of digital technologies on our lives and the ensuing importance of studying power dynamics and social justice within the digital realm. Rather than limiting observation to physical spaces, this method extends the ethnographic lens to the virtual world, allowing researchers to explore how marginalised communities navigate online spaces, challenge oppressive narratives, and mobilise for transformative change. The method provides a rich avenue for examining online interactions, digital identities, and online activism, illuminating the multifaceted ways digital platforms can reproduce existing power structures and act as sites of resistance and redefinition. In an age where digital interactions are integral to social life, digital ethnography within the transformative research paradigm offers a critical and timely perspective, bridging the virtual and the real in a quest for understanding and transformation.

viii **Arts-Based Methods:** Arts-based methods, which encompass a wide range of creative expressions such as storytelling, visual arts, theatre, or poetry (Wang et al., 2017), are emerging as potent tools for data collection within the transformative research paradigm. Unlike traditional research approaches, these methods facilitate a unique and emotive pathway for participants to express their experiences, emotions, and aspirations. By fostering creativity and embracing alternative ways of knowing and sharing knowledge, arts-based methods enable marginalised individuals to communicate their stories and perspectives in ways that are both transformative and accessible. This approach not only acknowledges but celebrates the complexity and diversity of human experience, and it can resonate on a deeply personal level that transcends conventional language barriers. By engaging with arts-based methods, researchers are able to tap into the rich tapestry of lived realities of marginalised communities, challenging dominant narratives and creating a platform for dialogue and reflection. Through the lens of art, the abstract and the personal become intertwined, fostering a deeper understanding and empathy that can inspire transformative change. In the hands of both researchers and participants, art becomes more than mere aesthetics; it becomes a medium for connection, empowerment, and social transformation.

ix **Participatory Video:** Participatory video is an innovative and empowering data collection method that actively involves community members in creating and analysing video footage (Rose & Cardinal, 2018). Within the transformative research paradigm, this method allows marginalised communities to use video as a multifaceted tool for self-expression, advocacy, and tangible social change. Rather than merely being subjects of research, participants are trained in video recording and editing techniques, enabling them to document their own experiences, issues, and aspirations. This democratisation of the storytelling process shifts the control of narrative and representation into the hands of those who have lived the experiences being depicted, amplifying their voices and promoting social justice. Moreover, the process of engaging in video-making fosters a sense of collective agency, helping participants not only gain valuable skills but also build confidence and camaraderie. By facilitating a platform for transformative dialogue and action, participatory video goes beyond mere documentation and becomes an active instrument in the quest for empowerment, empathy, and social transformation. It captures the reality of lived experiences while providing a vibrant visual medium through which those experiences can resonate and effect change.

x **Narrative Inquiry:** Narrative inquiry is a qualitative research method uniquely situated to capture the complexity of individuals' lived experiences and stories, focusing on what is told and how it's told (Adhikari, 2021). Within the transformative research paradigm, this method elevates the voices of marginalised individuals, providing a space where they can share their personal stories, challenge dominant discourses, and navigate intricate power dynamics. By delving into these personal narratives, narrative inquiry transcends mere factual recounting, unveiling deeper insights into social injustices, human emotions, relationships, and cultural norms. It recognises storytelling's inherent power and transformative potential, turning individual experiences into opportunities for collective learning. The detailed and nuanced analysis of individual narratives uncovers common themes and patterns that may otherwise remain obscured, allowing researchers to synthesise these into a broader understanding of social phenomena. Furthermore, the empathetic connections fostered through narrative inquiry humanise research, transforming personal stories into shared pathways for understanding, compassion, and transformative action. Narrative inquiry extends an invitation to see the world through others' eyes, enriching the research landscape with profound human connections and insights.

Therefore, the choice of data collection methods within the transformative research paradigm should reflect its goals of challenging power dynamics, promoting social justice, and empowering marginalised communities. In-depth interviews, focus groups, Photovoice, participatory mapping, observational methods, document analysis, digital ethnography, arts-based methods, participatory video and narrative inquiry are among the methodologies that can effectively capture the lived experiences, insights, and aspirations of marginalised individuals and communities. These methods provide opportunities for the co-creation of knowledge, the amplification of marginalised voices, and the identification of strategies for transformative action.

## 4.10 Data Analysis and Interpretation in Transformative Research

Data analysis methods within the transformative research paradigm are pivotal in synthesising, interpreting, and making sense of the collected data, imbuing them with a unique power to effect change. These methods go beyond mere statistical or thematic analysis; they delve into patterns, themes, and deeper connections that resonate with the transformative goals of challenging existing power dynamics, promoting social justice, and fostering transformative change. Analysing transformative data involves a sensitive, rigorous, and creative process that aligns the technical aspects of data analysis with ethical considerations and social commitments. This alignment ensures that the analysis resonates with the experiences and voices of marginalised communities, honouring their complexity and nuance. The selection of relevant data analysis methods is tailored to the research questions and context, enabling a rich, contextual understanding that connects individual experiences to broader social and cultural dynamics. This section's detailed exploration of ten specific methods showcases the diversity and adaptability of data analysis techniques within the transformative research paradigm, each contributing uniquely to the transformative agenda. By skilfully navigating these methods, researchers are equipped to uncover hidden truths, challenge prevailing narratives, and actively contribute to social change, ensuring that research is not just an academic exercise but a powerful tool for real-world impact.

i **Thematic Analysis:** Thematic analysis within the transformative research paradigm is a powerful and flexible qualitative data analysis method that concentrates on discerning and investigating recurring themes or patterns within the data (Braun & Clarke, 2012). Through a systematic and iterative coding and categorisation process, researchers immerse themselves in the data to extract underlying meanings and experiences, often related to power dynamics, social inequalities, and opportunities for transformative change. Unlike a more conventional approach that might focus purely on the surface content, thematic analysis in the transformative research context delves into the subtleties of social dynamics, recognising the multifaceted interactions between individuals, institutions,

*Transformative Paradigm and Methodological Alignment* 111

and ideologies. Organising the data into coherent themes allows for a nuanced exploration of how oppression, marginalisation, and inequality manifest in the participants' lived experiences. The themes that emerge not only provide insights into the immediate subject of study but also contribute to a broader understanding of social justice, acting as a catalyst for challenging existing oppressive structures and promoting empowerment and change within marginalised communities.

ii **Content Analysis:** Content analysis in the context of the transformative research paradigm is a rigorous method that systematically categorises and analyses textual or visual data, emphasising uncovering underlying power structures, ideologies, and discourses (Kleinheksel et al., 2020). Unlike a neutral or descriptive approach, content analysis within this paradigm is employed with a critical lens, probing media representations, policy documents, or other texts to identify and challenge hidden biases, stereotypes, or oppressive narratives. It moves beyond mere surface-level examination of content, delving into the ways language and imagery may be used to reinforce social inequalities, marginalise certain groups, or maintain existing power dynamics. By dissecting these elements, content analysis provides a deeper understanding of the sociocultural context in which they occur, revealing what is being communicated and how and why. This method facilitates a critical engagement with the data, enabling researchers to identify opportunities for transformative strategies, challenging dominant discourses, and ultimately contributing to the broader goals of social justice and empowerment within the transformative research paradigm.

iii **Discourse Analysis:** Discourse analysis within the transformative research paradigm is a complex and insightful method that delves into how language constructs, represents and shapes social realities and power dynamics. Rather than treating language as a neutral conduit for transmitting information, discourse analysis recognises that language is an active force that can either reinforce or challenge systems of oppression and inequality (Zajda, 2020). This method involves carefully examining language use, context, and underlying ideologies and assumptions that inform how people speak and write (Moser et al., 2013). Researchers employing discourse analysis look at how particular words, phrases, and rhetorical structures are used to legitimise or resist certain power relations, societal norms, and values. This critical examination of discourse goes beyond merely identifying patterns or themes in the text and actively interrogates how language contributes to the maintenance or transformation of social injustices. By unearthing these hidden aspects of discourse, researchers can contribute to transformative efforts, shedding light on how language can be harnessed to create counter-narratives, inspire resistance, and drive positive social change.

iv **Narrative Analysis:** Narrative analysis is a method that centres on the analysis of the structure, content, and meaning of individual or collective stories (Smith, 2016), recognising the profound influence of storytelling in shaping lived experiences and societal perceptions. Rather than treating narratives as mere data, this approach acknowledges the power and agency of storytelling, allowing researchers to delve into personal narratives' complexities and understand how they reflect, shape, or contest societal power dynamics and normative beliefs. Analysing narratives within this transformative lens goes beyond mere thematic identification; it actively engages with the ways in which stories can either perpetuate or challenge oppressive systems and stereotypes. By honouring and scrutinising the narrative form, researchers can amplify marginalised voices, fostering an environment in which alternative narratives and counter-stories are co-created and celebrated. This, in turn, can contribute to a broader understanding of social injustices and a collective commitment to promoting social justice and transformative change.

v **Qualitative Comparative Analysis (QCA):** QCA within the transformative research paradigm serves as a nuanced tool to explore the multifaceted interplay of factors that contribute to social injustices or facilitate transformative change. Unlike simplistic linear analyses, QCA recognises that social phenomena often result from complex combinations of conditions rather than isolated variables (Thomann & Ege, 2020). By employing a systematic approach to compare and contrast various cases, researchers utilising QCA can identify specific configurations of conditions that lead to particular outcomes. This analysis enables a richer understanding of the underlying mechanisms and contextual variables that drive transformative processes, moving beyond mere correlations to uncover causal complexity. Within the transformative research framework, QCA becomes particularly powerful as it aligns with the paradigm's goals of challenging power dynamics and promoting social justice. It allows for an in-depth examination of how diverse factors interact and merge to shape societal structures and experiences, thereby offering insights that can inform strategies for systemic change and empowerment.

vi **Critical Discourse Analysis (CDA):** CDA functions as a data analysis method, playing a pivotal role in the transformative research paradigm. CDA critically investigates language use and discursive practices as an analytical tool, delving into the underlying power dynamics, ideologies, and concealed meanings that shape social realities (Wodak, 2014). Within the framework of transformative research, CDA acts as a catalyst to deconstruct dominant narratives and examine how language can either reinforce or challenge social inequalities. By engaging with texts or discourses through this critical perspective, researchers are empowered to pinpoint the complexities of language and its role in perpetuating systems of oppression. This analysis exposes hidden biases and illuminates paths toward transformative change. The focus on more inclusive and equitable language use emphasises the potential of CDA to disrupt conventional discursive practices, thereby aligning with the paradigm's core goals of advocating social justice and fostering societal transformation.

vii **Visual Analysis:** Visual analysis is a method that centres on the examination and interpretation of visual data, including photographs, videos, and artwork, recognising the profound impact that visuals have in conveying social realities and confronting established narratives (Kruse & Steinbrecher, 2010). Within the transformative research paradigm, visual analysis grants researchers the ability to delve into the meanings and symbolism ingrained in visual portrayals, thereby shedding light on how power manifests visually. This approach offers a nuanced perspective, enabling researchers to discern the visual strategies that either strengthen or contest existing power dynamics. By dissecting the visual elements, researchers can advocate for alternative and more equitable representations, fostering an environment conducive to transformative change. The adoption of visual analysis within transformative research underscores the method's capacity to explore beyond textual information, tapping into a rich visual landscape that can amplify voices, challenge stereotypes, and contribute to the overarching goals of social justice and transformation.

viii **Participatory Data Analysis:** Participatory data analysis is a collaborative approach that includes participants or community members in the data analysis process, embodying the principles of inclusiveness and the co-creation of knowledge (Kortuem et al., 2014) that are central to the transformative research paradigm. By inviting participants to engage in workshops or discussions during the analysis phase, this method not only democratises the research process but also fosters empowerment by giving voice to diverse perspectives that can inform and enrich the interpretation of findings. The participatory nature of this analysis amplifies the agency of marginalised communities in shaping research conclusions, thereby reinforcing the validity and relevance of the results. Additionally, community members' involvement enhances the research's transformative potential, forging a path that can lead to more socially just and impactful outcomes. participatory data analysis thus stands as a robust method within transformative research, facilitating a more authentic and community-centred approach to understanding and addressing complex social issues.

ix **Intersectional Analysis:** Intersectional analysis, building on the key concept of intersectionality within the transformative paradigm, serves as a nuanced method for analysing data by exploring how various social identities intersect and shape individuals' experiences (Christensen & Jensen, 2012). Within the transformative research paradigm, this approach provides a comprehensive perspective that recognises social inequalities' complexity and multifaceted nature. It examines how power operates across different dimensions, such as race, gender, class, sexuality, and disability, weaving a complex web of oppression and privilege. By employing an intersectional lens, researchers can delve into the unique challenges and experiences faced by individuals or communities situated at the crossroads of these intersecting identities. The insights gleaned from intersectional analysis illuminate the intricate dynamics of social inequalities and guide the development of informed and targeted strategies that aim to promote social justice and transformative change. This method adds depth and sensitivity to the research, helping to foster a more inclusive and empathetic understanding of the social world.

### 4.10.1 Transformative Justification of the Data Analysis Methods

All the data analysis methods discussed above are transformative in nature because they align with the goals and principles of the transformative research paradigm. These methods enable researchers to challenge power dynamics, promote social justice, and contribute to transformative change in several ways.

First, these data analysis methods facilitate the amplification of marginalised voices. By carefully analysing qualitative data, such as in-depth interviews, narratives, or focus group discussions, researchers can highlight the perspectives and experiences of individuals and communities who have been historically marginalised or silenced. This process of centring marginalised voices challenges dominant narratives disrupts power imbalances, and promotes a more inclusive understanding of social realities. Second, the data analysis methods allow for critical examination of power relations and systems of oppression. Through techniques such as thematic analysis, content analysis, discourse analysis, and CDA, researchers can uncover how power operates, how ideologies are reinforced or challenged, and how discursive practices shape social inequalities. By critically analysing data, researchers can bring to light the ways in which power dynamics perpetuate social injustices, ultimately paving the way for transformative interventions and social change.

Furthermore, these data analysis methods provide opportunities for the identification of transformative strategies and pathways for change. By exploring patterns, themes, and connections within the data, researchers can identify promising practices, resistance strategies, and alternative narratives that challenge oppressive systems. This knowledge can inform advocacy efforts, policy recommendations, and community-led initiatives aimed at dismantling structural inequalities and promoting social justice. Moreover, many of the data analysis methods mentioned emphasise participatory and collaborative approaches. By involving participants or community members in the data analysis process, researchers empower marginalised communities, recognise their expertise, and ensure that their perspectives shape the interpretation of findings. This participatory approach aligns with the transformative principle of empowering marginalised communities, fostering agency, and promoting the co-creation of knowledge.

Therefore, all the data analysis methods discussed are transformative in nature as they contribute to challenging power dynamics, promoting social justice, and fostering transformative change. These methods centre marginalised voices, critically examine power relations, identify transformative strategies, and embrace participatory approaches. By employing these transformative data analysis methods, researchers can generate knowledge that uncovers social injustices and paves the way for transformative interventions, advocacy, and collective action towards a more equitable and just society.

## 4.11 Critiques and Debates in Transformative Research

Like any research paradigm, transformative research is subject to critiques and debates within the scholarly community. These critiques and debates revolve around various aspects of the transformative paradigm, including its theoretical foundations, methodological approaches, and potential limitations. Here, we will discuss some of the key critiques and debates in transformative research.

A critique of the transformative paradigm centres around the potential subjectivity and researcher bias that may arise (Gough & Madill, 2012; Romm, 2015). Critics argue that the paradigm's emphasis on social justice and transformative change may lead to a predetermined agenda that influences the research process and outcomes. They highlight the need for researchers to critically reflect on their own biases and ensure transparency in their methods to address these concerns. It is essential for researchers to be aware of their positionality and actively engage in reflexivity throughout the research process, acknowledging their own perspectives and potential influence on data collection, analysis, and interpretation. By embracing transparency and reflexivity, researchers can navigate these challenges and minimise bias, ensuring a more robust and inclusive research process.

Another debate within the transformative paradigm revolves around the validity and generalisability of findings (Kukull & Ganguli, 2012). Critics argue that the paradigm's emphasis on context-specific understandings and the unique experiences of marginalised communities may limit the generalisability of research findings to broader populations. They contend that the focus on individual contexts and rich descriptions may compromise the ability to draw universal conclusions. On the other hand, proponents argue that the transformative paradigm aims to uncover contextual nuances and challenge dominant knowledge frameworks, prioritising depth of understanding over generalisability. They advocate for the importance of rich, context-specific analyses that contribute to broader theoretical understandings and inform context-sensitive interventions.

Transformative research is concerned with power dynamics, but debates arise regarding the power dynamics within the research process itself. Critics argue that power imbalances may persist between researchers and participants despite the transformative goals (Mertens, 2007, 2012). They emphasise the need to critically examine and address potential power differentials, ensuring that research is conducted ethically and empoweringly. This includes actively involving participants in decision-making processes, respecting their agency, and fostering genuine collaboration. Proponents recognise the importance of navigating power dynamics and advocate for research methodologies that prioritise participant empowerment, knowledge co-creation, and power redistribution within research partnerships.

Within the transformative paradigm, debates arise around how researchers can effectively navigate their identities, biases, and privileges. Critics argue that researchers must be vigilant in critically examining their own positionality and acknowledge the potential impact on research outcomes. They assert that researchers should be aware of their social location and privileges' influence on data collection, analysis, and interpretation. Open dialogue and ongoing reflexivity are necessary to mitigate potential biases and ensure ethical research practices. Proponents highlight the importance of self-reflection, acknowledging and embracing the situatedness of the researcher, and engaging in a continuous process of reflexivity to improve the quality and validity of research conducted within the transformative paradigm.

An ongoing debate centres around striking a balance between research rigour and the transformative goals of social justice. Critics argue that an overemphasis on social justice may compromise traditional standards of scientific rigour, potentially undermining the credibility of research findings. They caution against sacrificing rigour in pursuit of transformative objectives. Proponents, however, assert that transformative research can achieve rigorous methodologies while remaining committed to challenging power dynamics and promoting social justice. They advocate for the integration of rigorous research methods, including systematic data collection, transparency, validity checks, and robust analysis techniques, within a transformative framework. Balancing rigour and social justice requires thoughtful methodological choices, critical reflexivity, and an understanding that both aspects are vital to ensuring the credibility and impact of research conducted within the transformative paradigm.

It is important to note that these critiques and debates are inherent in the broader research landscape, not exclusive to the transformative paradigm. Engaging in these discussions contributes to the ongoing development and refinement of transformative research methodologies, addressing potential limitations and ensuring the ethical and impactful implementation of the paradigm.

## 4.12 Balancing Research Rigour and Social Justice in Transformative Research

Balancing research rigour and social justice is a crucial consideration for transformative researchers. It involves conducting high-quality research while remaining committed to addressing power imbalances, promoting social equity, and advocating for transformative change. Here are some key strategies that transformative researchers can employ to achieve this balance:

- ***Reflexivity and Positionality:*** Transformative researchers should engage in ongoing reflexivity, critically examining their own positionality, biases, and privileges. This self-awareness helps researchers navigate their role in

the research process and mitigate potential biases. By acknowledging and addressing their own power and position, researchers can promote social justice by ensuring that their actions and decisions align with transformative principles.
- **Ethical Considerations:** Ethical research practices are essential in transformative research. Researchers must prioritise participants' well-being, autonomy, and agency, particularly in marginalised communities. This involves obtaining informed consent, protecting privacy and confidentiality, and ensuring participant safety. Ethical considerations include acknowledging potential power imbalances between researchers and participants and actively empowering marginalised communities throughout the research process.
- **Rigorous Methodologies:** Transformative researchers should employ rigorous methodologies to ensure the trustworthiness of their research findings. This includes utilising appropriate sampling techniques, systematic data collection methods, and robust analysis techniques. By adhering to rigorous methodologies, researchers enhance the credibility of their work and contribute to the overall body of knowledge in the field of transformative research.
- **Collaborative and Participatory Approaches:** Emphasising collaboration and participatory approaches is crucial for balancing research rigour and social justice. Engaging participants as active collaborators in the research process can help challenge power imbalances and promote social equity. By involving participants in decision-making, analysis, and interpretation of data, researchers ensure that the research reflects the perspectives and priorities of the communities being studied.
- **Addressing Structural Inequalities:** Transformative research goes beyond individual experiences and seeks to address systemic and structural inequalities. Researchers should strive to understand and address the underlying causes of social injustices identified in their research. This may involve advocating for policy changes, raising awareness, or collaborating with stakeholders to bring about transformative change at a systemic level.
- **Collaboration with Community Organisations:** Collaborating with community organisations and advocacy groups can enhance the social justice impact of transformative research. Working closely with these organisations ensures that research findings are relevant, actionable, and have a greater potential for transformative change. By aligning research goals with the priorities and needs of the communities being studied, researchers can strengthen the social justice outcomes of their work.

Based on this, it is essential to note that balancing research rigour and social justice requires intentional and conscientious efforts from transformative researchers. By integrating reflexivity, ethical considerations, rigorous methodologies, participatory approaches, and a focus on addressing structural inequalities, researchers can contribute to both scholarly rigour and meaningful social justice outcomes within the transformative research paradigm.

## 4.13 Summary

This chapter explored the transformative paradigm within research, focusing on its philosophical foundations, key concepts, methodological designs, and considerations for aligning research questions with transformative goals. The chapter discussed the evolution of the transformative paradigm and its commitment to transformative change and social justice. I delved into the epistemological, ontological, axiological, and methodological underpinnings that shape the transformative paradigm, highlighting the importance of understanding these philosophical foundations for comprehending its distinctive nature. Additionally, the chapter examined various methodological designs suitable for implementing transformative research, such as action research, PAR, participatory case study, and CBAR. We discussed the relevance of these designs in empowering marginalised communities, challenging power dynamics, and promoting social justice. Furthermore, I explored factors to consider when aligning research questions with transformative research, emphasising the importance of reflexivity, social justice orientation, and community engagement. The place of data collection methods, data analysis methods, and the critical debates and critiques surrounding transformative research were presented. Lastly, the chapter sheds light on the delicate balance between research rigour and social justice, highlighting strategies for achieving this balance through ethical considerations, rigorous methodologies, reflexivity, participatory approaches, and addressing structural inequalities.

# 5 Postcolonial Indigenous Paradigm and Methodological Alignment

**Chapter Synopsis**

This chapter delves into the postcolonial indigenous paradigm (PCIP) and its methodological alignment, comprehensively exploring its historical context, philosophical foundations, key concepts, and assumptions. The chapter examines the evolution of this paradigm, highlighting its significance in the research. It further explores methodological designs, data collection methods, and data analysis within the postcolonial indigenous research framework, emphasising the importance of aligning research questions with its principles. Additionally, the chapter addresses critiques, debates, and the ethical considerations of conducting research in this paradigm, focusing on the delicate balance between empowerment and respecting indigenous rights and protocols. The introductory paragraph sets the stage for a comprehensive exploration of the PCIP, laying the foundation for an in-depth understanding of its theoretical underpinnings and methodological approaches.

## 5.1 Concept Postcolonial Indigenous Paradigm

The PCIP arises within the context of the historical and ongoing effects of colonialism on indigenous communities. It acknowledges and challenges the oppressive legacy of colonisation, recognising the profound social, cultural, political, and economic disruptions experienced by indigenous peoples worldwide. This paradigm seeks to reclaim indigenous identities, knowledge, and sovereignty while critiquing the dominant colonial narratives that have marginalised and eroded indigenous cultures (Chilisa & Phatshwane, 2022).

Postcolonialism emerged as a response to the legacy of colonial domination and the need to challenge the power dynamics inherent in the colonial relationship (Ndlovu-Gatsheni, 2013). In the indigenous context, this paradigm recognises the unique experiences and struggles of indigenous peoples, who have historically faced dispossession, forced assimilation, cultural genocide, and systemic inequalities. It also acknowledges that colonialism is not a thing of the past but continues to shape indigenous realities in various forms. Therefore, examining the context of colonisation, the PCIP seeks

DOI: 10.4324/9781003484066-5

to decolonise research, methodologies, and knowledge production (Chilisa, 2012). It recognises that traditional research approaches have often been Eurocentric and have perpetuated colonial narratives, further marginalising indigenous communities. In response, this paradigm aims to centre indigenous perspectives, knowledge systems, and ways of knowing by challenging the dominant power structures and hierarchies that marginalise indigenous peoples. It advocates for recognising indigenous self-determination, cultural revitalisation, and restoring indigenous rights and sovereignty. Essentially, the paradigm emphasises the importance of engaging in respectful and reciprocal research relationships with indigenous communities, involving them as active participants in the research process and ensuring that research aligns with their needs, priorities, and values.

Hence, the concept of the PCIP requires acknowledging the historical and ongoing impacts of colonisation on indigenous peoples. This paradigm seeks to empower indigenous communities, celebrate their rich cultural heritage, and work towards social justice and equity by recognising and challenging the oppressive structures that persist. It represents a crucial shift in research and scholarship, promoting inclusivity, decolonisation, and recognising indigenous knowledge and perspectives as integral to understanding the world.

## 5.2 The Evolution of the Postcolonial Indigenous Paradigm

The evolution of the PCIP reflects a dynamic and ongoing process of understanding and responding to the complex challenges faced by indigenous peoples in the aftermath of colonialism. This paradigm has evolved over time in response to changing social, political, and academic landscapes and through indigenous communities' continuous contributions and resilience. The origins of the PCIP can be traced back to the emergence of postcolonial studies in the mid-20th century, which aimed to critique and challenge the lasting impacts of colonialism. Scholars such as Linda Tuhiwai Smith, Vine Deloria Jr and Bagele Chilisa could be linked to its emergence (Chilisa, 2019; O'Neal, 2015; Smith et al., 2018). Postcolonial indigenous paradigms challenge dominant Western frameworks, engage in knowledge co-creation with indigenous communities, and aim to address the legacies of colonisation and cultural erasure (Chilisa & Phatshwane, 2022). However, within indigenous scholarship and activism, indigenous peoples' specific context and experiences began to be foregrounded and given distinct attention.

The initial stages of the paradigm focused on articulating the historical injustices faced by indigenous communities, shedding light on the systemic violence, cultural erasure, and dispossession they endured. Scholars and activists worked to counter prevailing colonial narratives that painted indigenous peoples as inferior or disappeared altogether. Indigenous communities asserted their resilience and agency by reclaiming their own stories, cultures, and identities. Over time, the paradigm expanded to incorporate a deeper understanding of indigenous knowledge systems, epistemologies, and ontologies. Indigenous scholars such as Linda Tuhiwai Smith, Vine Deloria Jr and Bagele Chilisa articulated the importance of recognising and valuing indigenous ways of knowing, advocating for cultural revitalisation, and self-determination toward challenging the dominant Eurocentric knowledge paradigms that had marginalised indigenous knowledge. This evolution highlighted the need to decolonise research methodologies, education systems, and institutions and to centre indigenous perspectives and voices in academia.

The PCIP also recognised the importance of intersectionality, acknowledging the diversity within indigenous communities and the overlapping forms of oppression faced by indigenous women, LGBTQ+ individuals, disabled individuals, and other marginalised groups. This intersectional lens expanded the paradigm's scope and provided a more nuanced understanding of power dynamics and inequalities within indigenous contexts. This is to justify that ongoing political struggles and legal advancements have influenced the evolution of the paradigm. Land rights movements, treaty negotiations, and the United Nations Declaration on the Rights of Indigenous Peoples (UNDRIP) have shaped the discourse and provided frameworks for indigenous self-determination and sovereignty. These developments have contributed to the paradigm's emphasis on indigenous empowerment, self-governance, and the restoration of indigenous rights.

Today, the PCIP continues to evolve, driven by dialogues, collaborations, and activism. It embraces diverse indigenous perspectives and challenges researchers and institutions to engage in meaningful, ethical, and respectful relationships with indigenous communities. By centring indigenous knowledge, experiences, and aspirations, this paradigm strives for social justice, healing, and revitalising indigenous cultures and identities. Hence, the PCIP reflects a transformative journey that continues to shape research, activism, and policymaking. It stands as a testament to the resilience and determination of indigenous peoples to assert their rights, reclaim their voices, and challenge the structures of power that perpetuate colonial legacies.

## 5.3 Key Concepts and Assumptions

Key Concepts and Assumptions within the PCIP play a vital role in shaping its theoretical framework and guiding principles. These concepts and assumptions are essential for understanding the paradigm's unique perspective and its focus on decolonisation, empowerment, and the restoration of indigenous rights and knowledge. In this section, the key concepts and assumptions that underpin the PCIP are discussed.

i **Decolonisation:** Decolonisation is a central concept within the PCIP. It refers to the process of challenging and dismantling the colonial structures, systems, and ideologies that continue to impact indigenous communities (Ndlovu-Gatsheni, 2018). Decolonisation involves questioning and critiquing the power dynamics, cultural erasure, and historical injustices imposed by colonial forces. It encompasses the restoration of indigenous self-determination, the revitalisation of indigenous cultures and languages, and the recognition and respect for indigenous knowledge systems.

ii **Cultural Revitalisation:** Cultural revitalisation is another key concept within the PCIP. It emphasises the importance of reclaiming, preserving, and strengthening indigenous cultural practices, languages, and traditions. Cultural revitalisation involves restoring and celebrating indigenous identities, fostering a sense of pride and connection to cultural heritage. It recognises that the erasure and suppression of indigenous cultures during colonisation have had profound impacts and that reclaiming and revitalising cultural practices is essential for healing, resilience, and the empowerment of indigenous communities.

iii **Self-Determination:** Self-determination is a fundamental concept within the PCIP. It refers to the inherent right of indigenous peoples to govern themselves and make decisions that impact their communities, lands, and resources. Self-determination recognises that indigenous communities possess distinct political, social, and cultural systems and should have the authority to determine their futures. This concept challenges the imposition of external governance structures and promotes indigenous autonomy, sovereignty, and the right to shape their own destinies (Katmo, 2016).

iv **Sovereignty:** Sovereignty is closely related to the concept of self-determination within the PCIP (Graham & Wiessner, 2011). It refers to indigenous peoples' inherent authority, jurisdiction, and control over their lands, resources, and governance. Sovereignty recognises that indigenous nations have a unique political status and rights that should be respected and protected. It challenges the historical and ongoing infringements on indigenous sovereignty and advocates for the restoration of indigenous land rights, self-governance, and decision-making powers.

v **Cultural Continuity:** Cultural continuity is a concept that recognises the importance of maintaining and nurturing indigenous cultural practices, knowledge systems, and intergenerational transmission (Graham & Wiessner, 2011). It acknowledges that indigenous cultures and traditions are living and evolving, passed down from generation to generation. Cultural continuity emphasises the connection to ancestral knowledge, the interplay between past and present, and the role of cultural practices in shaping indigenous identities, resilience, and well-being.

Furthermore, assumptions within the PCIP include acknowledging the historical injustices and ongoing impacts of colonisation on indigenous communities. It assumes that indigenous knowledge systems are valid and valuable, deserving of recognition and respect within academic and societal contexts. The paradigm assumes that research and scholarship should be conducted collaboratively and culturally sensitively, with meaningful engagement and participation of indigenous communities. It also assumes that social justice, equity, and the restoration of indigenous rights are crucial for healing, empowerment, and the transformation of power dynamics.

These key concepts and assumptions shape the PCIP, providing a framework for understanding the complexities of indigenous experiences, centring indigenous knowledge and perspectives, and challenging colonial legacies. They guide research, activism, and policy-making efforts to foster decolonisation, cultural revitalisation, self-determination, and the recognition of indigenous sovereignty and rights.

## 5.4 The Philosophical Foundations of the Postcolonial Indigenous Paradigm

The philosophical foundations of the PCIP are crucial in shaping its theoretical framework and guiding principles, encompassing various aspects, including epistemology, ontology, axiology, and methodology. Understanding these philosophical underpinnings provides insight into indigenous peoples' unique worldview and knowledge systems within the PCIP and plays a significant role in shaping research, activism, and the reclamation of indigenous identities and knowledge. This section conducted a detailed analysis of each of these philosophical dimensions, illuminating their significance in crafting a cohesive understanding of the complex interplay between indigenous thought and postcolonial contexts.

### 5.4.1 Epistemology of the Postcolonial Indigenous Paradigm

The epistemology of the PCIP serves as a radical challenge to Eurocentric knowledge systems, acknowledging and valuing indigenous ways of knowing that have historically been marginalised (Mawere & Awuah-Nyamekye, 2015; Tripathy, 2009). Unlike Western models, which often rely on written and compartmentalised methodologies, the paradigm is deeply embedded in indigenous communities' cultural traditions, oral histories, and lived experiences. It emphasises the importance of oral transmission, fostering intergenerational connections and presenting a holistic worldview that sees all elements of existence as interconnected. The wisdom and expertise of indigenous elders and traditional knowledge holders are respected and elevated within this paradigm, acknowledging them as invaluable contributors to knowledge production. This shift away from Eurocentric dominance creates a platform for the integration and validation of indigenous knowledge systems, countering the epistemic violence that has silenced these voices in the past. The PCIP is not merely an alternative way of thinking; it is a corrective and inclusive approach that aims to enrich the global intellectual landscape and establish a more equitable space for diverse perspectives.

### 5.4.2 Ontology of the Postcolonial Indigenous Paradigm

The ontology of the PCIP represents a fundamental shift from the dualistic and hierarchical frameworks often found in Western thought, challenging conventional categorisations and separations such as those between mind and body or subject and object. Instead, it embraces a relational ontology, foregrounding the interconnectedness and interdependence of all beings, encompassing humans, non-human entities, and the very fabric of the environment (Romm, 2014). This ontology celebrates the reciprocal relationships between humans and the natural world, drawing attention to concepts of kinship, land-based spirituality, and the continuity of existence across past, present, and future generations. By rejecting Cartesian separations and promoting a holistic understanding of existence, the PCIP brings to the fore a worldview that acknowledges the symbiotic relationships and interplay between all living entities. It seeks to restore a sense of balance, harmony, and respect that transcends the often fragmented and mechanistic perspectives prevalent in conventional Western ontologies.

### 5.4.3 Axiology of the Postcolonial Indigenous Paradigm

The axiology of the PCIP is deeply rooted in the ethical values that govern relationships, research, and activism within indigenous contexts (Dube et al., 2013; Walter, 2016). These values, such as respect, reciprocity, and relationality, set a moral framework that recognises indigenous peoples' inherent rights and sovereignty. This axiological stance is not merely theoretical; it actively promotes social justice, equity, and self-determination, challenging and working to dismantle the colonial power dynamics that have historically oppressed indigenous communities. By emphasising ethical engagement and advocacy, the paradigm aims to restore indigenous rights and foster cultural revitalisation, standing as a guidepost for interaction with and within indigenous contexts. Within the framework of this paradigm, the axiological foundations extend to concrete practices in research and intellectual pursuits. Ethical research practices are paramount, with an emphasis on engaging with indigenous communities in a manner that honours their traditions, wisdom, and autonomy. This includes the protection of indigenous knowledge and intellectual property, recognising them not as objects to be mined but as sacred and collective wisdom to be respected and preserved. The PCIP's axiology acts as a beacon, directing scholars, activists, and communities toward a path that respects indigenous integrity and sovereignty, encourages responsible engagement, and sets the stage for a more equitable and culturally sensitive approach to indigenous relations and studies.

### 5.4.4 Methodology of the Postcolonial Indigenous Paradigm

The methodology of the PCIP represents a profound shift towards decolonising research practices by centring indigenous voices, perspectives, and priorities (Bowe et al., 2015; Held, 2019). This approach emphasises community-based and participatory research methods that involve indigenous communities and empower them, fostering collaboration, reciprocity, and mutual learning. Unlike traditional methodologies that may objectify or misrepresent indigenous cultures, the PCIP promotes indigenous research protocols, ensuring informed consent and employing culturally sensitive data collection, analysis, and interpretation techniques. It acknowledges that building trust and forging meaningful relationships with indigenous communities is foundational to the research process, requiring respect for their cultural protocols and an unwavering commitment to the ethical representation of findings. By realigning research practices with the principles of self-determination, cultural revitalisation, and recognition of indigenous knowledge as valid and valuable, the methodology of the PCIP not only challenges conventional academic practices but also sets a new ethical standard, contributing to a more inclusive, respectful, and empowering academic and societal landscape.

## 5.5 Methodological Designs in Postcolonial Indigenous Research

The methodological designs employed within the PCIP are crucial in ensuring culturally sensitive and community-centred research. These designs recognise indigenous communities' unique context, knowledge systems, and priorities, aiming to decolonise research approaches and empower indigenous voices. This section explores various methodological designs suitable for postcolonial indigenous research, highlighting their strengths, limitations, and ethical considerations. By employing these designs, researchers can engage meaningfully with indigenous communities and generate knowledge that respects and reflects indigenous perspectives and experiences.

i *Participatory Action Research (PAR):* PAR is an innovative research design and a powerful tool for implementing the PCIP. The framework recognises indigenous communities as sovereign and knowledgeable entities with unique insights and wisdom (Doucet et al., 2022). PAR aligns with this perspective by treating indigenous communities as experts in their own experiences, actively involving them at every stage of the research process. The emphasis on collaborative identification of research questions, designing methodologies, and data interpretation resonates with the PCIP's commitment to self-determination, cultural revitalisation, and the recognition of indigenous knowledge. By fostering reciprocal and transformative relationships, PAR helps dismantle traditional power dynamics that may marginalise indigenous voices, instead promoting empowerment, capacity-building, and social change. The prioritisation of community engagement, shared decision-making, and actionable knowledge within PAR (Doucet et al., 2022) is intrinsically linked to the core principles of the PCIP, serving as a methodological manifestation of the paradigm's commitment to ethical, respectful, and inclusive research and activism. In this way, PAR is not merely compatible with the paradigm but vital to its realisation, helping to bridge the gap between theory and practice in the quest for justice, equity, and indigenous sovereignty.

ii **Community-Based Participatory Research (CBPR):** CBPR is a design that is deeply aligned with the principles of the PCIP, emphasising collaboration, community agency, and the equitable distribution of power in research. Unlike traditional research methodologies that may perpetuate hierarchical dynamics, CBPR actively involves community members as equal partners, recognising their expertise and addressing community-identified research priorities and needs (Gullion & Tilton, 2020; Omodan, 2022a). This reflects the PCIP's commitment to valuing indigenous ways of knowing, cultural protocols, and self-determination. CBPR's focus on shared decision-making and reciprocal relationships resonates with the paradigm's emphasis on respect, reciprocity, and relationality, fostering trust and long-term partnerships beyond transactional engagements. By allowing for the co-creation of knowledge and the translation of research findings into tangible community outcomes, CBPR facilitates the integration of indigenous knowledge systems and the implementation of culturally sensitive solutions. It serves as a methodological embodiment of the paradigm, bridging theory and practice and contributing to dismantling colonial legacies within research, paving the way for a more inclusive, respectful, and empowered approach to working with indigenous communities.

iii **Two-Eyed Seeing:** Two-eyed seeing is an integrative design that perfectly aligns with the principles of the PCIP, as it seeks to combine indigenous knowledge with Western scientific knowledge, recognising the inherent value and complementarity of both perspectives (Reid et al., 2021). While Western paradigms often approach research through specialised and compartmentalised lenses, indigenous epistemologies offer holistic insights. Two-eyed seeing bridges these paradigms, emphasising the importance of integrating indigenous ways of knowing with Western methodologies, reflecting the PCIP's commitment to valuing and validating indigenous knowledge systems. By encouraging respectful dialogue and collaboration, two-eyed seeing facilitates the synthesis of diverse knowledge systems, fostering meaningful cross-cultural exchanges and addressing research gaps that might otherwise persist. This approach doesn't just recognise the contributions of indigenous knowledge but actively seeks to harmonise it with Western approaches, creating a more comprehensive understanding of complex issues. In doing so, two-eyed seeing serves as a methodological embodiment of the PCIP's principles, helping to counterbalance the historical marginalisation of indigenous voices, fostering equity, and providing a tangible means of implementing the PCIP within research, education, and community engagement.

iv **Ethnographic Research:** Ethnographic research, with its emphasis on immersive and contextually aware inquiry, aligns with the principles of the

PCIP in several key ways. Unlike distant or purely analytical approaches, ethnography involves immersing oneself within a community or cultural context, seeking to understand experiences, beliefs, and practices from an insider's perspective. This aligns with PCIP's emphasis on valuing indigenous knowledge and recognising the inherent complexity and richness of indigenous cultures. By engaging in participant observation, building genuine relationships, conducting interviews, and analysing cultural artefacts, ethnographic research strives to move beyond surface-level insights to capture the nuanced lived experiences of indigenous communities. The method respects and acknowledges the importance of cultural context and embraces the multiplicity of perspectives within indigenous knowledge systems (Desta, 2009). When implemented with sensitivity and awareness, ethnographic research can serve as a valuable tool within the PCIP, fostering a deeper understanding of indigenous cultures and histories. It does so by centring indigenous voices and experiences, respecting cultural protocols, and contributing to dismantling colonial narratives, thus aligning the research process with the ethical and epistemological foundations of the PCIP.

v **Indigenous Feminist Research:** Indigenous Feminist Research offers a methodological design that is both resonant with and vital to the implementation of the PCIP. This approach actively integrates indigenous worldviews and feminist principles, aiming to redress and understand the complex intersections of identity, including gender, culture, colonisation, and more, as they shape the experiences of indigenous women, Two-Spirit, and LGBTQ+ individuals (Chilisa & Ntseane, 2014). Where traditional research might overlook or oversimplify these intersections, Indigenous Feminist Research brings them to the forefront, recognising the unique contributions, knowledge, and challenges that exist within these communities. By centring these voices and perspectives, this methodology aligns with the PCIP's emphasis on inclusivity, respect, and self-determination while simultaneously working to decolonise gender roles and promote gender equity within indigenous contexts. Indigenous Feminist Research doesn't merely align with the principles of PCIP; it acts as an essential avenue for exploring aspects of indigenous experiences that might otherwise remain obscured or misunderstood. Focusing on these specific intersections of identity helps broaden and deepen the PCIP, contributing to a more comprehensive and nuanced understanding of indigenous communities and supporting the larger goals of justice, equity, and self-determination within the postcolonial context.

vi **Action Research:** As a design that seeks to intertwine research and transformative action, Action Research is highly relevant and compatible with the PCIP principles. Unlike conventional research that may take a more passive or observational stance, Action Research is committed to active engagement and collaboration with communities, embodying the ethos of the PCIP's emphasis on self-determination, community agency, and inclusivity. Within the indigenous context, Action Research enables the community to identify critical issues, co-design interventions, and collaborate in achieving sustainable change, ensuring that the research process is tailored to the community's unique needs, history, and cultural context. It recognises indigenous communities not merely as subjects of study but as vital partners and active agents in the research process, thereby empowering them and honouring their knowledge, experiences, and aspirations. This cyclical process of reflection, planning, action, and evaluation (Coghlan, 2019) resonates with the holistic and interconnected worldviews often present in indigenous epistemologies. By facilitating a more equitable and participatory research relationship, Action Research supports the implementation of the PCIP by fostering a research process that both respects indigenous values and effectively promotes transformative community change.

vii **Participatory Research:** Participatory research is an approach that inherently aligns with the PCIP by shifting the dynamics of research to a more collaborative and community-centred process. This method resonates with the PCIP's call for self-determination, empowerment, and respectful engagement with indigenous communities. It acknowledges and honours the richness of indigenous knowledge, understanding that the community's expertise is essential for addressing their specific research questions and needs. Participatory Research provides a space for inclusive decision-making and co-learning, cultivating an environment where researchers' and community members' insights and wisdom are valued (Ohly et al., 2023). This approach challenges traditional research hierarchies and creates a more balanced and meaningful research partnership by ensuring equitable power dynamics and fostering mutual respect. The ultimate goal of participatory research in the context of the PCIP is not merely to gather information but to facilitate a process where the research itself becomes an instrument of empowerment, social justice, and community transformation. The focus on co-creation, inclusivity, and direct relevance to indigenous communities provides a concrete pathway for implementing the PCIP, allowing for research that reflects, respects, and advances indigenous peoples' complex realities, aspirations, and values.

## 5.6 Aligning Research Questions with the Postcolonial Indigenous Paradigm

When aligning research questions with the PCIP, several factors should be considered to ensure the questions are culturally sensitive, community-centred, and respectful of indigenous knowledge and perspectives. These factors are essential for fostering meaningful engagement with indigenous communities and generating research aligning with decolonisation and empowerment principles. Two key factors to consider are the recognition of indigenous worldviews and the incorporating community priorities and needs.

*Postcolonial Indigenous Paradigm and Methodological Alignment* 129

Firstly, recognising indigenous worldviews is crucial when formulating research questions within the PCIP. This involves acknowledging and valuing indigenous ways of knowing, being, and relating to the world. Research questions should incorporate indigenous epistemologies, ontologies, and axiologies, considering the interconnectedness of all aspects of life, the importance of oral traditions and storytelling, and the spiritual and cultural dimensions of indigenous knowledge systems. For example, a research question aligned with this factor could be:

**Example:** How does the revitalisation of indigenous storytelling traditions contribute to the cultural resilience and empowerment of indigenous youth?

Secondly, aligning research questions with the PCIP necessitates incorporating community priorities and needs. Engaging in respectful and reciprocal relationships with indigenous communities is essential, involving them in the research process from the outset. Research questions should be co-developed with community members, ensuring they address relevant and meaningful issues to the community. For instance, a research question aligned with this factor could be:

**Example:** What are the community-identified strategies for improving healthcare access and outcomes for indigenous elders in collaboration with local healthcare providers?

By considering these factors and developing research questions that recognise indigenous worldviews and incorporate community priorities, researchers can align their work with the PCIP. This alignment facilitates the production of research that respects indigenous knowledge, values, and aspirations while promoting self-determination, cultural revitalisation, and social justice.

*5.6.1  Case Studies on How to Align Research Questions With the Postcolonial Paradigm*

---

**Case Study 1:   Researching Indigenous Food Sovereignty in Collaboration with a Community**

**Research Question:** How does the revitalisation of traditional food practices contribute to indigenous food sovereignty and well-being in a specific community?

In this case study, researchers seek to align their research question with the PCIP by centring indigenous knowledge, community engagement, and the promotion of self-determination. They collaborate closely with an indigenous community to investigate the role of traditional food practices in achieving food sovereignty and overall well-being. The research question reflects the community's identified priorities and acknowledges their unique cultural context. The researchers engage in ongoing dialogue and consultations with community members, elders, and knowledge holders to co-develop the research question. They listen to the community's perspectives and experiences regarding the impacts of colonisation on their food systems and the significance of revitalising traditional food practices. By involving community members from the outset, the research question aligns with the community's goals and priorities for reclaiming food sovereignty. Throughout the research process, the researchers maintain a collaborative and participatory approach. They work closely with community members to collect and analyse data using culturally appropriate methods, such as interviews, community workshops, and land-based activities. The research findings are regularly shared with the community in a culturally respectful manner, ensuring transparency and reciprocity.

This case study demonstrates how aligning research questions with the PCIP involves active engagement with indigenous communities, respect for their knowledge systems, and the incorporation of community priorities and needs. By centring indigenous voices and perspectives, researchers can contribute to the community's self-determined goals of revitalising traditional food practices and achieving food sovereignty.

### Case Study 2: Examining Indigenous Language Revitalisation through Collaborative Research

**Research Question:** What are the community-driven strategies for revitalising indigenous languages and the impact of language revitalisation on cultural resilience and well-being?

This case study illustrates how research questions can be aligned with the PCIP by focusing on the revitalisation of indigenous languages and the associated impacts on cultural resilience and well-being. The research is conducted in collaboration with an indigenous community that seeks to reclaim and revitalise their endangered language as a means of cultural resurgence and empowerment. The researchers work closely with community language speakers, elders, and language revitalisation experts to co-develop the research question. Through extensive consultations and engagement, they understand the community's priorities and the significance of language revitalisation in reclaiming cultural identity, fostering intergenerational connections, and promoting community well-being. The research question reflects these community-driven goals and acknowledges the historical impacts of colonisation on indigenous languages. The research employs participatory methods such as language immersion programs, community language workshops, and interviews with language speakers to align with the PCIP. The researchers actively involve community members in data collection, analysis, and interpretation, respecting their cultural protocols and knowledge systems. The research findings are shared with the community, and recommendations for language revitalisation strategies are collaboratively developed. The research contributes to academic knowledge and provides valuable insights and resources for the community's language revitalisation efforts. By aligning the research question with the community's priorities and engaging in a collaborative research process, the study aligns with the principles of the PCIP, empowering the community in reclaiming and revitalising their language and cultural heritage.

### Case Study 3: Revitalising Indigenous Agricultural Practices for Rural African Empowerment

**Research Question:** How do community-driven strategies for revitalising indigenous agricultural practices impact the empowerment of rural African communities, fostering food security, preserving cultural heritage, and promoting overall well-being?

In this case study, researchers aim to align their investigation with the principles of community engagement, cultural preservation, and empowerment, drawing inspiration from successful approaches in indigenous food sovereignty and language revitalisation. The research question is carefully co-developed through dialogues, consultations, and partnerships with rural African communities. By actively involving community members, elders, and agricultural experts, the researchers ensure that the research question reflects the community's priorities and acknowledges the unique cultural context of the region. Similar to Case Study 1 and Case Study 2, researchers could work closely with local communities to collect and analyse data using culturally appropriate methods, including community workshops, interviews with traditional knowledge holders, and on-the-ground observations of agricultural practices. This may allow for an understanding of the historical impacts of colonisation on indigenous farming practices and how these practices are intertwined with cultural identity.

> These case studies exemplify how aligning research questions with the PCIP involves active collaboration, community engagement, and centring indigenous knowledge and priorities. By working in partnership with indigenous communities and incorporating their perspectives, researchers can conduct research that respects indigenous self-determination, promotes cultural revitalisation, and contributes to community empowerment.

## 5.7 Data Collection Methods in Postcolonial Indigenous Research

Data collection methods suitable for the PCIP are crucial in conducting culturally sensitive research, respecting indigenous knowledge systems, and centring indigenous voices and perspectives. These methods should align with the principles of the paradigm, fostering meaningful engagement with indigenous communities and generating data that accurately represent their experiences and aspirations. In this section, we will explore a range of data collection methods suitable for the PCIP, discussing their strengths, considerations, and ethical implications. By employing these methods, researchers can gather data that reflects the richness and diversity of indigenous knowledge and experiences.

- **Oral Histories and Storytelling:** Oral histories and storytelling are deeply ingrained methodologies within indigenous cultures and, therefore, serve as especially fitting methods for collecting data within the framework of the PCIP (Rieger et al., 2023). They are not just means of information gathering; they represent ways of knowing, understanding, and connecting that resonate with indigenous worldviews. These methods prioritise indigenous voices and narratives, allowing for transmitting, preserving, and revitalising cultural knowledge, history, and lived experiences. Unlike some Western research methods that might objectify or extract information, oral histories and storytelling promote active engagement, dialogue, and relationship-building with community members, elders, and knowledge-keepers. Researchers adopting these methods must do so with the utmost cultural sensitivity, respecting indigenous protocols and ensuring that the process aligns with community values and consent practices. This alignment with community values fosters trust and creates a space where rich, nuanced, and authentic data can be collected. By embracing oral histories and storytelling, researchers can align with the principles of the PCIP, capturing indigenous communities' depth, resilience, and cultural richness in a way that respects and amplifies indigenous epistemologies and ontologies. It also serves as a powerful counter-narrative to the historical marginalisation and silencing of indigenous voices, contributing to a more inclusive and culturally responsive research landscape.

- **Participatory Mapping and Visual Methods:** Participatory mapping and visual methods, when used thoughtfully, align strongly with the principles of the PCIP, making them suitable for collecting data within this framework. These methods acknowledge and honour indigenous communities' deeply rooted connections with their land, place, and territory. Rather than viewing the land merely as a physical space, these approaches understand it as a living entity intertwined with culture, history, spirituality, and identity. Through collaborative activities like community mapping or visual art creations, indigenous people can visually express their spatial relationships, traditional knowledge, and cultural landscapes, conveying complex ideas and connections that might be lost or misinterpreted in textual forms. This collaborative process promotes community engagement and empowerment and ensures that diverse perspectives are integrated. The emphasis on cultural sensitivity, ownership, control over data, and obtaining proper consent is vital to maintain ethical integrity and align with the community's values. The tangible and meaningful representations that emerge from participatory mapping and visual methods provide rich data and become tools for advocacy, education, and cultural preservation. They transcend the conventional barriers of language and allow for a more nuanced understanding of indigenous knowledge and relationships to the land, encapsulating aspects that are central to the PCIP and affirming the validity and vitality of indigenous epistemologies.
- **Indigenous Research Protocols:** Indigenous research protocols serve as vital tools for aligning research practices with the PCIP, and their adoption is highly suitable for collecting data within indigenous contexts. These protocols act as guidelines that reflect the unique cultural practices, values, ethics, and aspirations of individual indigenous communities. Researchers affirm indigenous peoples' sovereignty, agency, and dignity by respecting and adhering to these protocols. Rather than imposing an external research agenda, they engage in ongoing dialogue and consultation with community members, recognising their expertise and knowledge. This includes understanding ceremonies, traditional knowledge access, data collection, and sharing guidelines specific to each community. Such an approach nurtures a more authentic and enriched understanding and ensures that the research is conducted with integrity, sensitivity, and reciprocity. It dismantles the hierarchical and extractive tendencies often present in conventional research, instead fostering collaborative, respectful, and mutually beneficial relationships. In this way, indigenous research protocols align with the principles of the PCIP, contributing to the validation, preservation, and revitalisation of indigenous knowledge systems and paving the way for empowering and culturally resonant research.
- **Photovoice and Digital Storytelling:** Photovoice and digital storytelling align well with the PCIP as suitable methods for collecting data

(Rieger et al., 2021; Vining & Finn, 2023). These approaches prioritise indigenous perspectives, enabling participants to express themselves through photographs, audio recordings, or videos. Unlike traditional text-based methods, they allow for a richer and more nuanced exploration of lived realities, cultural nuances, and complex issues within indigenous communities. By empowering participants to control the creation and dissemination of their stories, these methods reinforce the principles of self-determination, agency, and autonomy central to PCIP. The collaborative nature of photovoice and digital storytelling requires researchers to engage with participants on equal footing, offering training and support and ensuring informed consent and privacy. These actions reflect the broader paradigmatic commitment to reciprocal relationships, respectful engagement, and equitable power distribution. Furthermore, these visual and auditory methods often resonate more strongly with indigenous ways of knowing, which may prioritise oral and visual transmission. Photovoice and digital storytelling can effectively capture, preserve, and amplify indigenous knowledge and voices by providing alternative communication and knowledge-sharing mediums, bridging cultural gaps and fostering mutual understanding and respect.

- **Community-Based Surveys:** When conducted within the PCIP framework, Community-based surveys can serve as suitable methods for collecting data from indigenous communities (Kaplan et al., 2004). The collaborative design and implementation of these surveys are the key to this alignment. By working closely with community members to develop questions that reflect community priorities, values, and cultural contexts, researchers adhere to the principles of respect, reciprocity, and relationality that underpin the PCIP. Ensuring that survey questions are culturally appropriate and that local languages and cultural protocols are incorporated demonstrates a commitment to respecting and validating indigenous ways of knowing. This approach counters traditional research dynamics that may marginalise or overlook indigenous perspectives, promoting instead a sense of agency and empowerment within the community. Moreover, community-based surveys allow for the broad and diverse inclusion of voices within the community, fostering a more holistic and nuanced understanding of the issues being explored. By prioritising community engagement, acknowledging the inherent rights and wisdom of indigenous peoples, and emphasising shared responsibility in the research process, community-based surveys align with the principles of self-determination and inclusivity essential to the PCIP, thus making them a suitable tool for data collection in this context.
- **Focus Group Discussion:** Focus group discussions are often employed within the PCIP framework, especially when they are carefully designed to align with indigenous values and principles. In this approach, a diverse group of community members gathers to discuss specific topics, enabling the collective sharing of knowledge, perspectives, and insights

(Redman-MacLaren et al., 2014). Such collaborative dialogue encourages the participants to explore complex issues in a culturally resonant manner, emphasising relationality, respect, and reciprocity. By facilitating these communal conversations, focus group discussions acknowledge and honour the collective wisdom of indigenous communities, recognising that knowledge is often communally held rather than individually owned. This method also allows for the nuanced exploration of collective memories, shared experiences, and community-defined priorities. Moreover, when guided by culturally sensitive facilitation and framed within indigenous protocols, focus group discussions can create a safe and respectful space that encourages honest and open communication. This fosters a deeper understanding of community needs, aspirations, and cultural contexts, making focus group discussions a powerful tool for collecting relevant and meaningful data to indigenous communities within the postcolonial paradigm.

- **Interviews:** Interviews are a valuable data collection method within the PCIP as they provide a platform for in-depth conversations and exploring individuals' perspectives, experiences, and knowledge (Gardner, 2010). Interviews allow researchers to engage directly with community members, Elders, and knowledge holders to gain insights into various aspects of indigenous cultures, histories, and contemporary issues. Here, we will discuss the use of interviews as a data collection method within the PCIP, highlighting its strengths, considerations, and ethical implications. The following are some of the notable interviews applicable to this paradigm:

    a *Semi-Structured Interviews:* Semi-structured interviews are commonly used in Postcolonial indigenous research as they allow for flexibility while maintaining a general focus on specific research questions or topics. These interviews typically follow a predetermined interview guide, but they also allow for organic conversation and the exploration of unanticipated themes. Semi-structured interviews provide the opportunity to delve deeply into community members' lived experiences, perspectives, and knowledge. They enable researchers to gain rich qualitative data, capture personal narratives, and understand the complexity and diversity of indigenous perspectives. It is important for researchers to approach these interviews with cultural sensitivity, respect, and a willingness to listen actively. Informed consent, confidentiality, and voluntary participation are key ethical considerations in conducting interviews.

    b *Elder Interviews:* Engaging in interviews with elders holds particular significance within the PCIP. Elders are esteemed knowledge-keepers who possess deep cultural knowledge, traditional practices, and historical insights. Conducting interviews with elders allows for the transmission of intergenerational knowledge and the documentation of cultural heritage. It is essential to approach these interviews with the utmost respect, honouring cultural protocols and valuing the elders' wisdom.

Researchers should build relationships, seek guidance on appropriate interview methods, and be mindful of the time, energy, and potential emotional labour required from elders. Elder interviews contribute to preserving and passing on indigenous knowledge and ensuring that their voices and perspectives are included in research.

c *Group Interviews:* Group interviews, also known as focus groups, involve bringing together community members to discuss specific topics or research questions. Group interviews provide a platform for participants to share their perspectives, engage in dialogue, and collectively build upon each other's insights. They can be particularly useful for capturing diverse viewpoints, identifying common themes, and fostering community engagement. Researchers should ensure that group dynamics are respectful and inclusive, allowing for everyone to contribute. Cultural protocols, confidentiality, and informed consent are essential in conducting group interviews. Researchers should also be aware of potential power dynamics and facilitate an environment where all participants feel comfortable expressing their thoughts.

d *Key Informant Interviews:* Key informant interviews involve engaging with individuals with specialised knowledge or expertise on specific topics within the community. These individuals may include community leaders, cultural practitioners, scholars, or professionals with insights relevant to the research questions. Key informant interviews allow researchers to gain in-depth knowledge from those with deep understanding and experience. Approaching these interviews and respecting the interviewee's time and expertise is important. Researchers should be prepared to listen actively, ask relevant questions, and establish trust and rapport with the key informants. Confidentiality and voluntary participation should be upheld throughout the process.

## 5.8 Data Analysis and Interpretation in Postcolonial Indigenous Research

Data analysis methods within the PCIP are essential for interpreting and making sense of the data collected in a culturally sensitive and community-centred manner. These methods should align with the paradigm's principles, emphasising the inclusion of indigenous perspectives, respect for indigenous knowledge systems, and the promotion of self-determination. Employing these methodologies requires an awareness of and adherence to indigenous communities' unique cultural, historical, and social contexts. This involves recognising and valuing the richness of indigenous epistemologies and ensuring that the analysis does not inadvertently perpetuate colonial biases. Seven data analysis methods suitable for the PCIP include thematic analysis, narrative analysis, participatory analysis, grounded theory, critical discourse analysis, content analysis, and visual analysis. By exploring their strengths, considerations, and ethical implications, researchers can produce a research report that uncovers insights and contributes to the empowerment and well-being of indigenous communities, thus fulfilling the intention of the PCIP to create meaningful, respectful, and reciprocal research outcomes.

- ***Narrative Analysis:*** Narrative analysis focuses on the examination and interpretation of stories, personal narratives, and other forms of storytelling within the collected data (Esin, 2011). This method enables researchers to explore and understand indigenous communities' complex and nuanced realities by identifying recurring themes, patterns, and meanings embedded within the narratives. Unlike more rigid analytical approaches, narrative analysis appreciates the cultural nuances, metaphors, and symbols employed in storytelling, recognising their significance within indigenous contexts. This understanding is integral to the PCIP, which emphasises respect for indigenous knowledge systems and including indigenous perspectives. Narrative analysis allows for a deeper understanding of indigenous communities' lived experiences, identities, and cultural resilience, providing insights that may not be accessible through other means. By approaching narrative analysis with cultural sensitivity, respecting indigenous protocols, and ensuring that participants' voices and perspectives are accurately represented, researchers can craft analyses that align with the principles of the paradigm. This method thus contributes to a more inclusive and respectful research process, emphasising the co-creation of knowledge and honouring indigenous ways of knowing and being.
- ***Indigenous Knowledge Systems Analysis:*** Indigenous knowledge systems analysis involves the exploration and interpretation of indigenous ways of knowing, being, and relating to the world within the collected data, making it a suitable approach within the PCIP. Unlike Western analytic models that might impose external frameworks, this method is deeply grounded in indigenous knowledge systems' unique epistemologies and ontologies. By identifying and analysing indigenous concepts, values, and principles that emerge from the data, researchers recognise, validate, and centre indigenous knowledge within the research findings. This approach aligns with the paradigm's principles by emphasising the inclusion of indigenous perspectives and the promotion of self-determination. Furthermore, it necessitates engagement with indigenous scholars, community members, and knowledge-keepers in the analysis process. Their collaboration ensures that the interpretation is authentic and culturally sensitive and respects their expertise and contributions. In essence, indigenous knowledge systems analysis fosters a research environment that is collaborative, reciprocal, and empowering, reflecting the cultural integrity and complexity of indigenous communities and contributing to the broader project of decolonising academia.
- ***Thematic Analysis:*** Thematic analysis involves identifying and analysing patterns, themes, and categories within the collected data (Braun & Clarke, 2012; Omodan, 2020). This method allows researchers to identify

the dataset's common threads and overarching concepts. Thematic analysis is flexible and can be applied to various types of qualitative data, such as interviews, focus groups, or textual documents. Researchers should be mindful of the cultural context when conducting thematic analysis within the PCIP, ensuring that the themes identified align with indigenous perspectives and experiences. It is important to involve community members in the analysis process, seeking their input and validating the identified themes.

- **Community Validation and Interpretation:** Community validation and interpretation involve sharing the research findings with the community and seeking their input and feedback. This method allows community members to contribute their perspectives, interpretations, and additional insights to the analysis process. Researchers facilitate community dialogues, workshops, or sharing sessions to ensure that the findings resonate with community members and accurately reflect their experiences. This collaborative approach promotes ownership, reciprocity, and community empowerment in the interpretation of the data. Researchers must approach community validation and interpretation with cultural sensitivity, acknowledging the authority of community members in shaping the meaning of the research findings.
- **Indigenous Research Frameworks**: Indigenous research frameworks provide a guiding framework for analysing and interpreting data within the PCIP. These frameworks often draw upon indigenous epistemologies, ontologies, and axiologies, providing a culturally appropriate lens for analysis. Examples of Indigenous Research Frameworks include the two-eyed seeing approach, Indigenous Feminist frameworks, or community-specific frameworks developed in collaboration with indigenous communities. Employing Indigenous Research Frameworks ensures that the analysis process is rooted in indigenous perspectives, values, and knowledge systems. Researchers should work closely with community members, elders, and indigenous scholars to apply these frameworks and interpret the data in a culturally respectful manner.
- **Counter-Narrative Analysis:** Counter-narrative analysis challenges dominant narratives and power structures by foregrounding alternative perspectives and experiences within the collected data (Lundholt & Boje, 2018). This method involves identifying narratives that challenge stereotypes, disrupt colonial narratives, or challenge hegemonic discourses. Counter-narrative analysis allows for the amplification of marginalised voices and the exploration of resistance, agency, and resilience within indigenous communities. Researchers should be mindful of power dynamics and ethical considerations when conducting counter-narrative analysis, ensuring that participants' consent and confidentiality are protected and that their narratives are not further retraumatised or exploited.
- **Intersectional Analysis:** Intersectional analysis recognises the complex intersections of identity, power, and oppression within the collected data.

This method involves examining how different forms of identity, such as gender, race, class, and sexuality, intersect and shape individuals' experiences and perspectives (Christensen & Jensen, 2012). Intersectional analysis highlights the unique challenges and strengths of different marginalised groups within indigenous communities, acknowledging that multiple axes of oppression intersect to shape individuals' lives. Researchers should approach intersectional analysis with cultural sensitivity, recognising the diversity and intersectionality within indigenous communities and avoiding generalisations or essentialisations.

- **Discourse Analysis:** Discourse analysis is a valuable data analysis method within the PCIP as it allows researchers to examine the language, narratives, and power dynamics present in the collected data (Moser et al., 2013; Zajda, 2020). Discourse analysis focuses on how language is used to construct meaning, shape identities, and perpetuate social structures. Within the PCIP, discourse analysis can help uncover and challenge dominant narratives, colonial ideologies, and the impacts of power dynamics on indigenous communities.

## 5.9 Critiques and Debates in Postcolonial Indigenous Research

Critiques and debates in postcolonial indigenous research reflect the ongoing discussions and complexities surrounding this field's approach, methods, and ethical considerations. While the PCIP seeks to challenge colonial legacies, centre indigenous perspectives, and promote self-determination, it is not without its critiques and areas of debate. Here, we will extensively discuss some key critiques and debates in postcolonial indigenous research.

i **Essentialism vs. Intersectionality:** One debate centres around the tension between essentialism and intersectionality within postcolonial indigenous research. Essentialism refers to the tendency to view indigenous peoples as a homogeneous group, overlooking the diversity, complexities, and intersectional identities within indigenous communities. Critics argue that essentialism can perpetuate stereotypes and fail to recognise the unique experiences and challenges faced by different indigenous groups. On the other hand, intersectionality emphasises the need to consider the intersecting identities, such as gender, class, and sexuality, that shape indigenous experiences. This debate calls for researchers to navigate the balance between acknowledging shared experiences while respecting the diversity and intersectionality within indigenous communities.

ii **Representation and Authenticity:** A significant critique in postcolonial indigenous research revolves around issues of representation and authenticity. Indigenous communities have long been subjected to misrepresentation and appropriation, raising concerns about how research conducted within the paradigm can reproduce these dynamics. Critics argue that researchers may unintentionally reinforce colonial power structures, tokenise indigenous voices, or exoticise indigenous cultures. The challenge lies in ensuring that research is conducted in a way that respects indigenous self-determination, accurately represents indigenous perspectives, and promotes authentic collaborations. Researchers must prioritise building genuine relationships, engaging in ongoing dialogue, and seeking community input and validation to address these concerns.

iii **Ethical Considerations and Power Dynamics:** Ethical considerations and power dynamics are central to critiques in postcolonial indigenous research. Critics highlight the potential for research to perpetuate harm, extract knowledge without reciprocity, or exploit indigenous communities. The power imbalance between researchers and indigenous communities can influence the research process, including formulating research questions, data collection, and analysis. Addressing these critiques requires researchers to engage in self-reflection, ongoing dialogue, and an understanding of the historical context of colonialism. Researchers should prioritise community-driven research, informed consent, data ownership, and reciprocal relationships to ensure ethical research practices.

iv **Researcher Positionality and Indigenous Knowledge Systems:** Debates exist regarding the role of researchers' positionality and the integration of indigenous knowledge systems in postcolonial indigenous research. Some argue that non-indigenous researchers should not engage in research on indigenous topics, while others emphasise the importance of allyship and collaboration. The integration of indigenous knowledge systems raises questions about the appropriation and commodification of indigenous knowledge. Researchers must engage in reflexive practices, acknowledge their positionality, and work in genuine partnership with indigenous communities, recognising indigenous knowledge as valid and valuable.

v **Decolonisation and research outcomes:** Another debate revolves around the extent to which research conducted within the PCIP can contribute to decolonisation and transformative change. Critics argue that research outcomes often fail to address the systemic issues and power imbalances inherent in colonial structures. They stress the need for research to go beyond documentation and contribute to tangible and meaningful actions for indigenous self-determination and social justice. Researchers must continuously reflect on the transformative potential of their research, engaging with community members in co-creating knowledge and actively supporting indigenous-led initiatives for decolonisation.

These critiques and debates within postcolonial indigenous research highlight the complexities, challenges, and ongoing discussions surrounding this field. Engaging with these critiques promotes critical reflexivity, accountability, and the pursuit of ethical, inclusive, and empowering research practices. Researchers must approach their work with cultural sensitivity, engage in open dialogue with indigenous communities, and actively work towards challenging power imbalances and colonial legacies within the research process. By addressing these critiques, researchers can contribute to developing a more ethical, inclusive, and impactful postcolonial indigenous research paradigm.

## 5.10 Balancing Empowerment and Ethical Issues in Postcolonial Indigenous Research

Balancing empowerment and ethical issues in postcolonial indigenous research is crucial to ensure that research conducted within this paradigm respects indigenous self-determination, promotes positive outcomes for communities, and upholds ethical standards. It requires researchers to navigate power dynamics, prioritise community engagement, and work towards research that empowers indigenous communities while maintaining ethical integrity. Here, we will discuss strategies and considerations for achieving this balance.

1 *Community Engagement and Collaboration*

   Meaningful community engagement and collaboration are fundamental to balancing empowerment and ethical issues in postcolonial indigenous research. Researchers should approach research as a collaborative partnership with indigenous communities, involving community members in all stages of the research process. This includes co-developing research questions and methods and interpreting findings. Researchers empower communities to actively shape research processes and outcomes by valuing indigenous knowledge and perspectives.

2 *Informed Consent and Ownership*

   Respecting the autonomy and self-determination of indigenous communities requires obtaining informed consent and recognising the ownership of indigenous knowledge and data. Researchers should clearly communicate the research's purpose, risks, and benefits to potential participants, ensuring their free and informed consent. Consent processes should be culturally appropriate, including providing information in local languages, using visual aids, and considering literacy levels. Researchers should also establish protocols for data ownership, ensuring that indigenous communities have control over how their data is stored, used, and shared.

3 *Reflexivity and Self-Reflection*

   Researchers must engage in reflexive practices, acknowledging their positionality, biases, and power dynamics within the research process. Reflexivity involves critically examining one's own role, assumptions, and potential impacts on the research. Researchers should actively question and challenge their own perspectives, seeking input from indigenous community members and incorporating their feedback to ensure research is conducted in a culturally sensitive and ethical manner.

4 **Reciprocity and Benefit Sharing**
Reciprocity is a foundational principle in balancing empowerment and ethical issues. Researchers should prioritise reciprocity by ensuring that research benefits indigenous communities. This can be achieved by providing community members with meaningful and timely feedback on research findings, offering capacity-building opportunities, and supporting community-led initiatives for positive change. Researchers should also consider how their research can address community-identified priorities and support indigenous self-determination.

5 **Cultural Sensitivity and Protocols**
Cultural sensitivity is vital in navigating ethical considerations in postcolonial indigenous research. Researchers should familiarise themselves with and respect indigenous cultural protocols, customs, and traditions. This includes understanding appropriate behaviour, engaging in ongoing cultural learning, and seeking guidance from indigenous community members and cultural advisors. Researchers should also consider the potential impacts of their research on indigenous cultural practices, spiritual beliefs, and intellectual property, taking steps to avoid cultural appropriation and promote cultural revitalisation.

6 **Ethical Review and Accountability**
Adhering to ethical review processes and accountability mechanisms is essential in balancing empowerment and ethical issues. Researchers should ensure that their research is reviewed by an ethics board that includes indigenous representation or engages indigenous research ethics committees. This ensures that research aligns with ethical guidelines and respects indigenous rights, protocols, and cultural sensitivities. Researchers should also be transparent about their methodologies, limitations, and potential impacts and be accountable to indigenous communities by reporting back to them in a culturally appropriate and accessible manner.

## 5.11 Summary

This chapter delved into the PCIP, exploring its context, philosophical foundations, key concepts, and evolution. The methodological designs suitable for postcolonial indigenous research were discussed, emphasising participatory and action research approaches. I highlighted the importance of aligning research questions with the paradigm, considering factors such as community engagement, cultural sensitivity, and intersectionality. The chapter explored various data collection methods, including oral histories, participatory mapping, and interviews, suitable for capturing indigenous knowledge and experiences. Additionally, it discussed seven data analysis methods, such as narrative analysis, discourse analysis, and indigenous knowledge systems analysis, that allow for a comprehensive exploration of the data within the PCIP. The chapter addressed critiques and debates in postcolonial indigenous research, emphasising the need for cultural sensitivity, ethical considerations, and the promotion of indigenous self-determination. Lastly, it examined how to balance empowerment and ethical issues in research, emphasising community engagement, informed consent, reciprocity, and cultural sensitivity. In summary, by employing these approaches and considerations, researchers can contribute to research that respects indigenous perspectives, challenges colonial legacies and promotes positive outcomes for indigenous communities.

# 6 Pragmatism Paradigm and Methodological Alignment

**Chapter Synopsis**

This chapter comprehensively presents the pragmatism paradigm, weaving a multifaceted exploration that spans its inception, evolution, and key aspects. By delving into the underlying philosophical foundations, including epistemology, ontology, and axiology, the chapter provides insights into the methodological designs and alignment with various research questions within the paradigm. Attention is also given to data collection and analysis techniques and the prominent debates that characterise this field. Further, the chapter sheds light on the alignment of the pragmatism paradigm with qualitative and mixed-methods research, considering the practicalities involved in employing this approach. This extensive examination provides readers with a thorough understanding of pragmatism and its methodological alignment.

## 6.1 Concept of Pragmatism Paradigm

Unlike other paradigms that seek eternal truths, pragmatism focuses on the practical consequences and usefulness of beliefs and theories. The paradigm emphasises experience, experimentation, and the resolution of doubts through practical application, offering a distinctive and flexible approach that is well-suited to various fields, including scientific inquiry, ethical discussions, and even art criticism (Goldkuhl, 2012). The pragmatic paradigm has paved the way for a more inclusive and dynamic way of thinking, rejecting rigid frameworks and embracing reality's complexity and multifaceted nature. The core tenet of pragmatism is the alignment of knowledge with action, a belief that concepts and theories should be evaluated based on their practical impact and usefulness in real-world situations (Brierley, 2017). This principle encourages a more flexible and adaptive approach to understanding phenomena, fostering the selection of methods and techniques most appropriate for addressing specific research questions. pragmatism's emphasis on practical application serves as a unifying thread, tying together various disciplines and research methodologies. By focusing on the "what works" principle (Kelly & Cordeiro, 2020), the pragmatism paradigm pushes the boundaries

DOI: 10.4324/9781003484066-6

of traditional philosophical thought and opens new avenues for problem-solving and innovation.

Pragmatism's integrative nature allows it to bridge different philosophical traditions, including positivism and interpretivism. Recognising that multiple perspectives can provide valuable insights into a research problem, it does not strictly adhere to a single philosophical stance. This inclusiveness enables researchers to draw from various theoretical backgrounds and methodological approaches, fostering a more holistic and nuanced understanding of the subject matter. By allowing for a synthesis of often conflicting paradigms, pragmatism reflects a sophisticated worldview that acknowledges the complexity of human understanding and the multiplicity of valid ways to explore and explain the world.

In the context of research, pragmatism has emerged as an influential paradigm, providing a framework that accommodates diverse methods and techniques. It is particularly favoured in mixed-methods research, where both qualitative and quantitative approaches are employed harmoniously (Morgan, 2013). By prioritising the research question and employing the most suitable means to answer it, pragmatism encourages a problem-centred orientation that can adapt to the demands and complexities of any given study. The flexibility and responsiveness to the context make pragmatism a versatile tool in the researcher's arsenal, aligning scholarly inquiry with pragmatic considerations and real-world applications. That is, the proponents of pragmatism emphasise its practical utility and responsiveness to real-world challenges, viewing these apparent weaknesses as strengths. In an increasingly complex and interconnected world, the pragmatism paradigm continues to resonate with researchers and scholars and demonstrates its enduring relevance and vital role in modern intellectual discourse.

### 6.2 The Evolution of Pragmatism Paradigm

Pragmatism emerged in the late 19th century, primarily in the United States, as a philosophical approach that emphasises the practical consequences and usefulness of beliefs and theories (Kaushik & Walsh, 2019). Its roots can be traced back to Charles Sanders Peirce, who introduced the term in the 1870s, laying the foundation for a philosophical tradition that values practicality over abstract theorising (Shields, 1998). William James, a contemporary of Peirce, played a significant role in popularising and expanding upon the ideas of pragmatism (Pihlström, 2007). James saw pragmatism as a bridge between scientific empiricism and religious belief, emphasising the real-world application of ideas.

John Dewey further positioned the pragmatism paradigm, especially in the field of education. Dewey's emphasis on experiential learning and the connection between knowledge and action has had a lasting impact on modern educational practices (Yinkore & Mgbomo, 2022). However, during the mid-20th century, pragmatism faced a decline in influence, overshadowed by Logical Positivism and other philosophical movements. The late 20th century saw a resurgence of interest in Pragmatic ideas, partly driven by a growing recognition that practical and contextual factors shape human understanding and behaviour. Philosophers like Richard Rorty helped reintegrate pragmatism into contemporary philosophical discourse (Kloppenberg, 1996; Pettegrew, 2000).

The renewed interest in pragmatism extended beyond philosophy, influencing various disciplines such as sociology, anthropology, and political science. Pragmatism's inclusive and integrative nature allowed researchers in these fields to explore complex social phenomena with more nuanced and comprehensive perspectives. This interplay between qualitative and quantitative approaches reflected pragmatism's core principles of adaptability and contextual understanding. Pragmatism has found new relevance in the digital age, resonating with the needs of a rapidly changing technological landscape. Its focus on practical application, adaptability, and continuous learning has influenced areas such as human–computer interaction, information systems, and digital ethics. By emphasising context and practical engagement, pragmatism offers valuable insights into the challenges and opportunities of our increasingly interconnected world.

Pragmatism continues to face criticism despite its resurgence, particularly for its perceived lack of theoretical coherence and philosophical depth. Some argue that its inherent flexibility can lead to inconsistencies, while others value this adaptability as a strength. These ongoing debates contribute to the dynamism of the pragmatism paradigm, reflecting its continued relevance and complexity. As a living philosophy, pragmatism is likely to continue evolving, adapting to new challenges and opportunities, and remaining a vital part of intellectual discourse and practical application. Its rich history and multifaceted development underscore its enduring impact, demonstrating the power of a philosophy that bridges theory and practice, offering a flexible and robust approach to understanding the world.

### 6.3 Key Concepts and Assumptions

The pragmatism paradigm represents a unique philosophical stance that emphasises practical application, contextual understanding, and the integration of thought and action. Emerging as a significant intellectual movement in the late 19th century, pragmatism has shaped various fields, challenging traditional dichotomies between theory and practice, objectivity and subjectivity. Key to pragmatism's influence is a set of core concepts and assumptions that distinguish it from other philosophical paradigms. These principles guide the pragmatic approach, fostering a flexible, problem-solving orientation that values experience, collaboration, and adaptability. The following discussion delves into these foundational ideas, exploring what makes pragmatism a compelling and enduring paradigm. Here's a discussion of some of them:

  i ***Practical Consequences as the Criterion of Meaning:*** Pragmatism's emphasis on practical consequences is not merely an evaluation of ideas but a defining feature of its philosophy. It is about acknowledging that the significance of a belief or theory lies in its applicability to real-world situations and its ability to drive meaningful action (Pinales & Rivas, 2005). Pragmatism sees ideas as tools, and like any tool, their value is measured by their effectiveness in accomplishing a task or solving a problem. This focus shifts the philosophical inquiry from abstract speculation to a more grounded, applicable terrain. It recognises that concepts are not static entities but dynamic constructs that evolve with experience and practice. By concentrating on what works, pragmatism encourages flexibility, adaptability, and a close engagement with the complexities of the lived world.

ii **Anti-Essentialism:** Anti-essentialism in pragmatism is the rejection of fixed, universal truths or underlying essences (Sayer, 1997). This stance recognises the fluidity and complexity of existence and steers away from the pursuit of absolute certainty. According to this view, knowledge is provisional, context-dependent, and ever-changing. It underscores the notion that our understanding of the world is not about discovering static truths but about interacting with an evolving, dynamic reality. This rejection of essentialism fosters a more open, tolerant approach, allowing for multiple perspectives and acknowledging the human experience's uncertainty and ambiguity.

iii **Experiential Learning:** Pragmatism's emphasis on experiential learning represents a shift from traditional, often abstract educational practices to a more engaged, interactive process (Schank, 2010). It posits that knowledge is not something to be passively received but actively constructed through experience, experimentation, and reflection. John Dewey, one of pragmatism's leading figures, applied this idea to educational theory, advocating for a learning environment that encourages exploration, creativity, and critical thinking. Experiential learning is not just about acquiring information; it's about developing skills, attitudes, and values that enable individuals to navigate and shape the world effectively.

iv **Integration of Thought and Action:** The integration of thought and action is a cornerstone of pragmatism, rejecting the traditional dichotomy that separates the intellectual from the practical. In the pragmatic view, thinking is not an isolated activity but is intrinsically connected to doing. Ideas are seen as tools for guiding action, and action, in turn, shapes and refines thinking. This interplay creates a dynamic, reciprocal relationship where thought and action continually inform and transform each other. It encourages an engaged, problem-solving approach that values both theoretical insight and practical application.

v **Pluralism and Tolerance:** Pluralism is a defining feature of pragmatism, reflecting its commitment to diversity, inclusivity, and tolerance (Rydenfelt, 2020). Rather than seeking a single definitive answer, pragmatism acknowledges the validity of multiple perspectives and approaches. This pluralistic stance encourages dialogue, collaboration, and a willingness to recognise and engage with complexity. It fosters an intellectual climate that values differences, respects individuality and encourages creative, cross-disciplinary thinking. Pluralism in pragmatism is not merely a theoretical position but a practical orientation that shapes how we interact with others, approach problems, and navigate the multifaceted challenges of modern life.

vi **Instrumentalism:** Instrumentalism in pragmatism views concepts and theories as instruments or tools for understanding and interacting with the world (Riga, 2020). This perspective reframes knowledge from a representation of reality to a means of engaging with and manipulating it. It recognises that our theories, models, and concepts are not mirrors reflecting an objective world but constructs that enable us to predict, control, and make sense of our experience. Instrumentalism encourages a flexible, adaptive approach, valuing ideas for their utility and efficacy rather than their correspondence to an absolute truth.

vii **Fallibilism:** Fallibilism is the acknowledgement that all knowledge is fallible, imperfect, and subject to revision. It's an acceptance of the inherent uncertainty and limitations of human understanding. Pragmatism embraces fallibilism, recognising that our beliefs and theories are always provisional, open to questioning, and capable of being wrong. This stance fosters humility, curiosity, and a willingness to change our minds in the face of new evidence or better arguments. It encourages a continual process of inquiry, learning, and growth, recognising that the pursuit of knowledge is not about reaching final answers but about engaging in an ongoing, dynamic process of exploration and discovery.

viii **Contextualism:** Contextualism in pragmatism emphasises the importance of context in shaping understanding and action (Pranowo, 2020). It recognises that meanings, values, and practices are not fixed but vary depending on the specific situation, culture, or historical moment. This emphasis on context encourages a nuanced, sensitive approach to inquiry, valuing the particular over the universal, the situated over the abstract. It fosters an attentiveness to the unique, complex factors that shape each situation, encouraging a flexible, adaptive approach that recognises the diversity and complexity of human experience.

ix **Problem-Solving Orientation:** Pragmatism's focus on problem-solving reflects its commitment to practical engagement with the world (Farjoun et al., 2015). It directs attention to specific, concrete problems and emphasises the need for practical solutions. This problem-solving orientation encourages a close connection between theory and practice, recognising that intellectual inquiry is not an isolated, abstract endeavour but an engaged, purposeful activity to understand and address real-world challenges. It fosters a dynamic, interactive approach that values creativity, collaboration, and the continual refinement of ideas through testing, reflection, and revision.

x **Emphasis on Community and Collaboration:** The focus on community and collaboration reflects pragmatism's social, communal orientation

(Bruce & Bloch, 2013). Knowledge is seen not as a private possession but as a shared enterprise shaped by interaction, dialogue, and cooperation. This communal perspective recognises the interconnectedness of human experience, valuing relationships, empathy, and social responsibility. It fosters an ethos of collaboration, encouraging the pooling of diverse perspectives, skills, and experiences to create more comprehensive, robust solutions to shared problems.

xi **Rejection of the Fact-Value Dichotomy:** The rejection of the fact-value dichotomy is an integral aspect of the pragmatism paradigm, challenging the traditional separation of objective facts from subjective values (Doughney, 2005). Pragmatism posits that facts and values are intertwined, shaping, and influenced by one another. This stance recognises that our perception of facts is often guided by our values, beliefs, and cultural context, while our understanding of facts informs our values. The implication extends to research, ethics, decision-making, and education, advocating for a more holistic and reflective approach that acknowledges the intricate connections between rationality and emotion, science and morality. By dispelling the fact-value dichotomy, pragmatism fosters a more complex, multidimensional understanding of human knowledge and experience, allowing for a more integrated, human-centred approach to inquiry and action.

## 6.4 The Philosophical Foundations of the Pragmatism Paradigm

The pragmatism paradigm is grounded in an intricate philosophical framework that intricately interweaves various domains of thought. At its core lie four key philosophical foundations: epistemology, ontology, axiology, and methodology. Together, these pillars form the structure upon which pragmatism builds its approach to understanding, interpreting, and engaging with the world. Each aspect embodies specific principles and perspectives that reflect pragmatism's commitment to practical consequences, flexibility, and the integration of diverse viewpoints. These foundations define the paradigm and guide its application across various fields and disciplines. The following sections delve into these critical aspects of pragmatism, shedding light on how they shape and inform this distinctive philosophical approach.

### 6.4.1 Epistemology of the Pragmatism Paradigm

Epistemology in the pragmatism paradigm focuses on the nature, origin, and scope of knowledge, and it presents a departure from traditional epistemological stances. Pragmatic epistemology emphasises the practical consequences of belief and the use of knowledge as a tool for problem-solving and action (Farjoun et al., 2015). It rejects the idea that there are fixed, universal truths to be discovered and instead asserts that knowledge is dynamic, provisional, and context-dependent (Korte & Mercurio, 2017). Ideas and beliefs are evaluated based on their efficacy in dealing with specific problems, and truth is considered to be what works best in the way of belief at a particular time. This epistemological perspective recognises that knowledge is not merely a reflection of an external reality but a construct that enables individuals to navigate and interact with their world.

The implications of pragmatism's epistemological stance are far-reaching, influencing research methodologies, educational practices, and ethical considerations. In research, it supports the use of multiple methods, recognising that different approaches may be needed to address complex, real-world issues. In education, it fosters an emphasis on experiential learning, critical thinking, and the integration of theory and practice. Ethically, it encourages reflection on how knowledge is used and its impact on society. Overall, pragmatic epistemology offers a flexible, adaptive framework that aligns with the complexities of modern life, emphasising action, results, and continuous inquiry. It bridges the divide between theoretical and practical knowledge, fostering a more engaged, responsive approach to understanding and interacting with the world.

### 6.4.2 Ontology of the Pragmatism Paradigm

Ontology in the pragmatism paradigm refers to the nature of reality and being, and it plays a vital role in shaping the pragmatic approach to understanding the world. Unlike traditional ontological stances that may assert a singular, objective reality, pragmatism sees reality as something that is continuously shaped through human actions and experiences. It recognises that reality is not a static entity waiting to be discovered but is constructed and reconstructed through interactions, interpretations, and interventions (Creswell & Clark, 2017). According to Maarouf (2019), the pragmatic ontological perspective emphasises reality's fluidity, complexity, and context dependence, allowing for a more nuanced and multifaceted understanding of the world.

The ontological stance of pragmatism has profound implications for research, policymaking, and ethics. This research supports the use of varied methods and approaches, reflecting the belief that different contexts and questions may require different ways of understanding. In policymaking, it fosters a more adaptable, responsive approach that recognises the complexity of social issues and the interplay of multiple factors. Ethically, it encourages a focus on the practical consequences of actions and decisions, considering how they shape and reshape reality. By emphasising the dynamic, constructed nature of reality, pragmatism's ontological perspective offers a flexible, open-ended framework that recognises the multifaceted nature of existence and the importance of context, interpretation, and action in shaping our understanding and engagement with the world. It opens doors to a richer, more complex view of reality that aligns with contemporary life's diverse, interconnected nature.

### 6.4.3 Axiology of the Pragmatism Paradigm

Axiology in the pragmatism paradigm deals with values, ethics, and aesthetics, reflecting the paradigm's emphasis on practical consequences and human-centred inquiry. Unlike some philosophical worldviews that may seek to separate facts from values, pragmatism recognises that values are integral to human experience and cannot be easily disentangled from our understanding of the world. The pragmatic approach to axiology emphasises the role of values in shaping actions, decisions, and interpretations, acknowledging that they are not merely personal preferences but deeply ingrained aspects of culture, society, and individual identity (Maarouf, 2019). It fosters a reflective, critical engagement with values, encouraging individuals to examine how they influence and are influenced by their interactions with the world.

The axiological stance of pragmatism has significant implications for research, education, policymaking, and professional practice. Research calls attention to values' role in shaping questions, methods, and interpretations, encouraging transparency and reflexivity. In education, it fosters a more holistic approach that integrates ethical considerations into learning and emphasises the development of values alongside knowledge and skills. In policymaking and professional practice, it supports a more empathetic, human-centred approach that recognises the importance of values in shaping decisions and actions. By emphasising the interplay of values, facts, and actions, pragmatism's axiological perspective offers a nuanced, integrated framework that recognises the complexity of human experience and fosters a more thoughtful, responsible engagement with the world. It encourages an ongoing dialogue between values and actions, fostering a dynamic, responsive approach to life's challenges and opportunities.

### 6.4.4 Methodology of the Pragmatism Paradigm

Methodology within the pragmatism paradigm is characterised by flexibility, adaptability, and a focus on practical outcomes. Pragmatism's methodological approach is not confined to a specific set of approaches, techniques or methods but rather emphasises the selection of methods that best suit the research question and context (Foster, 2023). Pragmatist researchers are often guided by what works best in a particular context rather than adhering to rigid philosophical or ethical stances (Kaushik & Walsh, 2019). It allows for mixing qualitative and quantitative methods, recognising that different approaches may be necessary to fully understand complex phenomena. The core principle in pragmatic methodology is the pursuit of useful knowledge that addresses real-world problems rather than adherence to a particular theoretical or philosophical stance. This orientation encourages researchers to be creative, reflective, and open to diverse methods that align with the needs and goals of their inquiry.

The implications of pragmatism's methodological stance extend across various fields and disciplines, influencing how research is conducted, interpreted, and applied. In research, it supports a more integrative, interdisciplinary approach that can capture the multifaceted nature of contemporary issues. In education, it fosters a focus on experiential learning, critical thinking, and integrating theory and practice. In policymaking and professional practice, it encourages a problem-solving orientation that emphasises practical solutions and responsiveness to context. Overall, the methodological perspective of pragmatism offers a flexible, dynamic framework that supports a more engaged, practical approach to inquiry and action. It recognises the complexity of modern life and seeks to bridge the gap between theory and practice, fostering a more responsive, effective engagement with the challenges and opportunities of the contemporary world.

### 6.4.5  Pragmatism Paradigm and Qualitative Research

The pragmatism paradigm represents a distinctive philosophical stance that emphasises the fluid nature of reality, the integration of values and facts, and the importance of practical consequences. It offers a flexible, adaptive framework that aligns with the complexities and nuances of human experience. One of the key areas where pragmatism's influence is strongly felt is in the realm of qualitative research. Qualitative research seeks to delve into the intricacies of human behaviour, beliefs, and interactions, exploring phenomena in their natural context (Savin-Baden & Major, 2023). This approach resonates with the core principles of pragmatism, which values human-centred inquiry, adaptability, and a focus on real-world problems. The alignment between pragmatism and qualitative research goes beyond mere methodological considerations, reflecting a shared commitment to understanding the multifaceted nature of existence. The pragmatism paradigm profoundly informs and enriches qualitative research from the way questions are formulated to the ethical considerations that guide the research process. This section will explore these connections in detail, shedding light on how the pragmatism paradigm shapes qualitative research and fosters a more engaged, responsive approach to inquiry. It will delve into the alignment between these two approaches, highlighting their shared emphasis on context, flexibility, ethics, and practical relevance.

- **Alignment with Qualitative Inquiry:** The pragmatism paradigm aligns seamlessly with the qualitative research approach, creating a symbiotic relationship that emphasises reality's complexity and multifaceted nature. This alignment is rooted in pragmatism's acknowledgement that human experience and interpretation shape reality, a view that resonates with the qualitative research's objective to explore human experiences, beliefs, and behaviours in depth. Both approaches reject a one-size-fits-all perspective, embracing instead a flexible, adaptive methodology that allows for a nuanced exploration of human phenomena. Whether it's understanding social dynamics, individual perceptions, or cultural influences, pragmatism encourages the use of qualitative methods that delve into the rich and intricate fabric of human existence. This marriage between pragmatism and qualitative research offers a robust framework for considering the perspectives and meanings that individuals attach to their experiences, thus fostering a more comprehensive and empathetic understanding of the human condition.

- **Emphasis on Human-Centred Inquiry:** The emphasis on human-centred inquiry within the pragmatism paradigm finds a synergistic partner in the goals of qualitative research. Unlike paradigms that view individuals as passive receptors of an objective reality, pragmatism sees people as active constructors of meaning, engaging with and shaping their world. Qualitative research echoes this sentiment, employing tools like in-depth interviews, participant observation, and narrative analysis to explore the complexities of how individuals interpret and interact with their surroundings. This focus on understanding the human experience from the inside out, recognising the intricate interplay of context, subjectivity, and meaning, is at the heart of both approaches. By emphasising the complexity and dynamism of human experience, pragmatism and qualitative research develop a rich, multifaceted exploration of life as it is lived, seen, and understood by those experiencing it, elevating the voices and perspectives that might otherwise remain unheard.

- **Integration of Values and Ethics: The** integration of values and ethics in the pragmatism paradigm aligns with and enriches the ethical considerations inherent in qualitative research. Pragmatism's axiological stance goes beyond mere adherence to ethical guidelines, recognising that the very nature of research is intertwined with values and ethical considerations, such as consent, confidentiality, and the potential effects on participants. This perspective resonates with qualitative researchers' commitment to approaching their subjects with empathy, respect, and responsibility. The pragmatism paradigm encourages a reflective, thoughtful engagement with these ethical dimensions, acknowledging that research is not merely a technical exercise but a human endeavour filled with moral implications. This shared ethical orientation between pragmatism and qualitative research transcends mere compliance with rules, fostering a more profound, human-centred understanding and practice of research. It reminds researchers to always see their subjects as people, not objects, and to approach their work with an awareness of the deeper values and ethical responsibilities that underpin the pursuit of knowledge.

- **Adaptability and Problem-Solving Orientation**: The pragmatism paradigm's adaptability and focus on problem-solving find a harmonious counterpart in qualitative research's flexible and iterative nature. Unlike rigid methodologies that adhere strictly to a predetermined path, pragmatism, and qualitative research embrace a cyclical inquiry process. This process is characterised by continuous refinement in data collection and analysis, adapting to emerging insights and the intricate realities of the subject matter. Pragmatism's emphasis on practical solutions and constant inquiry fuels this dynamism, supporting a research approach that is theoretically robust and anchored in the real world's complexities. This synergy fosters a research process that is responsive, adaptable, and committed to producing insights that are not merely abstract but practically relevant and applicable. It is a confluence that transcends traditional boundaries, embracing the multifaceted nature of human existence and the ever-evolving quest for knowledge while focusing on solving real-world problems and enriching human understanding.

In summary, the pragmatism paradigm and the qualitative research approach are deeply interconnected, sharing a commitment to understanding human experience in its complexity, recognising the interplay of values and facts, and embracing a flexible, problem-solving orientation. Together, they offer a rich, responsive framework for exploring the multifaceted nature of human life, bridging the gap between theory and practice, and fostering a more thoughtful, engaged approach to research.

### 6.5 Pragmatism Paradigm and Mixed-Methods Research

The pragmatism paradigm has emerged as an essential philosophical underpinning in contemporary research methodologies, reflecting a flexible and adaptive approach that transcends traditional dichotomies between qualitative and quantitative research. In particular, the pragmatism paradigm resonates profoundly with mixed-methods research, combining qualitative and quantitative methods to offer a more comprehensive perspective on research problems (McBeath, 2023). The alignment between pragmatism and mixed-methods research is not merely a methodological coincidence but reflects more profound philosophical affinities that recognise reality's multifaceted and context-dependent nature. Pragmatism's focus on problem-solving, its embrace of complexity, its ethical considerations, and its commitment to human-centred inquiry all find a natural counterpart in the principles and practices of mixed-methods research. This synergy between the pragmatism paradigm and mixed-methods research opens up new horizons for inquiry, providing researchers with a robust and versatile framework to investigate complex phenomena. The following sections present this alignment's key facets, delving into how the pragmatism paradigm informs and enriches mixed-methods research, enhancing both its theoretical depth and practical relevance.

Here's an exploration of the pragmatism paradigm and its relevance with mixed-methods research, discussed over four full paragraphs:

- **Combination of Qualitative and Quantitative Approaches:** The pragmatism paradigm's adaptability and focus on problem-solving find a harmonious counterpart in qualitative research's flexible and iterative nature. Unlike rigid methodologies that adhere strictly to a predetermined path, pragmatism research embraces a cyclical inquiry process. This process is characterised by continuous refinement in data collection and analysis, adapting to emerging insights and the intricate realities of the subject matter. Pragmatism's emphasis on practical solutions and continuous inquiry fuels this dynamism, supporting a research approach that is theoretically robust and anchored in the real world's complexities. This synergy fosters a research process that is responsive, adaptable, and committed to producing insights that are not merely abstract but practically relevant and applicable. It is a confluence that transcends traditional boundaries, embracing the multifaceted nature of human existence and the ever-evolving quest for knowledge while focusing on solving real-world problems and enriching human understanding.

- **Problem-Centred Orientation:** The pragmatism paradigm's problem-centred orientation is at the heart of its alignment with mixed-methods research. Unlike other paradigms emphasising theoretical purity or methodological consistency, pragmatism is committed to addressing real-world challenges and finding practical solutions. This emphasis on solving problems rather than merely understanding or describing them resonates deeply with the mixed-methods research approach, which seeks to explore complex issues from various perspectives. By leveraging both qualitative insights and quantitative measurements, mixed-methods research under the pragmatism paradigm can navigate the intricate facets of a problem, providing a well-rounded view that facilitates actionable conclusions. The ability to integrate diverse methods in response to the complexity of the research problem ensures that the inquiry is not only academically rigorous but also tied to the lived realities of the subjects. This connection between theory and practice, understanding and action, positions mixed-methods research within the pragmatism paradigm as a vital tool for researchers aiming to make a tangible difference in the world, transforming research from an abstract exercise into a vehicle for real change and practical interventions.

- **Emphasis on Context and Complexity:** Pragmatism's nuanced recognition of reality's complexity and context-driven nature is a cornerstone in its alignment with mixed-methods research. By embracing the intricate web of human experience, social constructs, and individual perspectives, the pragmatism paradigm offers a scaffold for mixed-methods research to conduct a multidimensional examination. This approach moves beyond reductionist or binary views, allowing researchers to employ qualitative and quantitative techniques to explore phenomena from various angles, considering what is happening and why and how it is happening within a specific context. The combination of methods provides a richer, more complex picture that reflects the multifaceted nature of reality, acknowledging that human experiences cannot be neatly compartmentalised or oversimplified. Instead, the pragmatism paradigm encourages a comprehensive and empathetic understanding that appreciates the interplay of factors and forces that shape human behaviour and social phenomena.

This focus on context and complexity enhances the research's depth and breadth and fosters a more authentic and human-centred perspective that resonates with the lived experiences of individuals and communities.
- **Ethical Consideration and Human-Centred Inquiry:** The pragmatism paradigm's emphasis on ethical consideration and human-centred inquiry aligns with mixed-methods research, enhancing its moral dimension. Unlike research approaches that may objectify or distance the researcher from their subjects, pragmatism infuses the research process with an acute sense of empathy, responsibility, and recognition of the human condition. This emphasis on ethics and values serves as a guiding compass in mixed-methods research, ensuring that the methodology is analytically rigorous and morally grounded. It recognises research subjects not merely as data sources but as active, conscious participants in constructing meaning whose dignity, autonomy, and well-being are central to the research process. The pragmatism paradigm elevates mixed-methods research beyond mere methodological exercise to a reflective, ethical practice by fostering a humanistic approach sensitive to participants' rights and needs. This focus on humanity adds depth and sincerity to the research, ensuring that it is not just intellectually robust but also ethically sound, aligning the pursuit of knowledge with a broader commitment to social responsibility and human compassion.

Therefore, the pragmatism paradigm's characteristics of flexibility, problem-solving orientation, emphasis on complexity, and ethical consideration align seamlessly with the mixed-methods research approach. It fosters a more holistic, responsive, and human-centred approach, allowing researchers to explore complex phenomena with both depth and breadth.

### 6.6 Methodological Designs in Pragmatism Paradigm

Unlike traditional paradigms that may firmly align with either qualitative or quantitative research, pragmatism embraces a pluralistic approach. It advocates for the integration of diverse methods guided by the research questions rather than strict philosophical adherence. This adaptability allows researchers under the pragmatism paradigm to navigate complex, real-world issues with a problem-solving orientation. The various research designs suitable for implementing the pragmatism paradigm resonate with this flexibility, offering innovative and comprehensive approaches that meld qualitative and quantitative insights. The suitability of these designs is not just in their methodological blend but also in their alignment with the core principles of pragmatism, including ethical consideration, human-centred inquiry, context sensitivity, and an unwavering focus on practical applicability. The following section presents specific research designs that embody the pragmatism paradigm, justifying their alignment and discussing their unique contributions. Understanding these designs is critical for researchers seeking to implement the pragmatism paradigm effectively, ensuring that the research is theoretically robust, practically relevant, empathetic, and ethically sound.

Here are some research designs that are suitable for implementing the pragmatism paradigm, each discussed in a full paragraph:

i **Explanatory Sequential Design:** The explanatory sequential design is emblematic of the pragmatism paradigm's commitment to fluidity and adaptability in research. Comprising two phases, according to Subedi (2016), the design begins with the collection and analysis of quantitative data, forming an empirical foundation that is subsequently expanded and enriched through qualitative data collection and analysis. This phased approach embodies pragmatism's principle of selecting methods that best address the research question, not limiting the inquiry to a singular methodological approach. It recognises the complexity of human experiences and social phenomena, utilising both numerical analysis and narrative insights to generate a multidimensional understanding. The explanatory sequential design's ability to balance these diverse methods and facilitate their complementary interaction ensures a more holistic and practical engagement with the research problem. It allows for nuanced explorations that resonate with pragmatism's focus on problem-solving and real-world applicability, making it an apt choice for researchers operating within the pragmatism paradigm.

ii **Convergent Design:** The convergent design represents another powerful manifestation of the pragmatism paradigm, illustrating the paradigm's willingness to embrace diverse methods in a harmonious fashion. The convergent design ensures that statistical analysis and human insights are equally prioritised by simultaneously collecting qualitative and quantitative data but analysing them separately (Noyes et al., 2019). This dual focus is then synthesised at the interpretation stage, creating a multifaceted view reflecting pragmatism's recognition of reality's intricate, context-dependent nature. The design's inherent flexibility and commitment to a comprehensive understanding align perfectly with the pragmatic view that no single method can capture a complex phenomenon's dimensions. By emphasising the interplay between numerical and narrative data, the convergent design promotes a more empathetic and thorough exploration, reinforcing pragmatism's commitment to both the complexity of human experience and the practical relevance of research findings. It underscores the idea that the integration of different methods can lead to a more complete and actionable understanding of the subject under investigation.

iii **Transformative Design:** The transformative design exemplifies the pragmatism paradigm's emphasis on ethical responsibility and human-centred inquiry. Targeting marginalised or underrepresented populations, this design transcends mere methodological rigour to underscore social justice, empathy, and human dignity. Its alignment with pragmatism lies in its focus on values, ethics, and the lived experiences of individuals, resonating with pragmatism's commitment to the multifaceted reality of human experience. The transformative design goes beyond traditional research considerations to create a morally conscious framework that ensures an ethically sound exploration. It is not content with surface-level observations but seeks to empower and provide a voice to those often overlooked in research (Sangiorgi, 2011). Doing so aligns with pragmatism's principles and elevates the entire research process to a higher ethical plane. By engaging with the deeper social contexts and recognising the intrinsic value of every participant, the transformative design solidifies its suitability within the pragmatism paradigm, embodying a reflective, responsible, and profoundly human research approach.

iv **Embedded Design:** With its innovative approach to nesting one form of data within another, the embedded design beautifully aligns with the pragmatism paradigm's emphasis on adaptability and problem-solving orientation (Bastable et al., 2023). Embedding qualitative data within a primarily quantitative framework (or the reverse) ensures a multifaceted perspective on the research subject, reflecting the pragmatic understanding that reality is complex and multifarious. It supports pragmatism's goal of comprehensive understanding, adapting to the specific needs and contours of the research problem to provide insightful and practically relevant findings. The flexibility inherent in the embedded design allows researchers to explore different layers and dimensions of the phenomenon under investigation, aligning perfectly with the pragmatism paradigm's pluralistic stance. It embodies the pragmatic insistence on using the most suitable methods to illuminate the research question, regardless of strict adherence to traditional qualitative or quantitative boundaries. By enabling a more nuanced and context-sensitive approach, the embedded design complements pragmatism's aim to provide a rich, actionable understanding that is closely aligned with the real-world complexity and dynamism of human experience.

v **Action Research:** Action research, with its iterative and cyclical process of planning, acting, observing, and reflecting (Coghlan, 2019), epitomises pragmatism's commitment to addressing real-world problems and achieving practical solutions. This design is not a mere theoretical exercise but a purpose-driven approach to solve tangible problems or improve existing situations. Its alignment with the pragmatism paradigm is found in its orientation toward direct applicability and real-world change rather than abstract theorisation. Action research is guided by a pragmatic ethos that values the practical impact of research findings, emphasising their usability and relevance in everyday contexts. The shared focus on adaptability, continuous inquiry, and problem-solving orientation further strengthens the alignment between action research and pragmatism. It represents a hands-on approach that actively engages with the complexities of reality, seeking to generate insights that are not only insightful but also actionable.

In this way, action research stands as a suitable and robust design within the pragmatism paradigm, bridging the gap between theory and practice and contributing to meaningful and sustainable change.

vi **Case Study Research:** Case study research, characterised by its in-depth examination of a specific "case" within its real-world context (Scapens, 2004), aligns harmoniously with the pragmatism paradigm. The alignment is evident in its focus on context, subjectivity, and the intricate interplay of meanings, mirroring pragmatism's recognition of the multifaceted complexity of human experience. Unlike more rigid research designs, the case study approach allows for the flexibility to use mixed methods, offering both breadth and depth in understanding a phenomenon. This pluralistic approach complements pragmatism's inherently flexible and adaptive nature, which encourages the use of various methods to provide a more comprehensive understanding. The case study research design does not just seek to theoreticalise abstractly but to immerse in the particularities of a situation, aiming to extract general insights from the unique, often complex realities of individual cases. Its alignment with the pragmatism paradigm allows for a nuanced exploration of human phenomena, recognising the individuality of each case while seeking broader, actionable insights.

In summary, these designs support the flexibility, problem-solving orientation, ethical consideration, and human-centred inquiry that characterise the pragmatism paradigm. They provide tools to explore complex phenomena in context, using mixed methods to achieve practical, relevant, and applicable insights.

## 6.7 Aligning Research Questions with the Pragmatism Paradigm

Aligning research questions with the underlying paradigm of a study is a crucial step in ensuring the coherence and integrity of the research process. In the context of the pragmatism paradigm, this alignment takes on particular significance. Pragmatism's emphasis on practical applicability, ethical considerations, and the complex interplay of human experience necessitates research questions that are attuned to these dimensions. Crafting questions that resonate with this paradigm ensures that the inquiry is methodologically consistent and philosophically grounded. This alignment fosters a more meaningful engagement with the research subject, promoting a holistic understanding that is reflective of pragmatism's nuanced and adaptive stance. It sets the stage for a research process that is both rigorous and relevant, capable of yielding insights that are deeply connected to the real world and the multifaceted nature of human experience.

Aligning research questions with the pragmatism paradigm requires careful consideration and deliberate planning, as pragmatism's multifaceted nature influences the way in which research questions are formulated and investigated. Here's an exploration of this alignment and the factors that must be considered, along with examples:

1. **Flexibility and Adaptability:** Pragmatism emphasises flexibility in methodological choices. When formulating research questions within this paradigm, researchers should strive for adaptability and openness to multiple ways of knowing. The questions should not be confined to strict quantitative or qualitative methods but should allow for the integration of both, depending on what is most suitable to answer the research problem.

    **Examples:**
    Below are two examples that reflect the principle of flexibility and adaptability in formulating research questions within the pragmatism paradigm:

    i. **Exploring Workplace Motivation:** A researcher studying motivation in the workplace might ask: *What factors contribute to employee motivation, and how do these factors vary among different roles within the organization?* This question is designed to be flexible, allowing the researcher to employ both quantitative methods (such as surveys or statistical analysis) to identify common motivational factors and qualitative methods (like interviews or observations) to explore the specific experiences and perceptions of employees in various roles. Integrating both approaches would provide a comprehensive understanding of motivation within the organisation's context.

    ii. **Investigating Community Health Programs:** In a study aimed at understanding the effectiveness of community health programs, a researcher could pose the question: *How do community health programs impact overall health outcomes, and what are the community members' perceptions and experiences of these programs?* This research question is adaptable, embracing both quantitative methods (such as analysing health statistics and program success rates) and qualitative methods (like conducting focus group discussions with community members) to understand their experiences and perceptions. By combining both methods, the researcher can gain insights into the programs' measurable outcomes and the community members' lived experiences, leading to a more rounded understanding of the subject.

    In both examples, the research questions are crafted with an openness to multiple ways of knowing without confining them to strict quantitative or qualitative methods. This reflects the pragmatism paradigm's emphasis on flexibility and adaptability, allowing for a richer and more nuanced exploration of the research problem, depending on the most suitable methods to answer the question.

2. **Problem-Centred Focus:** In pragmatism, research often begins with a real-world problem or practical issue. The research questions should, therefore, be formulated with a clear focus on the practical and applicable rather

*Pragmatism Paradigm and Methodological Alignment* 161

than merely theoretical considerations. The questions must generate actionable insights that can lead to positive change or a deeper understanding of a concrete problem.

**Examples:**
Below are two examples that encapsulate a problem-centred focus within the pragmatism paradigm:

i **Improving Educational Outcomes in Low-Income Schools:** A researcher might ask: *What teaching strategies are most effective in improving literacy rates among elementary students in low-income schools, and how can these strategies be implemented across the district?* This question is focused on a concrete problem—low literacy rates—and aims to generate actionable insights, such as identifying effective teaching strategies that could lead to positive change within the district.

ii **Addressing Mental Health Issues in the Workplace:** In a study focusing on mental health in the corporate environment, the researcher could ask: *What are the primary causes of stress and burnout among employees in high-pressure industries, and what interventions can be designed to alleviate these issues?* This question targets a real-world problem—work-related stress and burnout—and seeks to understand the causes and possible solutions. The goal is to generate knowledge that could lead to the development of practical interventions for improving mental well-being in the workplace.

The research questions aim to address specific, tangible problems and create practical solutions in both examples. This aligns with the pragmatism paradigm's emphasis on problem-centred focus, reflecting the desire to conduct research that goes beyond theoretical exploration and leads to real-world impact and improvement.

3 **Ethical Considerations**: Pragmatism's axiological stance highlights the importance of values and ethics. Research questions within this paradigm should reflect a conscious consideration of ethical implications, including matters of consent, confidentiality, and the potential impact on participants. The focus should not just be on what can be done but also on what should be done.

**Examples:**
Here are two examples that illustrate the ethical considerations inherent in the pragmatism paradigm:

i Ethical Treatment of Prison Inmates: A researcher interested in the living conditions of prisoners might ask: *What are the current living conditions within maximum-security prisons, and how can improvements be made to align with international human rights standards?* This question is not just about discovering the facts but also about understanding what changes should be made to ensure the ethical treatment of inmates.

It considers both the practical aspects of living conditions and the ethical obligation to treat prisoners with dignity and humanity.

ii Data Privacy in Health Technology: In a study about personal health data management, a researcher could pose the question: **How do healthcare apps utilise personal health data, and what measures can be implemented to ensure data privacy and consent in accordance with ethical guidelines?** This question acknowledges the importance of technology in healthcare but strongly emphasises ethical considerations such as data privacy and user consent. It seeks to explore the usage of personal health data and the ethical boundaries that must be respected.

Both examples focus on subjects that have serious ethical implications. The research questions reflect a conscious consideration of these ethical aspects, aligned with the pragmatism paradigm's emphasis on the integration of values and ethics in research. They go beyond mere exploration of a phenomenon, taking into account the moral responsibilities and ethical considerations that guide what should be done.

4 **Complexity and Context:** The pragmatism paradigm recognises reality's complexity and context-dependent nature. Research questions should be formulated to acknowledge this complexity, seeking to explore phenomena nuanced and multifacetedly. This might involve recognising the interplay of various factors that contribute to a phenomenon and understanding how context shapes the experience or problem under study.

**Examples:**

Here are two examples that capture the essence of complexity and context within the pragmatism paradigm:

i **Urban Education Systems:** A researcher studying urban education systems may ask: **How do socioeconomic status, cultural background, and local educational policies interact to shape the educational outcomes in urban public schools?** This question recognises the complexity of urban education by considering the interplay of various factors such as socioeconomic status, culture, and policy. It seeks to understand how these elements interact within the specific context of urban settings to influence educational outcomes.

ii **Mental Health in the Workplace:** In a study about mental health in the workplace, a researcher could pose the question: **What are the psychological, organizational, and environmental factors that contribute to mental well-being among employees in technology startups, and how do they vary across different cultural and regulatory contexts?** This question acknowledges the multifaceted nature of mental well-being by exploring psychological, organisational, and environmental factors. It also emphasises the importance of context by considering how these factors may vary across different cultural and regulatory environments.

Both examples demonstrate the formulation of research questions that embrace complexity and context, aligned with the pragmatism paradigm's recognition of multifaceted reality. They aim to explore phenomena in a nuanced manner, acknowledging the interplay of various factors and understanding how context shapes the experience or problem under study. These examples show the applicability of pragmatism in addressing complex, real-world issues that cannot be reduced to simple binary constructs.

5 **Integration of Human Experience:** Lastly, as pragmatism emphasises human experience and interpretation, research questions should be framed in a way that allows for the exploration of human perceptions, beliefs, and experiences. This human-centred inquiry means that research questions should be crafted to probe into the human dimensions of the problem or phenomenon, taking into account the lived experiences of individuals.

**Examples:**
Here are two examples that encapsulate the integration of human experience within the pragmatism paradigm:

i **Impact of Climate Change on Coastal Communities:** A researcher interested in the human dimension of climate change might ask: *How do coastal communities perceive and adapt to the changing climate, and what are their lived experiences in dealing with rising sea levels and extreme weather events?* This question seeks to understand not just the physical effects of climate change but also the human responses, emotions, and adaptations, capturing the subjective experiences of individuals within these communities.

ii **Technology and Elderly Care**: In a study about technology's role in elderly care, a research question might be: *How do elderly individuals experience and interact with assistive technologies in their daily living, and what are the perceived benefits and challenges as narrated by both the elderly and their caregivers?* This question goes beyond mere functional aspects of technology to explore the human experience, understanding how technology integrates with or disrupts the daily lives of elderly individuals and those who care for them.

Both examples illustrate research questions crafted with a focus on human experience, seeking to delve into the individuals' perceptions, beliefs, and lived experiences. They align with the pragmatism paradigm's emphasis on human-centred inquiry, recognising that individuals are not just passive subjects but active participants in constructing meaning and interpreting their world. Such questions offer a more empathetic and nuanced understanding of the phenomena being studied.

In summary, aligning research questions with the pragmatism paradigm involves a thoughtful balance between methodological flexibility, problem-centred focus, ethical considerations, recognition of complexity, and a deep engagement with human experience. This alignment ensures that the research is methodologically sound, relevant, ethical, and attuned to the multifaceted nature of reality. It requires a more integrated and thoughtful approach that resonates with the core principles of pragmatism, facilitating research that can yield rich, comprehensive, and practically applicable insights.

### 6.7.1 Case Studies on How to Align Research Questions With Pragmatism Paradigm

Here are two case studies that demonstrate the alignment of research questions with the pragmatism paradigm:

---

**Case Study 1: Understanding Obesity Prevention Efforts**

Research Context: A public health department wants to study obesity prevention efforts in a community. They aim to understand both the statistical impact of interventions and the individual experiences of community members.

**Research Question:** "What is the statistical effectiveness of obesity prevention interventions within this community, and how do community members experience and perceive these efforts?"

**Alignment with Pragmatism**

This research question showcases the pragmatism paradigm by allowing for the combination of qualitative and quantitative methods (flexibility and adaptability), focusing on a real-world problem (problem-centred focus), considering community perspectives (integration of human experience), and addressing a public health issue with ethical implications (ethical considerations).

---

**Case Study 2: Analysing Education Technology in Rural Schools**

Research Context: An educational research team wants to explore how integrating technology in rural schools affects learning outcomes and student-teacher experiences. They recognise the multifaceted nature of technology integration and want to analyse it from different angles.

**Research Questions:** (1) How has the integration of technology in rural schools impacted student learning outcomes, as measured through standardised test scores and attendance? **(2)** What are the lived experiences, perceptions, and challenges students and teachers face in integrating technology into rural classrooms?

**Alignment with Pragmatism**

These questions embrace pragmatism by allowing for mixed methods (quantitative data on test scores, qualitative insights on experiences), focusing on practical challenges in education (problem-centred focus), considering the complex interplay of technology, education, and rural context (complexity and context), and putting the human experience at the centre (integration of human experience).

Both of these case studies reflect the principles of the pragmatism paradigm in formulating research questions. They allow for flexible methodologies, recognise complexity, focus on real-world problems, emphasise ethical considerations, and place the human experience at the core of the inquiry. These examples demonstrate how research questions can be crafted to align with pragmatism's unique approach to understanding the world.

## 6.8 Data Collection Methods in Pragmatism Paradigm

In the pragmatism paradigm, the approach to research is characterised by flexibility, practicality, and a focus on solving specific problems. Rooted in the belief that research methods should be tailored to the nature of the inquiry, pragmatism emphasises the use of any available techniques, tools, or procedures that facilitate understanding. Unlike other paradigms that adhere to strict philosophical or methodological guidelines, pragmatism allows researchers to employ a range of data collection methods, from quantitative surveys to qualitative interviews and even the innovative combination of both, known as mixed methods. This multiplicity and adaptability of methods align with the core principles of pragmatism and offer a comprehensive approach to research, providing diverse and multifaceted insights into the subject under investigation. Whether through observation, experimentation, or document analysis, the pragmatism paradigm enables a robust exploration of research questions, grounding the choice of methods in what is most relevant and effective for the specific inquiry.

Here's an overview of data collection methods that can be used in the pragmatism paradigm and how they are relevant:

i **Surveys and Questionnaires:** Surveys and questionnaires stand as versatile tools within the pragmatism paradigm, reflecting the philosophy's emphasis on flexibility and applicability. As methods designed to gather information from many participants align with pragmatic research's need for broad, generalisable data that can contribute to solving real-world problems. The inherent adaptability of surveys and questionnaires allows them to be tailored to specific research inquiries, whether aimed at quantifying attitudes on a large scale or understanding trends within a given population (Boeren, 2015; Rowley, 2014). Moreover, their compatibility with other methods amplifies the comprehensiveness of the research, enabling a multi-layered examination of the subject matter. In the pragmatism paradigm, where the choice of method is dictated by the nature and demands of the research question, surveys, and questionnaires serve as invaluable instruments, offering both breadth and depth in understanding and allowing for a synergistic approach that can enrich the overall picture.

ii **Interviews:** Interviews, whether structured or unstructured, play a crucial role in the pragmatism paradigm by offering an adaptable tool for gaining in-depth insights into individual perspectives. This method's flexibility aligns seamlessly with the pragmatic approach, as interviews can be tailored to suit a study's specific needs and objectives. Structured interviews provide a consistent framework that allows for comparability, while unstructured interviews offer a more open-ended exploration of respondents' thoughts and feelings. By facilitating a direct and often more nuanced understanding of the subject, interviews can capture the complexity of human experience in a way that other methods might not (Gardner, 2010). This adaptability to the research question makes interviews a valuable asset in pragmatic research, allowing researchers to delve deeply into their inquiries, whether seeking to understand a unique phenomenon or uncover broader trends, all within the accommodating and practical framework that defines the pragmatism paradigm.

iii **Observations:** Observations encompassing participant and non-participant methods epitomise the pragmatic approach's emphasis on flexibility and context-driven inquiry (Mirhosseini & Mirhosseini, 2020). Whether actively engaging in the environment as a participant or adopting a more detached stance as a non-participant observer, the researcher tailors the method to what best suits the research question and context. This choice reflects the pragmatic principle of employing whatever means will provide the most insightful data. Participant observations may provide an intimate insider's view, fostering empathy and understanding, while non-participant observations might offer an unbiased perspective, free from the influence of direct involvement. The ability to adapt and select the method of observation based on the specific needs and goals of the study aligns perfectly with the pragmatic paradigm, where the ultimate aim is to adopt the most effective approach to uncovering meaningful insights and understanding of the subject under investigation.

iv **Experiments:** Within the pragmatism paradigm, the use of experiments (Reif-Acherman, 2004), whether controlled in a laboratory or conducted in the field, emphasises the practical, problem-centred orientation of this research approach. Pragmatic researchers turn to experiments when they believe this method best aligns with their research question, unbound by rigid methodological constraints. This freedom to select the most appropriate experimental setting is a hallmark of the pragmatic approach. In a laboratory, researchers can control variables to pinpoint specific cause-and-effect relationships, while field experiments offer the advantage of studying phenomena in their natural context, often providing more ecologically valid results. The choice between these approaches is guided by what is deemed most suitable for the research needs and objectives, reflecting pragmatism's underlying philosophy that the value of any research method lies in its ability to facilitate understanding and solve real-world problems rather than adherence to a specific philosophical or methodological tradition.

v **Document Analysis:** Document analysis, encompassing the examination of existing texts, documents, media, or archival material, resonates strongly with the principles of the pragmatism paradigm (Danilovic, 2021). In a research approach that values practicality and adaptability, the utilisation of existing data offers a versatile method to extract relevant insights without necessarily collecting new primary data. Pragmatic researchers can explore historical records, policy documents, media content, or other textual resources to glean information pertinent to their research question. This method's alignment with the flexibility characteristic of pragmatism is evident in its ability to adapt to various research contexts and inquiries. Whether aiming to understand societal trends, organisational practices, or individual behaviours, document analysis provides a rich and varied source of data. In line with the pragmatic ethos, this method emphasises the best-fit approach, selecting and analysing documents in ways that most effectively answer the research question and contribute to a comprehensive and nuanced understanding of the subject matter.

In summary, the pragmatism paradigm's alignment with various data collection methods reflects its foundational principles of flexibility, practicality, and problem-centeredness. Unrestricted by rigid philosophical or methodological doctrines, pragmatism encourages researchers to craft their approach based on what best serves the research question. This may involve utilising, combining, or adapting diverse methods such as surveys, interviews, observations, experiments, and document analysis. By tailoring these tools to the specific needs and context of the inquiry, researchers can generate more robust and multidimensional insights. This holistic and adaptable approach empowers researchers to explore their subjects from different angles and depths, mirroring the complex reality of the phenomena under study. The pragmatism paradigm celebrates the creative and pragmatic fusion of methods driven by the quest for comprehensive and meaningful understanding.

## 6.9 Data Analysis and Interpretation in Pragmatism Paradigm

The pragmatism paradigm's orientation toward flexibility, practicality, and problem-centeredness significantly shapes the data analysis methods employed by researchers within this framework. Within this paradigm, data analysis is not confined to a singular method or technique but is instead guided by the specific research question and the context of the inquiry. The choice of data analysis methods in pragmatism reflects an acknowledgement of the multifaceted nature of reality and the need for diverse and flexible tools to uncover meaningful insights. This section explores the specific data analysis methods suitable for the pragmatism paradigm, including mixed-methods analysis, content analysis, discourse analysis, statistical analysis, thematic analysis, analytical software, grounded theory, and iterative analysis. Each method is discussed with justification of its relevance and alignment with the pragmatic paradigm, illustrating how they collectively contribute to a comprehensive and nuanced understanding of the subject under investigation.

i **Mixed-Methods Analysis:** Mixed-methods analysis is a quintessential approach within the pragmatism paradigm, reflecting its underlying commitment to flexibility and practicality. By synergistically combining quantitative and qualitative techniques, mixed-methods analysis allows researchers to glean a richer, more nuanced understanding of a phenomenon. Quantitative data can provide generalisable, statistical insights, while qualitative data adds depth and context, capturing the human aspects that numbers alone might miss. This fusion enables researchers to explore their subject from multiple angles, accommodating the complexity and multifaceted nature of real-world phenomena. The essence of pragmatism supports this blended approach, unbounded by rigid methodological constraints and driven by the desire to utilise different data types that provide complementary insights. In embracing mixed methods, the pragmatism paradigm demonstrates its core belief that the choice of research methods should be guided by what best serves the inquiry rather than adherence to a fixed philosophical stance.

ii **Content Analysis:** Content analysis embodies the adaptable and versatile nature of the pragmatism paradigm, serving as an essential tool in research that adheres to this approach. Whether utilised with qualitative or quantitative data, content analysis can be tailored to suit the specific research needs, allowing for an exploration that encompasses both the breadth and depth of the subject under investigation. This method's inherent flexibility resonates with the pragmatic view that methods should not be chosen for adherence to a specific ideology but rather for their practical applicability and relevance to the research question at hand. By systematically categorising and interpreting text or content (Huckin, 2003), researchers can uncover patterns, themes, and insights that align with their inquiry's objectives. This alignment between method and purpose, facilitated by content analysis, epitomises the pragmatism paradigm's core commitment to flexibility, practicality, and the pursuit of meaningful, real-world understanding.

iii **Discourse Analysis:** Discourse analysis, as a method of analysing data, fits seamlessly within the pragmatism paradigm, aligning with its fundamental principles of adaptability and utility in serving the research question. This approach focuses on the analysis of language, context, and the way meaning is constructed within various forms of communication (Moser et al., 2013). Unlike rigid methods that might look only at the surface structure of text, discourse analysis delves into the underlying social and cultural dynamics, recognising the complexity of human interaction and communication. This reflects the pragmatism paradigm's commitment to employing methods that can capture the multifaceted nature of reality. Discourse analysis provides a nuanced and comprehensive tool suitable for a wide range of research inquiries by allowing researchers to explore language within context and understand the interplay of various communicative elements. It embodies the pragmatic view that methods should be chosen for their ability to provide rich insights and deep understanding rather than mere adherence to a predetermined philosophical or methodological stance.

iv **Statistical Analysis:** Statistical analysis within the pragmatism paradigm reflects a willingness to embrace numerical and quantitative methods when the research question demands a generalisable or quantifiable understanding. Unlike paradigms that might strictly adhere to either qualitative or quantitative methodologies, pragmatism recognises the value of employing statistical methods if they are deemed the most suitable for addressing the research problem. This alignment with a problem-centred approach underscores the paradigm's flexibility and its focus on practical solutions. By employing statistical analysis, researchers can uncover patterns, relationships, and trends that might be essential to a comprehensive understanding of the phenomenon under investigation. The selection of this method is not based on a rigid philosophical alignment but is driven by the specific needs and context of the research question. In this way, statistical analysis exemplifies the pragmatism paradigm's commitment to choosing methods that best serve the inquiry, reinforcing its core principles of flexibility, practicality, and problem-centeredness.

v **Thematic Analysis:** Thematic analysis is a method particularly aligned with the pragmatism paradigm, especially when dealing with qualitative data. It offers a flexible and practical approach that resonates with pragmatism's core principles by enabling researchers to identify patterns and themes within the data (Braun & Clarke, 2012; Omodan, 2020). This method allows researchers to delve into complex human experiences and phenomena, seeking underlying themes that can provide insightful understanding. Unlike methods constrained by rigid methodological structures, thematic analysis supports an explorative and adaptive inquiry. It aligns with the pragmatic view that research methods should be chosen and moulded based on the needs of the study rather than a pre-established framework. By providing a tool that is both adaptable to various research contexts and capable of uncovering nuanced insights, thematic analysis embodies the pragmatism paradigm's commitment to flexibility, practicality, and the pursuit of meaningful comprehension of the subject under investigation.

vi **Use of Analytical Software:** The use of analytical software such as NVivo, SPSS, among others in the pragmatism paradigm, is emblematic of this approach's emphasis on practical solutions and efficiency. Pragmatic researchers are driven by the needs of their specific research question and the context of their inquiry, often leveraging technological tools that can aid in the analysis process. Whether dealing with complex statistical analysis or the intricate coding of qualitative data, these software tools enable researchers to manage, analyse, and interpret data with a level of precision and efficiency that manual methods might struggle to achieve. This use of technology is not merely a matter of convenience; it reflects the pragmatism paradigm's commitment to selecting methods and tools that facilitate a deeper, more accurate understanding of the phenomenon under investigation. It showcases the paradigm's openness to embracing modern tools that align with its core principles of practicality, flexibility, and problem-centeredness, ultimately serving the broader goal of robust and insightful inquiry.

vii **Grounded Theory:** Grounded theory, as a method of data analysis, aligns strongly with the pragmatism paradigm, resonating with its emphasis on flexibility, problem-centeredness, and real-world applicability. Unlike approaches that existing theories may confine, grounded theory allows for the inductive development of new theories that are rooted directly in the data itself (Noble & Mitchell, 2016). This enables researchers to build theories that specifically address the phenomena under study, especially if existing frameworks do not adequately explain or capture the complexities involved. By prioritising the data and allowing it to guide the theoretical construction, grounded theory reflects pragmatism's commitment to practical solutions that are intimately connected to the subject of inquiry. This approach does not merely seek to fit data into pre-established moulds but strives to understand and explain phenomena in a way that is both meaningful and directly relevant to the specific context. In this way, grounded theory embodies the core principles of pragmatism, prioritising flexibility, adaptability, and the pursuit of genuine insight that has tangible real-world significance.

viii **Iterative Analysis:** Iterative analysis, characterised by the ongoing process of analysing, revisiting, and reinterpreting data (Neale, 2021), finds a natural home within the pragmatism paradigm. This method recognises that understanding can deepen and evolve over time and that initial interpretations may require refinement or re-evaluation in light of new insights or broader contextual understanding. The iterative process is not a linear journey from data to conclusion; rather, it's a flexible and adaptive cycle that allows researchers to engage with the data from various angles and at different stages of the inquiry. This approach aligns perfectly with the pragmatism paradigm's core principles, emphasising flexibility, adaptability, and the recognition that complex real-world phenomena cannot always be captured or understood through a single, static analytical lens. By employing iterative analysis, pragmatic researchers demonstrate a commitment to a comprehensive and nuanced understanding, open to the dynamic nature of knowledge and the possibility that new insights can emerge through continuous engagement with the data. This reflects pragmatism's fundamental belief in practical, flexible, and problem-centred research methods that can respond to the multifaceted and evolving nature of the subject under investigation.

In summary, the suitability of these specific methods of data analysis in the pragmatism paradigm stems from their alignment with the paradigm's foundational principles. The choice of method is not dictated by adherence to a rigid philosophical or methodological stance but is driven by the nature of the research question and the context of the inquiry. Whether through blending different techniques, embracing technology, or fostering inductive theory-building, these methods reflect the pragmatism paradigm's essential commitment to flexibility, practicality, and problem-solving. They offer researchers a diverse toolkit that can be adapted to real-world research inquiries' multifaceted and often complex nature. However, there are still many methods not mentioned in this book.

## 6.10 Critiques and Debates in Pragmatism Paradigm

The pragmatism paradigm, known for its flexibility, adaptability, and focus on practical problem-solving, has gained recognition in various fields of research. However, it has not been without controversies and debates. While its proponents admire its non-committal stance to a single philosophical view and its ability to combine various research methods to create more robust insights, critics raise questions about its philosophical grounding, coherence, and ethical considerations. This section delves into the critiques and debates surrounding the pragmatism paradigm, exploring its underlying tensions, challenges, and the dialogues that continue to shape its role and definition in contemporary research.

- **Lack of Philosophical Commitment:** One notable critique of the pragmatism paradigm centres on its perceived lack of philosophical commitment (Talisse, 2013; Talisse, 2014). Pragmatism's inherent flexibility in method selection and its strong focus on problem-solving can lead some critics to view it as unanchored in a solid theoretical foundation. This absence of a clear philosophical stance might result in inconsistencies in interpretation, as researchers are free to choose, combine, or adapt methods based on what best serves the research question rather than adhering to a specific philosophical doctrine. While this adaptability is seen by many as a strength, allowing for a diverse and nuanced approach to research, detractors argue that it can lead to a superficial understanding of phenomena. Without a guiding philosophical framework, there may be a lack of cohesion and depth in the analysis, potentially undermining the validity and integrity of the research findings.

- **Potential Eclecticism:** The potential for eclecticism in the pragmatism paradigm emerges from its freedom to combine different methods and theoretical perspectives. While this flexibility is often hailed as one of pragmatism's key advantages, it has also given rise to concerns among some scholars. The fear is that this freedom might foster a "whatever works" approach, where methods are chosen and mixed without a coherent underlying rationale (Talisse, 2013). In such a scenario, the integration of various methods may not be guided by a consistent philosophical or theoretical foundation but rather by convenience or perceived utility. Critics argue that this could lead to a lack of rigour and coherence in the research, as the integration of disparate methods might not follow a logical or methodologically sound process. The concern here is that the pragmatism paradigm's adaptability could sometimes translate into a lack of discipline or clarity in research design, potentially compromising the depth, validity, or reliability of the findings.
- **Relativism:** The relativistic concerns associated with the pragmatism paradigm stem from its inherent flexibility and non-commitment to a specific philosophical or epistemological stance. This can lead to a perception that truth, within a pragmatic framework, becomes something negotiated, contextual, and contingent rather than absolute or universal. Critics argue that this approach to truth might undermine the ability to determine the validity and reliability of research findings. Without a fixed or absolute grounding, the criteria for judging the accuracy or credibility of research can become fluid and negotiable. This raises fundamental epistemological questions about the nature of knowledge and truth within the pragmatism paradigm, leading to debates about whether it provides a sufficiently robust framework for scientific inquiry. Proponents of pragmatism often counter that this flexible approach to truth reflects reality's complex and multifaceted nature, allowing for a more nuanced and context-sensitive understanding. Nonetheless, the concerns about relativism continue to be a focal point of critique and discussion within the scholarly community, reflecting broader debates about the nature of knowledge, objectivity, and scientific rigour.
- **Challenges in Integration:** Although praised for its ability to offer a multifaceted and comprehensive understanding, the use of mixed methods within the pragmatism paradigm poses challenges in integrating different types of data. The combination of quantitative and qualitative data requires

a thoughtful and balanced approach, recognising the inherent differences in these data types and the nuances they bring to understanding a phenomenon. The complexity of blending these distinct forms of information often leads to debates about the best practices and methodologies to achieve meaningful integration. Critics may argue that without clear guidelines, the process may result in an arbitrary or forced amalgamation that lacks coherence. Within the pragmatism paradigm, the challenge is to ensure that this integration is not only methodologically sound but also epistemologically consistent with the paradigm's core principles of flexibility, practicality, and problem-centeredness. The ongoing debates in this area reflect a broader dialogue about the nature of mixed-methods research, the epistemological assumptions underlying different data types, and the practical and philosophical challenges of integrating them in a way that enhances rather than diminishes the overall quality and depth of the research.

- ***Practicality vs. Depth:*** The pragmatism paradigm's emphasis on practicality and real-world applicability often draws criticism for the potential favour of surface-level solutions over in-depth theoretical exploration. While the focus on problem-solving is lauded by many as an essential aspect of pragmatism, allowing for research that is directly applicable to real-world issues, some scholars argue that this orientation might overshadow the importance of deeper understanding, conceptual analysis, and theory-building. Critics worry that the drive to provide immediate, practical solutions may lead researchers to bypass the complexities and nuances of a phenomenon in favour of more accessible but possibly superficial answers. In doing so, the rich theoretical insights and more profound understanding that often emerge from in-depth exploration might be neglected or undervalued. The debate around practicality versus depth reflects a broader tension within the research community about the roles and purposes of academic inquiry, raising questions about the balance between applied research with immediate utility and more fundamental, theory-driven exploration that may have longer-term significance.

- ***Identity and Definition:*** The identity and definition of the pragmatism paradigm have become subjects of scrutiny and debate among scholars, particularly due to its flexible and adaptable nature. Unlike paradigms with more rigid philosophical underpinnings, pragmatism's core principle of flexibility can make defining its boundaries and distinguishing it from other paradigms a complex endeavour. This fluidity and openness to various methodological approaches have led to questions about what precisely constitutes the pragmatism paradigm, its coherence, and even its legitimacy as a distinct paradigm. Critics may argue that this lack of clear definition might lead to inconsistencies, misunderstandings, or misapplications in research practice. Proponents of pragmatism often counter that its strength lies in its adaptability and responsiveness to specific research questions rather than adherence to a fixed set of rules or principles. However, the debates surrounding the identity and coherence of pragmatism

reflect underlying tensions about the nature and role of paradigms in research, the importance of philosophical grounding, and the balance between flexibility and structure in scientific inquiry.
- **Ethical Considerations:** The pragmatic approach's orientation towards what works best for a specific research question has raised concerns about potential oversights in broader ethical considerations (Pearson, 2014). Critics contend that the pragmatism paradigm's singular focus on practicality and efficiency may sometimes lead to conflicts with ethical principles, especially within complex and sensitive research contexts. For example, in the pursuit of the most practical or expedient research methods, considerations such as participant consent, confidentiality, or the potential harm to research subjects might be insufficiently addressed. The concern here is that the flexibility and adaptability that are hallmarks of the pragmatism paradigm could inadvertently lead to a de-emphasis on ethical rigour. Proponents of pragmatism would likely argue that ethical considerations are integral to any sound research practice, including within a pragmatic framework. Nonetheless, the tension between practicality and ethical considerations highlights a critical debate within the research community about how to balance the pursuit of effective research solutions with the commitment to uphold ethical standards and protect the rights and well-being of research subjects.

In summary, while offering a flexible and practical approach to research, the pragmatism paradigm faces various critiques and debates. Its strengths in terms of adaptability and problem-centeredness give rise to questions about its philosophical grounding, methodological rigour, epistemological stance, and ethical considerations. These debates reflect the complex nature of research paradigms and the ongoing dialogues that shape and refine our understanding of knowledge and inquiry in various fields.

## 6.11 Balancing Flexibility and Practicality in Pragmatism Paradigm

The pragmatism paradigm is rooted in the belief that research methods should be chosen based on the best answers to specific research questions. This approach combines flexibility and practicality, two core principles defining pragmatism's distinctive character. However, striking the right balance between these two principles can be a nuanced challenge. On the one hand, flexibility allows researchers to explore a problem from various angles, adapting their methods as needed to gain a rich understanding. On the other hand, practicality emphasises the real-world applicability and usefulness of research findings. While these principles can be complementary, balancing them effectively requires careful consideration and navigation. This section discusses the relationship between flexibility and practicality within the pragmatism paradigm, discusses the challenges and benefits of each, and provides insights into how researchers can thoughtfully balance these two essential aspects in their work.

The pragmatism paradigm uniquely blends flexibility and practicality, each contributing essential elements to the research process. Flexibility is about embracing a variety of methods, theoretical perspectives, and approaches to best serve the research question. This adaptability allows researchers to explore complex phenomena from various angles, providing a richer, more nuanced understanding. The advantage of this flexibility is that it enables diverse perspectives and responsiveness to unexpected changes or new insights during the research process. However, too much flexibility can lead to inconsistencies and a lack of focus, making it difficult to derive clear conclusions. Conversely, practicality within the pragmatism paradigm emphasises addressing specific problems or needs within a given context. Research findings become more directly applicable to real-world problems by focusing on practical solutions and providing clear direction and purpose. This emphasis on practicality can be valuable but also carries potential pitfalls, such as the risk of oversimplification or conflict with broader ethical considerations.

Striking the right balance between these two principles is a nuanced challenge. It's not about choosing one over the other but recognising how they can complement each other. Researchers can employ strategies to maintain a clear focus while allowing flexibility, continually reassessing and refining methods, utilising mixed-methods approaches for depth and breadth, and being transparent about decisions made in balancing these principles. Some researchers might lean too far into flexibility, leading to a "whatever works" approach that lacks coherence and rigour. Others may prioritise practicality, limiting the depth of understanding and overlooking ethical considerations. Therefore, navigating this balance requires careful planning, continuous reflection, and astute decision-making.

Therefore, balancing flexibility and practicality within the pragmatism paradigm ensures that the unique potential of this approach is fully realised. By thoughtfully blending these principles, researchers can create robust and comprehensive studies, contributing meaningful insights and solutions to the problems and contexts they aim to address. Fusing flexibility with practicality encapsulates the essence of pragmatism, enabling researchers to explore complex human experiences without being confined to a rigid methodological structure while ensuring real-world applicability and usefulness.

## 6.12 Summary

The chapter has presented the pragmatism paradigm, a research framework that emphasises adaptability, practicality, and problem-centred inquiry. Through an in-depth examination of various data collection and analysis methods, the chapter has illuminated how these techniques align with the core principles of pragmatism, reflecting its flexible and solution-driven nature. The critiques and debates surrounding the paradigm have also been addressed, highlighting potential pitfalls and challenges such as lack of philosophical commitment, eclecticism, and ethical considerations. In navigating these complex areas, the chapter has underscored the importance of balancing flexibility with practicality, ensuring that research under this paradigm remains coherent and ethically sound. By embracing both theoretical and practical concerns, the pragmatism paradigm offers a versatile and robust approach that can be tailored to a wide range of research questions and contexts.

# References

Adami, M. F., & Kiger, A. (2005). The use of triangulation for completeness purposes. *Nurse Researcher, 12*(4), 19–29. https://doi.org/10.7748/nr2005.04.12.4.19.c5956

Adhikari, S. P. (2021). Revealing the story of an individual through narrative inquiry: A methodological review. *Interdisciplinary Research in Education, 6*(1), 71–80.

Adil, M., Nagu, N., Rustam, A., & Winarsih, E. (2022). Interpretive paradigm on development of science and accounting research. *International Journal of Humanities Education and Social Sciences (IJHESS), 1*(4), 297–302. https://doi.org/10.55227/ijhess.v1i4.87

Aliyu, A. A., Bello, M. U., Kasim, R., & Martin, D. (2014). Positivist and non-positivist paradigm in social science research: Conflicting paradigms or perfect partners, *Journal of Management and Sustainability, 4*, 79, http://dx.doi.org/10.5539/jms.v4n3p79

Al-Saadi, H. (2014). Demystifying ontology and epistemology in research methods. *Research Gate, 1*(1), 1–10.

Anderson, E. M., Niska, J. R., & Niska, E. E. (2023). Factorial design. In Adam E. M. Eltorai, Jeffrey A. Bakal, David E. Wazer (Eds), *Translational radiation oncology* (pp. 327–330). Academic Press.

Antwi, S. K., & Hamza, K. (2015). Qualitative and quantitative research paradigms in business research: A philosophical reflection. *European Journal of Business and Management, 7*(3), 217–225.

Arghode, V. (2012). Qualitative and quantitative research: Paradigmatic differences. *Global Education Journal, 4*, 155–163.

Asamoah, M. K. (2014). Re-examination of the limitations associated with correlational research. *Journal of Educational Research and Reviews, 2*(4), 45–52.

Bahl, S., & Milne, G. R. (2007). 15 Mixed methods in interpretive research: An application to the study of the self concept. In Russell W. Belk (Ed.), *Handbook of qualitative research methods in marketing* (pp. 198–218). Edward Elgar Publishing.

Bais, A., & Amechnoue, K. (2023, May). An ex post facto study of global crisis impact on supply chain performance: Case of the automotive sector. In *2023 3rd international conference on Innovative Research in Applied Science, Engineering and Technology (IRASET)* (pp. 1–8). IEEE.

Balsiger, P., & Lambelet, A. (2014). Participant observation: How participant observation changes our view on social movements. In D. della Porta (Ed.), *Methodological practices in social movement research* (pp. 144–172). Oxford University Press.

Baporikar, N. (2015). Strategies for promoting research culture to support knowledge society. *International Journal of Information Communication Technologies and Human Development (IJICTHD)*, *7*(4), 58–72.

Bastable, E., Meng, P., Falcon, S. F., & McIntosh, K. (2023). Using an embedded mixed methods design to assess and improve intervention acceptability of an equity-focused intervention: A methodological demonstration. *Behavioral Disorders*, *48*(3), 201–211. https://doi.org/10.1177/0198742919880486

Bettany-Saltikov, J., & Whittaker, V. J. (2014). Selecting the most appropriate inferential statistical test for your quantitative research study. *Journal of Clinical Nursing*, *23*(11–12), 1520–1531. https://doi.org/10.1111/jocn.12343

Binns, M. G. (2023). *Relationship between the i-ready data and the standardized test data for Lakemore K-8 school* (Doctoral dissertation, St. Thomas University).

Bloemraad, I. (2013). The promise and pitfalls of comparative research design in the study of migration. *Migration Studies*, *1*(1), 27–46. https://doi.org/10.1093/migration/mns035

Boeren, E. (2015). Surveys as tools to measure qualitative and quantitative data. In Ellen Boeren (Ed.), *Handbook of research on scholarly publishing and research methods* (pp. 415–434). IGI Global.

Borkenau, P., & Ostendorf, F. (1990). Comparing exploratory and confirmatory factor analysis: A study on the 5-factor model of personality. *Personality and Individual Differences*, *11*(5), 515–524.

Borkovich, D. J., & Middle, G. A. (2022). Digital ethnography: A qualitative approach to inquiry in online spaces. *Proceedings of the International Association for Computer Information Systems-Europe*, 1–2.

Borrell, J., & Boulet, J. (2005). A critical exploration of objectivity and bias in gambling (and other) research. *International Journal of Mental Health and Addiction*, *2*(2), 25–39.

Braun, V., & Clarke, V. (2012). Thematic analysis. In H. Cooper, P. M. Camic, D. L. Long, A. T. Panter, D. Rindskopf, & K. J. Sher (Eds.), *APA handbook of research methods in psychology, vol. 2. Research designs: Quantitative, qualitative, neuropsychological, and biological* (pp. 57–71). American Psychological Association. https://doi.org/10.1037/13620-004

Breda, K. L. (2013). Critical ethnography. In *Routledge international handbook of qualitative nursing research* (pp. 230–241). Routledge.

Bridwell, S. D. (2013). A constructive-developmental perspective on the transformative learning of adults marginalized by race, class, and gender. *Adult Education Quarterly*, *63*(2), 127–146. https://doi.org/10.1177/0741713612447854

Brierley, J. A. (2017). The role of a pragmatist paradigm when adopting mixed methods in behavioural accounting research. *International Journal of Behavioural Accounting and Finance*, *6*(2), 140–154. https://doi.org/10.1504/IJBAF.2017.086432

Brown, M. J. (2019). Is science really value free and objective?: From objectivity to scientific integrity. In K. McCain, & K. Kampourakis (Ed.), *What is scientific knowledge?* (pp. 226–241). Routledge.

Bruce, B. C., & Bloch, N. (2013). Pragmatism and community inquiry: A case study of community-based learning. *Education and Culture*, *29*(1), 27–45.

Cardona-Rivera, R. E., Zagal, J. P., & Debus, M. S. (2020). Gfi: A formal approach to narrative design and game research. In *Interactive storytelling: 13th International conference on interactive digital storytelling, ICIDS 2020, Bournemouth, UK, November 3–6, 2020, Proceedings 13* (pp. 133–148). Springer International Publishing.

Carminati, L. (2018). Generalizability in qualitative research: A tale of two traditions. *Qualitative Health Research*, 28(13), 2094–2101. https://doi.org/10.1177/1049732318788379

Cavallo, A., Ris, M. D., & Succop, P. (2016). Correlational design. *How to Do Research: 15 Labs for the Social & Behavioral Sciences*, 46(7), 122–129.

Charlesworth, R., Hart, C. H., Burts, D. C., Thomasson, R. H., Mosley, J., & Fleege, P. O. (1993). Measuring the developmental appropriateness of kindergarten teachers' beliefs and practices. *Early Childhood Research Quarterly*, 8(3), 255–276.

Chilisa, B. (2012). Postcolonial indigenous research paradigms. *Indigenous Research Methodologies*, 98–127.

Chilisa, B. (2019). *Indigenous research methodologies*. Sage Publications.

Chilisa, B., & Ntseane, G. (2014). Resisting dominant discourses: Implications of indigenous, African feminist theory and methods for gender and education research. In *Rethinking gendered regulations and resistances in education* (pp. 23–38). Routledge.

Chilisa, B., & Phatshwane, K. (2022). *Qualitative research within a postcolonial indigenous paradigm* (pp. 225–235). SAGE Publications.

Christensen, A. D., & Jensen, S. Q. (2012). Doing intersectional analysis: Methodological implications for qualitative research. *NORA-Nordic Journal of Feminist and Gender Research*, 20(2), 109–125. https://doi.org/10.1080/08038740.2012.673505

Clark, A. M. (1998). The qualitative-quantitative debate: Moving from positivism and confrontation to post-positivism and reconciliation. *Journal of Advanced Nursing*, 27(6), 1242–1249.

Coghlan, D. (2019). *Doing Action Research in Your Own Organization*. Sage Publications Ltd. http://digital.casalini.it/9781526481719

Collins, L. M., Dziak, J. J., & Li, R. (2009). Design of experiments with multiple independent variables: A resource management perspective on complete and reduced factorial designs. *Psychological Methods*, 14(3), 202–224. https://doi.org/10.1037/a0015826

Comte, A. (1975). *Auguste Comte and positivism: The essential writings*. Transaction Publishers.

Conroy, T. (2017). A beginner's guide to ethnographic observation in nursing research. *Nurse Researcher*, 24(4), 10–14. https://doi.org/10.7748/nr.2017.e1472

Corradetti, C. (2012). The Frankfurt school and critical theory. *The Internet Encyclopedia of Philosophy*. 1–15. https://ssrn.com/abstract=2211197

Corry, M., Porter, S., & McKenna, H. (2019). The redundancy of positivism as a paradigm for nursing research. *Nursing Philosophy*, 20(1), e12230. https://doi.org/10.1111/nup.12230

Corus, C., & Saatcioglu, B. (2015). An intersectionality framework for transformative services research. *The Service Industries Journal*, 35(7–8), 415–429. https://doi.org/10.1080/02642069.2015.1015522

Creswell, J. W., & Clark, V. L. P. (2017). *Designing and conducting mixed methods research*. Sage Publications.

Crook, C., & Garratt, D. (2005). The positivist paradigm in contemporary social science research. *Research Methods in the Social Sciences*, 207–214.

Cunliffe, A. L., & Karunanayake, G. (2013). Working within hyphen-spaces in ethnographic research: Implications for research identities and practice. *Organizational Research Methods*, 16(3), 364–392. https://doi.org/10.1177/1094428113489353

Cuthbertson, L. M., Robb, Y. A., & Blair, S. (2020). Theory and application of research principles and philosophical underpinning for a study utilising interpretative phenomenological analysis. *Radiography, 26*(2), e94–e102. https://doi.org/10.1016/j.radi.2019.11.092

Danilovic, N. (2021). Application of the document analysis method in the social sciences. *Social Communications: Theory and Practice, 13*(2), 13–27.

Darawsheh, W. (2014). Reflexivity in research: Promoting rigour, reliability and validity in qualitative research. *International Journal of Therapy and Rehabilitation, 21*(12), 560–568. https://doi.org/10.12968/ijtr.2014.21.12.560

Darby, J. L., Fugate, B. S., & Murray, J. B. (2019). Interpretive research: A complementary approach to seeking knowledge in supply chain management. *The International Journal of Logistics Management, 30*(2), 395–413. https://doi.org/10.1108/IJLM-07-2018-0187

Davie, G., & Wyatt, D. (2021). Document analysis. In Grace Davie, & David Wyatt (Eds.), *The Routledge handbook of research methods in the study of religion* (pp. 245–255). Routledge.

Davies, C., & Fisher, M. (2018). Understanding research paradigms. *Journal of the Australasian Rehabilitation Nurses Association, 21*(3), 21–25.

De Carvalho, J., & Chima, F. O. (2014). Applications of structural equation modeling in social sciences research. *American International Journal of Contemporary Research, 4*(1), 6–11.

De Monticelli, R. (2018). The paradox of axiology. A phenomenological approach to value theory. *Phenomenology and Mind, 15*, 116–128.

Desta, A. (2009). *Comprehending Indigenous knowledge: An ethnographic study of knowledge processes within natural resource management.* London School of Economics and Political Science (United Kingdom).

Devi, R., Pradhan, S., Giri, D., Lepcha, N., & Basnet, S. (2022). Application of correlational research design in nursing and medical research. *Journal of Xi'an Shiyou University, Natural Sciences Edition, 65*(11), 60–69. https://doi.org/10.17605/OSF.IO/YRZ68

Dieronitou, I. (2014). The ontological and epistemological foundations of qualitative and quantitative approaches to research. *International Journal of Economics, Commerce and Management, 2*(10), 1–17.

Doucet, M., Pratt, H., Dzhenganin, M., & Read, J. (2022). Nothing about us without us: Using participatory action research (PAR) and arts-based methods as empowerment and social justice tools in doing research with youth 'aging out' of care, *Child Abuse & Neglect, 130*, 105358, https://doi.org/10.1016/j.chiabu.2021.105358

Doughney, J. (2005). Moral description: Overcoming the fact-value dichotomy in social research. *eCOMMUNITY: International Journal of Mental Health and Addiction, 2*(2), 6–12.

Dube, L., Ndwandwe, S., & Ngulube, P. (2013). Rowing upstream: Contextualising indigenous research processes and methodologies through the utilization of ethical principles. *Indilinga African Journal of Indigenous Knowledge Systems, 12*(1), 13–25.

Dyzenhaus, D. (1983). Positivism and validity. *South African Law Journal, 100*, 454.

Eatough, V., & Smith, J. A. (2017). Interpretative phenomenological analysis. In Stainton Rogers, Wendy Willig, Carla Stainton Rogers Wendy, & Willig Carla (Eds), *The Sage handbook of qualitative research in psychology* (pp. 193–209). Sage Publications Ltd.

Emmel, N. (2008). *Participatory mapping: An innovative sociological method.* https://eprints.ncrm.ac.uk/id/eprint/540/

Erciyes, E. (2020). Paradigms of inquiry in the qualitative research. *European Scientific Journal, ESJ, 16*(7), 181. http://dx.doi.org/10.19044/esj.2020.v16n7p181

Esin, C. (2011). Narrative analysis approaches. In Frost Nollaig (Ed.), *Qualitative Research methods in psychology: Combining core approaches* (92–117). McGraw-Hill Education.

Fallace, T., & Fantozzi, V. (2013). Was there really a social efficiency doctrine? The uses and abuses of an idea in educational history. *Educational Researcher, 42*(3), 142–150. https://doi.org/10.3102/0013189X13484509

Farjoun, M., Ansell, C., & Boin, A. (2015). PERSPECTIVE—Pragmatism in organization studies: Meeting the challenges of a dynamic and complex world. *Organization Science, 26*(6), 1787–1804. https://doi.org/10.1287/orsc.2015.1016

Fife-Schaw, C. (2012). Quasi-experimental designs. In C. Cuttler, R. S. Jhangiani, & D. C. Leighton (Eds.), *Research methods in psychology* (pp. 75–91). Kwantlen Polytechnic University.

Fitzgerald, T. (2004). Powerful voices and powerful stories: Reflections on the challenges and dynamics of intercultural research. *Journal of Intercultural Studies, 25*(3), 233–245. https://doi.org/10.1080/0725686042000315740

Foster, C. (2023). Methodological pragmatism in educational research: From qualitative-quantitative to exploratory-confirmatory distinctions. *International Journal of Research & Method in Education*, 1–16. https://doi.org/10.1080/1743727X.2023.2210063

Fowler, F. J. Jr (2013). *Survey research methods.* Sage Publications.

Frechette, J., Bitzas, V., Aubry, M., Kilpatrick, K., & Lavoie-Tremblay, M. (2020). Capturing lived experience: Methodological considerations for interpretive phenomenological inquiry, *International Journal of Qualitative Methods, 19*, 1609406920907254, https://doi.org/10.1177/1609406920907254

Fry, M., Curtis, K., Considine, J., & Shaban, R. Z. (2017). Using observation to collect data in emergency research. *Australasian Emergency Nursing Journal, 20*(1), 25–30. https://doi.org/10.1016/j.aenj.2017.01.001

Gardner, M. R. (2010). Conceptual, holistic, and pragmatic considerations for interviewing research participants. *Holistic Nursing Practice, 24*(3), 148–157.

Garlitz, D., & Zompetti, J. (2023). Critical theory as post-marxism: The Frankfurt school and beyond. *Educational Philosophy and Theory, 55*(2), 141–148. https://doi.org/10.1080/00131857.2021.1876669

Garrick, J. (1999). Doubting the philosophical assumptions of interpretive research. *International Journal of Qualitative Studies in Education, 12*(2), 147–156.

Goduka, N. (2012). From positivism to indigenous science: A reflection on world views, paradigms and philosophical assumptions. *Africa Insight, 41*(4), 123–138.

Godwin, A., Benedict, B., Rohde, J., Thielmeyer, A., Perkins, H., Major, J., … Chen, Z. (2021). New epistemological perspectives on quantitative methods: An example using Topological Data Analysis. *Studies in Engineering Education, 2*(1), 16–34. https://doi.org/10.21061/see.18

Goldkuhl, G. (2012). Design research in search for a paradigm: Pragmatism is the answer. In *Practical aspects of design science: European Design Science Symposium, EDSS 2011, Leixlip, Ireland, October 14, 2011, Revised Selected Papers 2* (pp. 84–95). Springer Berlin Heidelberg.

Gough, B., & Madill, A. (2012). Subjectivity in psychological science: From problem to prospect. *Psychological Methods, 17*(3), 374. https://psycnet.apa.org/doi/10.1037/a0029313

Goulding, C. (1999). Consumer research, interpretive paradigms and methodological ambiguities. *European Journal of Marketing, 33*(9/10), 859–873. https://doi.org/10.1108/03090569910285805

Graham, L. M., & Wiessner, S. (2011). Indigenous sovereignty, culture, and international human rights law. *South Atlantic Quarterly, 110*(2), 403–427. https://doi.org/10.1215/00382876-1162516

Guillemin, M., & Drew, S. (2010). Questions of process in participant-generated visual methodologies. *Visual Studies, 25*(2), 175–188. https://doi.org/10.1080/1472586X.2010.502676

Gullion, J. S., & Tilton, A. (2020). A decolonizing approach to community-based action research. In J. S. Gullion (Ed.), *Researching with*. (pp. 157–165). Brill.

Gustafsson, J. E. (2010). Longitudinal designs. In B. P. M. Creemers, & L. K. Pam (Eds.), *Methodological advances in educational effectiveness research* (pp. 91–115). Routledge.

Haase, R. F., & Ellis, M. V. (1987). Multivariate analysis of variance. *Journal of Counseling Psychology, 34*(4), 404.

Halfpenny, P. (2014). *Positivism and sociology (RLE social theory): Explaining social life*. Routledge.

Hardy, C., & Clegg, S. R. (2006). Some dare call it power. In S. R. Clegg, T. B. Lawrence, C. Hardy (Eds.), *Handbook of organization studies (nwe, completely revised second edition)*, (pp. 754–775). Sage Publications Ltd.

Harrell, F. E. (2015). Introduction to survival analysis. *Regression modeling strategies: With applications to linear models, logistic and ordinal regression, and survival analysis*, 399–422. https://doi.org/10.1007/978-3-319-19425-7_17

Harrison, H., Birks, M., Franklin, R., & Mills, J. (2017). Case study research: Foundations and methodological orientations. *Forum Qualitative Sozialforschung Forum: Qualitative Social Research, 18*(1). https://doi.org/10.17169/fqs-18.1.2655

Held, M. B. (2019). Decolonizing research paradigms in the context of settler colonialism: An unsettling, mutual, and collaborative effort, *International Journal of Qualitative Methods, 18*, 1609406918821574, https://doi.org/10.1177/1609406918821574

Hollstein, B. (2011). Qualitative approaches. In P. J. Carrington, & J. Scott (Eds.), *The SAGE handbook of social network analysis* (404–416). Sage Publications Ltd.

Holmes, A. G. D. (2020). Researcher positionality–A consideration of its influence and place in qualitative research–A new researcher guide. *Shanlax International Journal of Education, 8*(4), 1–10.

Huckin, T. (2003). Content analysis: What texts talk about. In Charles Bazerman, & Paul Prior (Eds), *What writing does and how it does it* (pp. 19–38). Routledge.

Hussein, M. E., Hirst, S., Salyers, V., & Osuji, J. (2014). Using grounded theory as a method of inquiry: Advantages and disadvantages. *The Qualitative Report, 19*(27), 1–15. Retrieved from http://nsuworks.nova.edu/tqr/vol19/iss27/3

Jackson, K. M., Pukys, S., Castro, A., Hermosura, L., Mendez, J., Vohra-Gupta, S., ... Morales, G. (2018). Using the transformative paradigm to conduct a mixed methods needs assessment of a marginalized community: Methodological lessons and implications, *Evaluation and Program Planning, 66*, 111–119, https://doi.org/10.1016/j.evalprogplan.2017.09.010

Järvinen, P. (2000). Research questions guiding selection of an appropriate research method. In *Proceedings of ECIS2000, 3–5 July* (pp. 124–131).

Johnson, E. S. (2020). Action research. In *Oxford research encyclopedia of education*. Oxford University Press.

Joseph, J. J., & Gandolfi, F. (2022). The servant leader as a critical pedagogue: Drawing lessons from critical pedagogy. *International Journal of Leadership in Education, 25*(1), 88–105. https://doi.org/10.1080/13603124.2019.1690702

Jukola, S. (2015). On the conditions for objectivity: How to avoid bias in socially relevant research. *Jyväskylä Studies in Education, Psychology and Social Research, 532*, 1–48.

Kaboub, F. (2008). Positivist paradigm. *Encyclopedia of counselling, 2*(2), 343.

Kalelioğlu, U. B. (2021). *Replicability: 21st century crisis of the positivist social sciences* (Doctoral dissertation, Hakan AKDAĞ). https://doi.org/10.38015/sbyy.1003103

Kaplan, S. A., Dillman, K. N., Calman, N. S., & Billings, J. (2004). Opening doors and building capacity: Employing a community-based approach to surveying, *Journal of Urban Health, 81*, 291–300, https://doi.org/10.1093/jurban/jth115

Karnieli-Miller, O., Strier, R., & Pessach, L. (2009). Power relations in qualitative research. *Qualitative Health Research, 19*(2), 279–289. https://doi.org/10.1177/1049732308329306

Karupiah, P. (2022). Positivism. In Islam, M.R., Khan, N.A., Baikady, R.(Eds.), *Principles of social research methodology* (pp. 73–82). Springer Nature Singapore.

Katmo, E. T. R. (2016). Postcolonial indigenous feminist paradigm as a strategy of self-determination: A reflection on Papua Mimika women in matrilineal tradition. *Journal Perempuan, 21*(3), 285–293.

Kaushik, V., & Walsh, C. A. (2019). Pragmatism as a research paradigm and its implications for social work research. *Social Sciences, 8*(9), 255. https://doi.org/10.3390/socsci8090255

Kelliher, F. (2011). Interpretivism d the pursuit of research legitimisation: An integrated approach to single case design. *Leading Issues in Business Research Methods, 1*(2), 123–131.

Kelly, L. M., & Cordeiro, M. (2020). Three principles of pragmatism for research on organizational processes. *Methodological Innovations, 13*(2), 2059799120937242. https://doi.org/10.1177/2059799120937242

Khatri, K. K. (2020). Research paradigm: A philosophy of educational research. *International Journal of English Literature and Social Sciences, 5*(5), 1435–1440.

Khosravi, S. H. (2011). Focus group, a data gathering method. *Iran Journal of Nursing, 23*(68), 19–30.

Kile, M. (2022). Uncovering social issues through photovoice: A comprehensive methodology. *HERD: Health Environments Research & Design Journal, 15*(1), 29–35. https://doi.org/10.1177/19375867211055101

Killam, L. (2013). *Research terminology simplified: Paradigms, axiology, ontology, epistemology and methodology*. Laura Killam.

Kim, Y. M. (2009). Validation of psychometric research instruments: The case of information science. *Journal of the American Society for Information Science and Technology, 60*(6), 1178–1191. https://doi.org/10.1002/Asi.21066

Kirk, R. E. (2009). Experimental design. In Maydeu-Olivares Alberto, & Millsap Roger E. (Eds.), *Sage handbook of quantitative methods in psychology* (23–45). Sage Publications Ltd.

Kivunja, C., & Kuyini, A. B. (2017). Understanding and applying research paradigms in educational contexts. *International Journal of Higher Education, 6*(5), 26–41. https://doi.org/10.5430/ijhe.v6n5p26

Kleinheksel, A. J., Rockich-Winston, N., Tawfik, H., & Wyatt, T. R. (2020). Demystifying content analysis. *American Journal of Pharmaceutical Education*, *84*(1), 7113. https://doi.org/10.5688/ajpe7113

Kler, B. K. (2010). Philosophically grounding tourism research in Malaysia. In Kadir Din, & Jabil Mapjabil (Eds.), *Tourism research in Malaysia: What, which way and so what?* (pp. 1–19). UUM Press.

Kloppenberg, J. T. (1996). Pragmatism: An old name for some new ways of thinking? *The Journal of American History*, *83*(1), 100–138. https://doi.org/10.2307/2945476

Konuralp, E. (2019). *On positivism and its methodological individualist revision*. Peter Lang AG.

Korte, R., & Mercurio, Z. A. (2017). Pragmatism and human resource development: Practical foundations for research, theory, and practice. *Human Resource Development Review*, *16*(1), 60–84. https://doi.org/10.1177/1534484317691707

Kortuem, G., Bourgeois, J., Van Der Linden, J., & Price, B. (2014). Participatory data analysis: A new method for investigating human energy practices. *CEUR Workshop Proceedings*, *1203*, 35–37.

Kruse, R., & Steinbrecher, M. (2010). Visual data analysis with computational intelligence methods. *Bulletin of the Polish Academy of Sciences. Technical Sciences*, *58*(3), 393–401.

Kuhn, T. S. (1997). *The structure of scientific revolutions* (Vol. 962). University of Chicago press.

Kuhn, T. S. (2012). *The structure of scientific revolutions*. University of Chicago Press.

Kukull, W. A., & Ganguli, M. (2012). Generalizability: The trees, the forest, and the low-hanging fruit. *Neurology*, *78*(23), 1886–1891. https://doi.org/10.1212/WNL.0b013e318258f812

Küsters, I. (2022). Narratives interview. In Nina Baur, & Jörg Blasius (Eds), *Handbuch Methoden der empirischen Sozialforschung* (pp. 893–900). Springer Fachmedien Wiesbaden.

Lee, E. S., & Whalen, T. (2007). Synthetic designs: A new form of true experimental design for use in information systems development. *ACM Sigmetrics Performance Evaluation Review*, *35*(1), 191–202. https://doi.org/10.1145/1269899.1254904

Lincoln, Y. S., & Guba, E. G. (1989). Ethics: The failure of positivist science. *The Review of Higher Education*, *12*(3), 221–240.

Lu, H., & Hodge, W. A. (2019). Toward multi-dimensional and developmental notion of researcher positionality. *Qualitative Research Journal*, *19*(3), 225–235. https://doi.org/10.1108/QRJ-D-18-00029

Lukka, K., & Kasanen, E. (1995). The problem of generalizability: Anecdotes and evidence in accounting research. *Accounting, Auditing & Accountability Journal*, *8*(5), 71–90.

Lundholt, M. W., & Boje, D. (2018). Understanding organizational narrative-counter-narratives dynamics: An overview of communication constitutes organization (CCO) and storytelling organization theory (SOT) approaches. *Communication & Language at Work*, *5*(1), 18–29.

Maarouf, H. (2019). Pragmatism as a supportive paradigm for the mixed research approach: Conceptualizing the ontological, epistemological, and axiological stances of pragmatism. *International Business Research*, *12*(9), 1–12.

MacRae, A. W. (2019). Descriptive and inferential statistics. In Andrew M. Colman (Ed.), *Companion encyclopedia of psychology* (pp. 1099–1121). Routledge.

Malaurent, J., & Avison, D. (2017). Reflexivity: A third essential 'R' to enhance interpretive field studies. *Information & Management, 54*(7), 920–933.

Mantzoukas, S. (2005). The inclusion of bias in reflective and reflexive research: A necessary prerequisite for securing validity. *Journal of Research in Nursing, 10*(3), 279–295. https://doi.org/10.1177/174498710501000305

Marsh, D., & Furlong, P. (2002). A skin not a sweater: Ontology and epistemology in political science. *Theory and Methods in Political Science, 2*(1), 17–41.

Marshall, G., & Jonker, L. (2010). An introduction to descriptive statistics: A review and practical guide. *Radiography, 16*(4), e1–e7. https://doi.org/10.1016/j.radi.2010.01.001

Marshall, G., & Jonker, L. (2011). An introduction to inferential statistics: A review and practical guide. *Radiography, 17*(1), e1–e6. https://doi.org/10.1016/j.radi.2009.12.006

Matusov, E., Marjanovic-Shane, A., Kullenberg, T., & Curtis, K. (2019). Dialogic analysis vs. discourse analysis of dialogic pedagogy: Social science research in the era of positivism and post-truth, *Dialogic Pedagogy: An International Online Journal, 7,* 20–62, https://doi.org/10.5195/dpj.2019.272

Mawere, M., & Awuah-Nyamekye, S. (Eds.). (2015). *Between rhetoric and reality: The state and use of indigenous knowledge in post-colonial Africa.* African Books Collective.

Maxcy, S. J. (2003). Pragmatic threads in mixed methods research in the social sciences: The search for multiple modes of inquiry and the end of the philosophy of formalism. In A. Tashakkori, & C. Teddlie (Eds.), *Handbook of mixed methods in social and behavioral research* (pp. 51–89). Sage.

McBeath, A. (2023). Mixed methods research: The case for the pragmatic researcher. In Sofie Bager-Charleson, & Alistair McBeath (Eds), *Supporting research in counselling and psychotherapy: Qualitative, quantitative, and mixed methods research* (pp. 187–205). Springer International Publishing.

McGregor, S. L., & Murnane, J. A. (2010). Paradigm, methodology and method: Intellectual integrity in consumer scholarship. *International Journal of Consumer Studies, 34*(4), 419–427. https://doi.org/10.1111/j.1470-6431.2010.00883.x

Mellinger, C. D., & Hanson, T. A. (2020). Methodological considerations for survey research: Validity, reliability, and quantitative analysis, *Linguistica Antverpiensia, New Series–Themes in Translation Studies, 19,* 172–190, https://doi.org/10.52034/lanstts.v19i0.549

Mertens, D. M. (2007). Transformative paradigm: Mixed methods and social justice. *Journal of Mixed Methods Research, 1*(3), 212–225. https://doi.org/10.1177/1558689807302811

Mertens, D. M. (2010). Transformative mixed methods research. *Qualitative Inquiry, 16*(6), 469–474. https://doi.org/10.1177/1077800410364612

Mertens, D. M. (2012). Transformative mixed methods: Addressing inequities. *American Behavioral Scientist, 56*(6), 802–813. https://doi.org/10.1177/0002764211433797

Migiro, S. O., & Magangi, B. A. (2011). Mixed methods: A review of literature and the future of the new research paradigm. *African Journal of Business Management, 5*(10), 3757–3764.

Minhat, H. S. (2015). An overview on the methods of interviews in qualitative research. *International Journal of Public Health and Clinical Sciences, 2*(1), 210–214.

Mirhosseini, S. A., & Mirhosseini, S. A. (2020). Collecting data through observation. *Doing qualitative research in language education* (pp. 61–84). https://doi.org/10.1007/978-3-030-56492-6_4

Moore, J. (2012). A personal insight into researcher positionality. *Nurse Researcher*, *19*(4), 11–14. https://doi.org/10.7748/nr2012.07.19.4.11.c9218

Morgan, D. L. (2013). *Integrating qualitative and quantitative methods: A pragmatic approach*. Sage publications.

Morgan, D. L. (2014). Pragmatism as a paradigm for social research. *Qualitative Inquiry*, *20*(8), 1045–1053. https://doi.org/10.1177/1077800413513733

Morley, C., Ablett, P., Noble, C., & Cowden, S. (Eds.). (2020). *The Routledge handbook of critical pedagogies for social work*. Routledge.

Morton, C., Anable, J., & Nelson, J. D. (2017). Consumer structure in the emerging market for electric vehicles: Identifying market segments using cluster analysis. *International Journal of Sustainable Transportation*, *11*(6), 443–459. https://doi.org/10.1080/15568318.2016.1266533

Moser, C., Groenewegen, P., Huysman, M. (2013). *Extending social network analysis with discourse analysis: Combining relational with interpretive data*. In: T. Özyer, J. Rokne, G. Wagner, A. Reuser (eds) *The Influence of Technology on Social Network Analysis and Mining. Lecture Notes in Social Networks* (pp. 547–561). Springer, Vienna. https://doi.org/10.1007/978-3-7091-1346-2_24

Murtagh, L. (2007). Implementing a critically quasi-ethnographic approach. *Qualitative Report*, *12*(2), 193–215.

Ndlovu-Gatsheni, S. (2013). Decolonial epistemic perspective and pan-African unity in the 21st century. Muchie Mammo, Lukhele-Olorunju Phindil, & Akpor Ogheneerobor B. (Eds), *The African Union ten years after* (pp. 385–409). Africa Institute of South Africa.

Ndlovu-Gatsheni, S. J. (2018). *Epistemic freedom in Africa: Deprovincialization and decolonization*. Routledge.

Neale, J. (2021). Iterative categorisation (IC) (part 2): Interpreting qualitative data. *Addiction*, *116*(3), 668–676. https://doi.org/10.1111/add.15259

Neubauer, B. E., Witkop, C. T., & Varpio, L. (2019). How phenomenology can help us learn from the experiences of others, *Perspectives on Medical Education*, *8*, 90–97, https://doi.org/10.1007/s40037-019-0509-2

Nickerson, C. (2022). Positivism in sociology: Definition, theory & examples. *Simply Psychology*. https://www.simplypsychology.org/positivism-in-sociology-definition-theory-examples.html

Noble, H., & Mitchell, G. (2016). What is grounded theory? *Evidence-Based Nursing*, *19*(2), 34–35. https://doi.org/10.1136/eb-2016-102306

Noyes, J., Booth, A., Moore, G., Flemming, K., Tunçalp, Ö, & Shakibazadeh, E. (2019). Synthesising quantitative and qualitative evidence to inform guidelines on complex interventions: Clarifying the purposes, designs and outlining some methods. *BMJ Global Health*, *4*(Suppl. 1), e000893. http://dx.doi.org/10.1136/bmjgh-2018-000893

Ochulor, C. L. (2005). Positivism as philosophy of science. *Global Journal of Humanities*, *4*(1), 1–4.

Ohly, H., Ibrahim, Z., Liyanage, C., & Carmichael, A. (2023). A scoping review of participatory research methods in agroecology studies conducted in South Asia. *Agroecology and Sustainable Food Systems*, *47*(2), 306–326. https://doi.org/10.1080/21683565.2022.2138674

Omodan, B. I. (2020). The vindication of decoloniality and the reality of COVID-19 as an emergency of unknown in rural universities. *International Journal of Sociology of Education*, 1–26. http://dx.doi.org/10.17583/rise.2020.5495

Omodan, B. I. (2022a). Transformative research in context: An argument of relevant methods. *South Africa international conference on education*. 26–28 October 2022. Pretoria.

Omodan, B. I. (2022b). A model for selecting theoretical framework through the epistemology of research paradigms. *African Journal of Inter/Multidisciplinary Studies*, 4(1), 275–285. https://doi.org/10.51415/ajims.v4i1.1022

O'Neal, J. R. (2015). "The right to know": Decolonizing native American archives. Scholars' Bank http://hdl.handle.net/1794/19360

Otoo, B. K. (2020). Declaring my ontological and epistemological stance. *The Journal of Educational Thought (JET)/Revue de la Pensée Éducative*, 53(1), 67–88. https://www.jstor.org/stable/27128291

Panayotova, P. (2020). Non-quantitative models: Comte and Durkheim. *Sociology and statistics in Britain, 1833–1979* (pp. 99–119). Palgrave Macmillan. https://doi.org/10.1007/978-3-030-55133-9_7

Panhwar, A. H., Ansari, S., & Shah, A. A. (2017). Post-positivism: An effective paradigm for social and educational research. *International Research Journal of Arts and Humanities*, 45(45), 253–259.

Paré, G. (2004). Investigating information systems with positivist case research. *Communications of the Association for Information Systems*, 13(1), 18.

Park, Y. S., Konge, L., & Artino, A. R. Jr (2020). The positivism paradigm of research. *Academic Medicine*, 95(5), 690–694. https://doi.org/10.1097/ACM.0000000000003093

Patel, M., & Patel, N. (2019). Exploring research methodology. *International Journal of Research and Review*, 6(3), 48–55.

Pearson, C. H. (2014). Does environmental pragmatism shirk philosophical duty? *Environmental Values*, 23(3), 335–352. https://doi.org/10.3197/096327114X13947900181879

Perdices, M. (2018). Null hypothesis significance testing, p-values, effects sizes and confidence intervals. *Brain Impairment*, 19(1), 70–80. https://doi.org/10.1017/BrImp.2017.28

Pervin, N., & Mokhtar, M. (2022). The interpretivist research paradigm: A subjective notion of a social context. *International Journal of Academic Research in Progressive Education and Development*, 11(2), 419–428. http://dx.doi.org/10.6007/IJARPED/v11-i2/12938

Pettegrew, J. (Ed.). (2000). *A pragmatist's progress?: Richard Rorty and American intellectual history* (No. 108). Rowman & Littlefield.

Pfadenhauer, M., & Knoblauch, H. (Eds.). (2018). *Social constructivism as paradigm?: The legacy of the social construction of reality*. Routledge.

Phillippi, J., & Lauderdale, J. (2018). A guide to field notes for qualitative research: Context and conversation. *Qualitative Health Research*, 28(3), 381–388. https://doi.org/10.1177/1049732317697102

Pihlström, S. (2007). Metaphysics with a human face: William James and the prospects of pragmatist metaphysics. *William James Studies*, 2. https://www.jstor.org/stable/26203703

Pinales, J. R., & Rivas, R. J. (2005). Relevance theory through pragmatic theories of meaning. In *Proceedings of the annual meeting of the Cognitive Science Society* (Vol. 27, No. 27).

Polit, D. F., & Beck, C. T. (2010). Generalization in quantitative and qualitative research: Myths and strategies. *International Journal of Nursing Studies, 47*(11), 1451–1458. https://doi.org/10.1016/j.ijnurstu.2010.06.004

Postone, M. (2017). Critical theory and the historical transformations of capitalist modernity. *The Palgrave handbook of critical theory* (pp. 137–163). https://doi.org/10.1057/978-1-137-55801-5_7

Potrac, P., Jones, R. L., & Nelson, L. (2014). Interpretivism. In Paul Potrac, Robyn L. Jones, & Lee Nelson (Eds), *Research methods in sports coaching* (pp. 31–41). Routledge.

Pranowo, P. (2020). The role of context in the interpretation of pragmatic meaning. *Retorika: Journal Bahasa, Sastra, dan Pengajarannya, 13*(2), 256–267. https://doi.org/10.26858/retorika.v13i2.12666

Prasad, A. (2015). Beyond positivism: Towards paradigm pluralism in cross-cultural management research. In Nigel Holden, Snejina Michailova, Susanne Tietze (Eds), *The Routledge companion to cross-cultural management* (pp. 198–207). Routledge.

Primecz, H., Romani, L., & Sackmann, S. A. (2009). Cross-cultural management research: Contributions from various paradigms. *International Journal of Cross Cultural Management, 9*(3), 267–274. https://doi.org/10.1177/1470595809346603

Procheş, Ş (2016). Descriptive statistics in research and teaching: Are we losing the middle ground? *Quality & Quantity, 50,* 2165–2174, https://doi.org/10.1007/s11135-015-0256-3

Quick, J., & Hall, S. (2015). Part three: The quantitative approach. *Journal of Perioperative Practice, 25*(10), 192–196.

Quist-Adade, C. (2019). *Symbolic interactionism: The basics*. Vernon Press.

Rahardja, U., Aini, Q., Graha, Y. I., & Lutfiani, N. (2019, December). Validity of test instruments. *Journal of Physics: Conference Series, 1364*(1), 012050. IOP Publishing. https://doi.org/10.1088/1742-6596/1364/1/012050

Raines, D. A. (2013). Research paradigms and methods. *Neonatal Network, 32*(6), 425–428. https://doi.org/10.1891/0730-0832.32.6.425

Ramsay-Jordan, N., Crenshaw, A., & Chestnutt, C. (2022). Examining purposeful researchable questions in mathematics education. *Journal of Honai Math, 5*(2), 127–146. https://doi.org/10.30862/jhm.v5i2.260

Rasid, R., Djafar, H., & Santoso, B. (2021). Alfred Schutz's perspective in phenomenology approach: Concepts, characteristics, methods and examples. *International Journal of Educational Research and Social Sciences (IJERSC), 2*(1), 190–201. https://doi.org/10.51601/ijersc.v2i1.18

Ratts, M. J. (2009). Social justice counseling: Toward the development of a fifth force among counseling paradigms. *The Journal of Humanistic Counseling, Education and Development, 48*(2), 160–172. https://doi.org/10.1002/j.2161-1939.2009.tb00076.x

Redman-MacLaren, M., Mills, J., & Tommbe, R. (2014). Interpretive focus groups: A participatory method for interpreting and extending secondary analysis of qualitative data. *Global Health Action, 7*(1), 25214. https://doi.org/10.3402/gha.v7.25214

Rehman, A. A., & Alharthi, K. (2016). An introduction to research paradigms. *International Journal of Educational Investigations, 3*(8), 51–59.

Reid, A. J., Eckert, L. E., Lane, J. F., Young, N., Hinch, S. G., Darimont, C. T., ... Marshall, A. (2021). "Two-eyed seeing": An Indigenous framework to transform fisheries research and management. *Fish and Fisheries, 22*(2), 243–261. https://doi.org/10.1111/faf.12516

Reif-Acherman, S. (2004). Heike Kamerlingh Onnes: Master of experimental technique and quantitative research, *Physics in Perspective, 6*, 197–223, https://doi.org/10.1007/s00016-003-0193-8

Reilly, R. C. (2010). Participatory case study. In A. J. Mills, G. Durepos, & E. Wiebe (Eds.), *Encyclopedia of case study research* (pp. 658–660). Sage.

Rieger, K. L., Bennett, M., Martin, D., Hack, T. F., Cook, L., & Hornan, B. (2021). Digital storytelling as a patient engagement and research approach with first nations women: How the medicine wheel guided our Debwewin journey. *Qualitative Health Research, 31*(12), 2163–2175.

Rieger, K. L., Horton, M., Copenace, S., Bennett, M., Buss, M., Chudyk, A. M., ...Schultz, A. S. (2023). Elevating the uses of storytelling methods within indigenous health research: A critical, participatory scoping review, *International Journal of Qualitative Methods, 22*, 16094069231174764, https://doi.org/10.1177/16094069231174764

Riga, F. (2020). Pragmatism—John Dewey. *Science education in theory and practice: An introductory guide to learning theory,* 227–239. https://doi.org/10.1007/978-3-030-43620-9_16

Rihoux, B. (2006). Qualitative comparative analysis (QCA) and related systematic comparative methods: Recent advances and remaining challenges for social science research. *International Sociology, 21*(5), 679–706. https://doi.org/10.1177/0268580906067836

Roberts, M., & Russo, R. (2014). *A student's guide to analysis of variance.* Routledge. https://doi.org/10.4324/9781315787954

Rogers, J., & Revesz, A. (2019). Experimental and quasi-experimental designs. In Jim McKinley, & Heath Rose (Eds), *The Routledge handbook of research methods in applied linguistics* (pp. 133–143). Routledge.

Rogers, M. (2012). Contextualizing theories and practices of bricolage research. *Qualitative Report, 17,* 7.

Romm, N. R. (2014). Indigenous ways of knowing and possibilities for re-envisaging globalization: Implications for human ecology. *Journal of Human Ecology, 48*(1), 123–133.

Romm, N. R. (2015). Reviewing the transformative paradigm: A critical systemic and relational (Indigenous) lens, *Systemic Practice and Action Research, 28,* 411–427, https://doi.org/10.1007/s11213-015-9344-5

Rose, E., & Cardinal, A. (2018). Participatory video methods in UX: Sharing power with users to gain insights into everyday life. *Communication Design Quarterly Review, 6*(2), 9–20.

Rowley, J. (2014). Designing and using research questionnaires. *Management Research Review, 37*(3), 308–330. Https://Doi.Org/10.1108/MRR-02-2013-0027

Ryan, A. B. (2006). Post-positivist approaches to research. In M. Antonesa (Ed.), *Researching and writing your thesis: A guide for postgraduate students* (pp. 12–26). MACE: Maynooth Adult and Community Education.

Ryan, G. (2018). Introduction to positivism, interpretivism and critical theory. *Nurse Researcher, 25*(4), 41–49. https://doi.org/10.7748/nr.2018.e1466

Ryan, P. (2015). Positivism: Paradigm or culture? *Policy Studies, 36*(4), 417–433. https://doi.org/10.1080/01442872.2015.1073246

Rydenfelt, H. (2020). Pragmatism, education and the problem of pluralism. *Rethinking Ethical-Political Education,* 197–207. https://doi.org/10.1007/978-3-030-49524-4_13

Sangiorgi, D. (2011). Transformative services and transformation design. *International Journal of Design, 5*(2), 29–40. https://hdl.handle.net/11311/968237

Sarton, G. (1952). Auguste Comte, historian of science: With a short digression on Clotilde de Vaux and Harriet Taylor. *Osiris, 10*, 328–357.

Savin-Baden, M., & Major, C. H. (2023). *Qualitative research: The essential guide to theory and practice.* Taylor & Francis.

Sayer, A. (1997). Essentialism, social constructionism, and beyond. *The Sociological Review, 45*(3), 453–487. https://doi.org/10.1111/1467-954X.00073

Scapens, R. W. (2004). Doing case study research. In C. Humphrey (Ed.), *The real life guide to accounting research* (pp. 257–279). Elsevier. https://doi.org/10.1016/B978-008043972-3/50017-7

Schaie, K. W. (2014). What can we learn from longitudinal studies of adult development?. In Susan Krauss Whitbourne (Ed.), *Successful aging* (pp. 133–158). Psychology Press.

Schank, R. C. (2010). The pragmatics of learning by doing. *Pragmatics and Society, 1*(1), 157–172. https://doi.org/10.1075/ps.1.1.10sch

Scholz, G. (2023). Roots of disputes over hermeneutics. *Семиотические исследования, 3*(1), 106–112. https://doi.org/10.18287/2782-2966-2023-3-1-106-112

Schutz, A. (1972). *The phenomenology of the social world.* Northwestern university press.

Schwartz-Shea, P. (2014). Interpretive social science. *The encyclopedia of political thought.* https://doi.org/10.1002/9781118474396.wbept0533

Sexton, K., Selevan, S. G., Wagener, D. K., & Lybarger, J. A. (1992). Estimating human exposures to environmental pollutants: Availability and utility of existing databases. *Archives of Environmental Health: An International Journal, 47*(6), 398–407. https://doi.org/10.1080/00039896.1992.9938381

Shah, S. R., & Al-Bargi, A. (2013). Research paradigms: Researchers' worldviews, theoretical frameworks and study designs. *Arab World English Journal, 4*(4), 252–264.

Sherwood, G. (2011). Data collectors' field journals as tools for research. *Journal of Research in Nursing, 16*(5), 466.

Shi, R., & Conrad, S. A. (2009). Correlation and regression analysis. *Annals of Allergy, Asthma & Immunology, 103*(4), S35–S41. https://doi.org/10.1016/S1081-1206(10)60820-4

Shields, P. (1998). Pragmatism as a philosophy of science: A tool for public administration. In J. D. White (Ed.), *Research in public administration* (pp. 195–225). JAI Press Inc.

Shipe, M. E., Deppen, S. A., Farjah, F., & Grogan, E. L. (2019). Developing prediction models for clinical use using logistic regression: An overview. *Journal of Thoracic Disease, 11*(Suppl. 4), S574. https://doi.org/10.21037%2Fjtd.2019.01.25

Smith, B. (2016). Narrative analysis. In Coyle Adrian, Lyons Evanthia Coyle Adrian, & Lyons Evanthia (Eds), *Analysing qualitative data in psychology* (Vol. 2, pp. 202–221). Sage Publications Ltd.

Smith, L. T., Tuck, E., & Yang, K. W. (Eds.). (2018). *Indigenous and decolonizing studies in education: Mapping the long view.* Routledge.

Spector, P. E. (2019). Do not cross me: Optimizing the use of cross-sectional designs. *Journal of Business and Psychology, 34*(2), 125–137. https://doi.org/10.1007/s10869-018-09613-8

# References

Stadler, F. (2015). The origins of logical empiricism—Roots of the Vienna Circle before the First World War. In: F. Stadler, *The Vienna Circle. Vienna Circle Institute Library* (pp. 1–25). Springer, Cham. https://doi.org/10.1007/978-3-319-16561-5_1.

Subedi, D. (2016). Explanatory sequential mixed method design as the third research community of knowledge claim. *American Journal of Educational Research, 4*(7), 570–577.

Sürücü, L., & Maslakci, A. (2020). Validity and reliability in quantitative research. *Business & Management Studies: An International Journal, 8*(3), 2694–2726. https://doi.org/10.15295/bmij.v8i3.1540

Swadener, B. B. (2005). *Power & voice in research with children* (Vol. 33). Peter Lang.

Talisse, R. B. (2013). *A pragmatist philosophy of democracy*. Routledge.

Talisse, R. B. (2014). Pragmatist political philosophy. *Philosophy Compass, 9*(2), 123–130.

Thanh, N. C., & Thanh, T. T. (2015). The interconnection between interpretivist paradigm and qualitative methods in education. *American Journal of Educational Science, 1*(2), 24–27.

Thomann, E., & Ege, J. (2020). *Qualitative comparative analysis (QCA) in public administration*. Oxford University Press. https://doi.org/10.1093/acrefore/9780190228637.013.1444

Tiselius, E. (2019). The (un-) ethical interpreting researcher: Ethics, voice and discretionary power in interpreting research. *Perspectives, 27*(5), 747–760. https://doi.org/10.1080/0907676X.2018.1544263

Tomkins, L., & Eatough, V. (2018). Hermeneutics: Interpretation, understanding and sense-making. In Catherine Cassell, Ann L. Cunliffe, & Gina Grandy (Eds), *SAGE handbook of qualitative business and management research methods* (pp. 185–200). Sage.

Tripathy, J. (2009). Postcolonialism and the Native American experience: A theoretical perspective. *Asiatic: IIUM Journal of English Language and Literature, 3*(1), 40–53.

Trott, C. D. (2016). Constructing alternatives: Envisioning a critical psychology of prefigurative politics. *Journal of Social and Political Psychology, 4*(1), 266–285. https://doi.org/10.5964/jspp.v4i1.520

Tuli, F. (2010). The basis of distinction between qualitative and quantitative research in social science: Reflection on ontological, epistemological and methodological perspectives. *Ethiopian Journal of Education and Sciences, 6*(1).

Tyson, K. B. (1992). A new approach to relevant scientific research for practitioners: The heuristic paradigm. *Social Work, 37*(6), 541–556. https://doi.org/10.1093/sw/37.6.541

Van Mersbergen, M., & Patrick, C. J. (2022). 10 Quantitative and physiological measures. *Language And Emotion, 1*, 201.

Vetter, V. M., Özince, D. D., Kiselev, J., Düzel, S., & Demuth, I. (2023). Self-reported and accelerometer-based assessment of physical activity in older adults: Results from the Berlin Aging Study II. *Scientific Reports, 13*(1), 10047. https://doi.org/10.1038/s41598-023-36924-5

Vining, R., & Finn, M. (2023). Why and how is photovoice used as a decolonising method for health research with Indigenous communities in the United States and Canada? A scoping review. *Nursing Inquiry*, e12605. https://doi.org/10.1111/nin.12605

Walter, M. (2016). Indigenous peoples, research and ethics. In Michael Adorjan, & Rose Ricciardell (Eds), *Engaging with ethics in international criminological research* (pp. 87–105). Routledge.

Wang, Q., Coemans, S., Siegesmund, R., & Hannes, K. (2017). Arts-based methods in socially engaged research practice: A classification framework. *Art/Research International: A Transdisciplinary Journal, 2*(2), 5–39. https://doi.org/10.18432/R26G8P

Wang, X., & Cheng, Z. (2020). Cross-sectional studies: Strengths, weaknesses, and recommendations. *Chest, 158*(1), S65–S71. https://doi.org/10.1016/j.chest.2020.03.012

Williamson, A., & Hoggart, B. (2005). Pain: A review of three commonly used pain rating scales. *Journal of Clinical Nursing, 14*(7), 798–804. https://Doi.Org/10.1111/J.1365-2702.2005.01121.X

Wodak, R. (2014). Critical discourse analysis. In Constant Leung, & Brian V Street (Eds), *The Routledge companion to English studies* (pp. 302–316). Routledge.

Yanow, D. (2017). Qualitative-interpretive methods in policy research. In Frank Fischer, & Gerald J. Miller (Eds), *Handbook of public policy analysis* (pp. 431–442). Routledge.

Yinkore, E. B., & Mgbomo, E. (2022). Bridging the gap between theory and practice in the Nigerian educational system: John Dewey's educational idea as paradigm. *GPH-International Journal of Educational Research, 5*(07), 19–27. https://doi.org/10.5281/zenodo.6954291

Young, T. J. (2015). Questionnaires and surveys. In Zhu Hua (Ed.), *Research methods in intercultural communication: A practical guide* (pp. 163–180). Wiley.

Yu, C. H. (2003). Misconceived relationships between logical positivism and quantitative research. In *Research methods forum [on-line], Retrieved September* (Vol. 2(2004), 33620–7750.

Zajda, J. (2020). Discourse analysis as a qualitative methodology. *Educational Practice and Theory, 42*(2), 5–21. https://doi.org/10.7459/ept/42.2.02

Zhai, Y., Li, D., Wu, C., & Wu, H. (2023). Spatial distribution, activity zone preference, and activity intensity of senior park users in a metropolitan area, *Urban Forestry & Urban Greening, 79*, 127761, https://doi.org/10.1016/j.ufug.2022.127761

Zuber-Skerritt, O. (2015). Participatory action learning and action research (PALAR) for community engagement: A theoretical framework. *Educational Research for Social Change, 4*(1), 5–25.

Zuber-Skerritt, O. (2018). An educational framework for participatory action learning and action research (PALAR). *Educational Action Research, 26*(4), 513–532. https://doi.org/10.1080/09650792.2018.1464939

Zwi, A. B., Grove, N. J., Mackenzie, C., Pittaway, E., Zion, D., Silove, D., & Tarantola, D. (2006). Placing ethics in the centre: Negotiating new spaces for ethical research in conflict situations. *Global Public Health, 1*(3), 264–277. https://doi.org/10.1080/17441690600673866

Zyphur, M. J., & Pierides, D. C. (2020). Statistics and probability have always been value-laden: An historical ontology of quantitative research methods, *Journal of Business Ethics, 167*, 1–18, https://doi.org/10.1007/s10551-019-04187-8

# Index

accountability 142
action research 98–99, 127–128, 158–159
adaptability 153–154
Analysis of Variance (ANOVA) 50
analytical software 170
anti-essentialism 147
arts-based methods 108–109

case study research 32, 62, 159; community development and indigenous land rights 104; diversity and inclusion, workplace 73–74; education technology, rural schools 164–165; employee job satisfaction 37; gender inequality, workplace 14–15; healthcare services and barriers 16–17; indigenous agricultural practices 131–132; indigenous food sovereignty 129–130; indigenous language revitalisation 130–131; indigenous youth, cultural identity and well-being 17; LGBTQ+-affirming mental health services 103; mobile banking on economic development 38; obesity prevention 164; online self-identity 72–73; reducing waste and recycling 17–18; student academic performance, technology on 36–37; teaching methodology on students 15–16; urbanisation and air quality 38–39; women's empowerment and microfinance 104–105; work-life balance 71–72
causality 34, 36–39
cause-and-effect relationships 15, 37–38, 44, 56
climate change, effect of 163

cluster analysis 49–50
collaborative research 90–91, 130–131
community-based action research (CBAR) 99
community-based participatory research (CBPR) 126
community-based surveys 134
community development 104
community engagement and collaboration 141
community health programs 160
community validation and interpretation 138
comparative analysis 81–82
comparative design 31
Comte, A. 24
constructivist paradigm 6, 63
content analysis 81, 111, 168–169
contextualism 148
contextual understanding 66
convergent design 157
correlational design 32
correlation analysis 48
counter-narrative analysis 138
critical discourse analysis (CDA) 112
critical ethnography 62–63, 97–98
critical paradigm 4–7, 87
critical theory 4, 87–89
cross-sectional design 30
cultural continuity 122
cultural revitalisation 122
cultural sensitivity 142

data privacy 162
decolonisation 121–122
deductive approach 28–29
descriptive statistics 30, 47–48
deterministic principles 28
Dewey, J. 145

## Index

dialogical analysis 82
digital ethnography 108
digital storytelling 133–134
digital tracking devices 44
discourse analysis 79–80, 111, 139, 169
diversity and inclusion, workplace 73–74
document analysis 76, 107–108, 167

education technology, rural schools 164–165
elder interviews 135–136
emancipation 90
embedded design 158
empiricism 27–28
employee job satisfaction 37
empowerment 102–103
essentialism 139
ethical review process 142
ethnographic observation 76–77
ethnographic research 126–127
ethnography 60
existing databases 45
experiential learning 147
experimental apparatus 44
experimental design 29
experiments 166–167
explanatory sequential design 157
ex post facto design 33

factor analysis 49
factorial design 32–33
fact-value dichotomy 149
fallibilism 148
field notes 77–78
focus groups 75–76, 106, 134–135

generalisability 34, 54–55
grounded theory 61, 80–81, 170
group interviews 136

human-centred inquiry 153, 156

in-depth interviews 105–106
indigenous: agricultural practices 131–132; feminist research 127; food sovereignty 129–130; knowledge systems analysis 137; land rights 104; language revitalisation 130–131; research frameworks 138; research protocols 133

inferential statistics 48
informed consent 141
instrumentalism 148
interpretative phenomenological analysis (IPA) 81
interpretive paradigm 4, 6, 8–10, 15, 19, 59–60; axiology of 68–69; balancing subjectivity 84–86; case study 62; concept of 63–64; contextual understanding 66; critical ethnography 62–63; data analysis and interpretation 78–82; data collection methods 74–78; epistemology of 67–68; ethical considerations 83–84; ethnography 60; evolution of 64–65; grounded theory 61; methodology of 69; multiple realities 65–66; narrative research 61–62; ontology of 68; phenomenology 60–61; qualitative and inductive methods 66–67; reflexivity and interpretation 66; reliability and validity 83; research questions 69–74; social construction 65; subjective meanings 65; subjectivity and generalisability 83; value-laden nature 67
interpretivist paradigm 7–8, 13, 15
intersectional analysis 98, 113–114, 138–139
intersectionality 91, 139
interviews 75, 135–136, 166
iterative analysis 170–171

James, W. 145

key informant interviews 136
Kuhn, T. S. 1–2

large sample sizes 41
LGBTQ+ affirming mental health services 103
LGBTQ+ youth 101
longitudinal design 30
low-income schools, educational outcomes 161

Maarouf, H. 150
mental health, workplace 161–163
microfinance 104–105
mixed-methods research 5, 57, 96–97, 145, 154–156, 168
mobile banking on economic development 38

multiple realities 65–66
Multivariate Analysis of Variance (MANOVA) 50–51

narrative analysis 79, 111–112, 137
narrative inquiry 109–110
narrative interviews 77
narrative research 61–62

obesity prevention 164
objectivity 21, 35, 40, 46
observational checklists 43–44
observational methods 107
observations 166
online self-identity 72–73
oppression 89–90
oral histories 132
oversimplification 52–53
ownership 141

paradigm compatibility 20
participant involvement 85
participant observation 75
participatory action learning action research (PALAR) 100
participatory action research (PAR) 97, 125–126
participatory case study 99
participatory data analysis 113
participatory mapping 106–107, 133
participatory research 90–91, 128
participatory video 109
peer review and collaboration 85
Peirce, C. S. 145
phenomenological analysis 80
phenomenology 60–61
philosophical commitment 171–172
photovoice 106, 133–134
physiological measures 43
pluralism 147–148
positionality 90
positivist paradigm 6, 23–24; axiology of 26–27; balancing objectivity and subjectivity 57–58; case study design 32; comparative design 31; contextual factors 54–55; correlational design 32; cross-sectional design 30; data analysis and interpretation 45–52; data collection methods 39–45; deductive approach 28–29; deterministic principles 28; empiricism 27–28; epistemology of 25–26; ethical considerations 56–57; evolution of 24–25; experimental design 29; ex post facto design 33; factorial design 32–33; generalisability 54–55; longitudinal design 30; methodology of 27; objectivity 27, 53; ontology of 26; oversimplification 52–53; power dynamics 55; quantitative methods 54; quasi-experimental design 30–31; realist ontology 28; reductionism 28, 52–53; researcher dominance 55; research questions 33–39; subjective experience 55–56; survey research design 29–30; true experimental design 31; universality 28; value-free/neutral stance 28; value neutrality 53–54
postcolonial indigenous paradigm (PCIP) 7; action research 127–128; axiology of 124; community-based participatory research 126; community engagement and collaboration 141; concept of 119–120; cultural continuity 122; cultural revitalisation 122; cultural sensitivity and protocols 142; data analysis and interpretation 136–139; data collection methods 132–136; decolonisation 121–122; decolonisation and research outcomes 140; epistemology of 123; essentialism vs. intersectionality 139; ethical considerations and power dynamics 140; ethical review and accountability 142; ethnographic research 126–127; evolution of 120–121; indigenous feminist research 127; informed consent and ownership 141; methodology of 124–125; ontology of 124; participatory action research 125–126; participatory research 128; reciprocity and benefit sharing 142; reflexivity and self-reflection 141; representation and authenticity 139–140; researcher positionality and indigenous knowledge systems 140; research questions 128–132; self-determination 122; sovereignty 122; two-eyed seeing 126
post-positivism 25
potential eclecticism 172
power dynamics 55, 89–90
power imbalance and representation 20
power relations 101–102

pragmatism paradigm 5, 7–10; action research 158–159; adaptability and problem-solving 153–154; anti-essentialism 147; axiology of 151; case study research 159; community and collaboration 148–149; concept of 144–145; context and complexity 155–156; contextualism 148; convergent design 157; data analysis and interpretation 168–171; data collection methods 165–167; embedded design 158; epistemology of 149–15; ethical consideration and human-centred inquiry 156; ethical considerations 174; evolution of 145–146; experiential learning 147; explanatory sequential design 157; fact-value dichotomy 149; fallibilism 148; flexibility and practicality 174–175; human-centred inquiry 153; identity and definition 173–174; instrumentalism 148; integration, challenges 172–173; integration of thought and action 147; methodology of 151–152; ontology of 150; philosophical commitment 171–172; pluralism and tolerance 147–148; potential eclecticism 172; practical consequences 146–147; practicality vs. depth 173; problem-centred orientation 155; problem-solving 148; qualitative and quantitative approach 154–155; qualitative research approach 152–153; relativism 172; research questions 159–165; transformative design 157–158; values and ethics 153
prison inmates, ethical treatment 161–162
problem-centred focus 160–161
problem-centred orientation 155
problem-solving 148, 153–154
psychometric tests 43

qualitative and inductive methods 66–67
qualitative comparative analysis (QCA) 112
qualitative inquiry 152–153
quantifiability 34, 40
quantitative analysis 46
quantitative methods 54
quasi-experimental design 30–31
questionnaires 42

rating scales 42–43
realist ontology 28
reciprocity 142
reductionism 28, 52–53
reflexive journals 77–78
reflexivity 57, 84; and interpretation 66; and positionality 90, 116–117; and self-reflection 141
regression analysis 49
relativism 172
reliability and validity 40–41
replicability 46
researcher bias 21
researcher dominance 55
researcher positionality 20
research ethics 19
research paradigm: axiology in 10–12; bias and objectivity 21; concept of 1–2; critical/transformative 6; data analysis and interpretation 21; epistemology in 8–9, 19; ethical considerations 19; historical development of 4–6; importance of 2–4; interpretivism/constructivism 6; methodology 12–13, 19; ontology in 9–10, 19; paradigm compatibility and integration 20; positivism 6; postcolonial indigenous paradigm 7; power dynamics and representation 20; pragmatism 7; researcher positionality 20; research questions and 13–18; theoretical frameworks 21

self-determination 122
semi-structured interviews 135
social construction 65
social justice 90, 102–103
sovereignty 122
standardisation 39–40
standardised tests 44–45
statistical analysis 169
statistical interpretation 46–47
storytelling 132
Structural Equation Modelling (SEM) 51
structural inequalities 102
student academic performance, technology on 36–37
Subedi, D. 157
subjective experience 55–56
subjective meanings 65
subjectivity 57–58

## Index 197

surveys 42; community-based 134; and questionnaires 165–166; research design 29–30
survival analysis 51

technology and elderly care 163
thematic analysis 79, 110–111, 137–138, 169–170
theoretical framework 21
tolerance 147–148
transformative change 91
transformative data analysis methods 114–115
transformative design 157–158
transformative paradigm 6, 10, 12; action research 98–99; axiology in 93–94; collaboration and participatory approach 117; community-based action research 99; and community organisations 117; concept of 87–88; critical ethnography 97–98; critiques and debates 115–116; data analysis and interpretation 110–115; data collection methods 105–110; emancipation and social justice 90; epistemology in 92–93; ethical considerations 92, 117; evolution of 88–89; intersectional analysis 98; intersectionality 91; methodology of 94; and mixed-methods research 96–97; ontology in 93; participatory action learning action research 100; participatory action research 97; participatory and collaborative research 90–91; participatory case study 99; power and oppression 89–90; and qualitative research 94–96; reflexivity and positionality 90, 116–117; research questions 100–105; rigorous methodologies 117; structural inequalities 117; transformative change 91
transparency 85–86
triangulation 57–58, 85
true experimental design 31
two-eyed seeing 126

universality 28
urban education systems 162
urbanisation and air quality 38–39

value-free/neutral stance 28
value-laden nature 67
value neutrality 53–54
values and ethics 153
Vienna Circle 24
visual analysis 113
visual methods 77, 133

women: empowerment 104–105; in leadership 15
work-life balance 71–72
workplace: diversity and inclusion 73–74; equality 71; gender inequality 14–15; mental health in 161–163; motivation 160

Zuber-Skerritt, O. 100